Lucy Moore was born in 1970 and educated in Britain and the US bef⸍ e reading history at Edinburgh University. Voted one of the ⸍enty young writers in Britain' by the *Independent on Sunday* in ⸍r books include the bestselling *Maharanis: The Lives & Times ⸍ Generations of Indian Princesses* (Viking, 2004) and the ⸍ed *Liberty: The Lives and Times of Six Women in Revolutionary* (HarperCollins, 2006).

erising... Like the champagne-immersed age she portrays, s book effervesces with the detail of this fascinating story.' Nicholson, *Evening Standard*

a decade it was! What goings-on – more violent, subversive otic than any of the parties, japes or shenanigans of our own Young Things... Moore has knitted the various diverse strands ⸍r impressively with an overview of the large cast of characters, attitudes, industries and statistics.' Anne de Courcy, *Daily Mail*

of anecdote, detail and colour... Fluid and elegant.' Marianne , *Independent*

of-control consumer spending? Unregulated banking system? ish need to drink and drug the jumpy self into oblivion? Check, k, check. We have been here before, and in a much worse state t the end of the "roaring" 1920s. If this book has a moral it is n the words of that balladeer of bad times Al Jolson, "you ain't seen nothing yet"' Kathryn Hughes, *Guardian*

'An especially well-timed history of the Roaring Twenties as the decade m⸍ from h⸍ high ⸍ boom to the bust of the Gr⸍

Anything Goes

A BIOGRAPHY OF THE ROARING TWENTIES

Lucy Moore

ATLANTIC BOOKS
LONDON

First published in hardback in Great Britain in 2008
by Atlantic Books, an imprint of Grove Atlantic Ltd.

This paperback edition published in Great Britain
in 2009 by Atlantic Books.

1 3 5 7 9 10 8 6 4 2

A CIP catalogue record for this book is
available from the British Library.

ISBN 978 1 84354 778 5

Designed and typeset in Filosofia by Lindsay Nash
Printed in Great Britain by CPI Bookmarque, Croydon

Atlantic Books
An imprint of Grove Atlantic Ltd
Ormond House
26–27 Boswell Street
London
WC1N 3JZ

www.atlantic-books.co.uk

xxxx

Contents

List of Illustrations

Al Capone and Henry Laubenheimer. © Hulton-Deutsch Collection/Corbis.

Izzy Einstein and Moe Smith. Time & Life Pictures/Getty Images.

Bessie Smith. Library of Congress, Prints & Photographs Division, Carl Van Vechten Collection.

Langston Hughes. James L. Allen Yale Collection of American Literature, Beinecke Rare Book and Manuscript Library.

The Louis Armstrong Hot Five. Roger-Viollet/Topfoto.

Scott and Zelda Fitzgerald. Courtesy of the F. Scott Fitzgerald Archive, Princeton University Library.

Cover of *The Beautiful and the Damned*. Courtesy of the F. Scott Fitzgerald Archive, Princeton University Library.

Scott, Zelda and Scottie. Courtesy of the F. Scott Fitzgerald Archive, Princeton University Library.

Gloria Swanson. Library of Congress, Prints & Photographs Division.

Theda Bara. Fox Films/The Kobal Collection.

Marion Davies. George Hurrell/The Kobal Collection.

Mary Pickford and Douglas Fairbanks. The Kobal Collection.

Charlie Chaplin. United Artists/The Kobal Collection.

Prologue

A HANDSOME YOUNG MAN stands on a sunny beach between his wife and his sister. It's late summer and the bathers frolicking in the shallows or shading themselves beneath striped parasols in the background are growing scarce. The two women are in pale knee-length dresses, their hair fashionably styled; one wears a cardigan against the sea wind. Harry Crosby stands out in his dark suit, his hands stuffed into his pockets and his face screwed up against the sun. The photograph was taken at Deauville in late September, 1929, but it has an astonishingly contemporary feel.

The three figures probably look more normal to us than they would have done to an onlooker at the time the photograph was taken. So many of the things that would have marked them out as modernists in the eyes of their peers are now taken for granted. When I look at it I have to pinch myself to remember that Harry being bareheaded, at a time when no gentleman went outside without a hat, was a daring declaration of freedom, and that the black silk gardenia he sports in his lapel was a deliberate subversion of the genteel buttonhole and a badge of his alliance with the avant-garde. Knowing the story behind this photograph provides us with clues about the world in which Harry and his family lived, a world of growth and social upheaval on an unprecedented scale – a world which, in its self-conscious modernity and its brash enthusiasms, was startlingly similar to our own.

The Crosbys were American aristocracy, living in Europe on vast wealth accumulated on Wall Street, although Harry affected to despise the conventional milieu from which he sprang and delighted in shocking it when he could. Despite their Establishment roots, Harry Crosby and his companions were prophets of a new age. Today there is nothing unusual in divorce but in 1929 it was still a scandal. On this day at the beach, Harry's sister announced that she was divorcing her husband. Harry's wife, Caresse, had left her first husband to marry him, branding them both outlaws from respectable society. Their example heralded a future when divorce would be commonplace.

Harry's eccentric dress and behaviour also marked them out. Like fellow members of the Lost Generation, Harry had responded to the atrocities he had seen as an ambulance driver in the French trenches during the First World War with reckless hedonism, fuelled by the American age of plenty in which he was living. He was promiscuous, he was profligate, he drank too much, he took drugs, he drove dangerously fast, he died young. Harry Crosby may have felt part of a tiny, forward-thinking elite during his lifetime, but his story is all too familiar today.

I've been interested in the 1920s in America for many years, but what made me decide to write about it now was an increasingly powerful sense of recognition. So many aspects of the Jazz Age recall our own: political corruption and complacency; fear of outsiders; life-changing technologies; cults of youth, excess, consumerism and celebrity; profit as a new religion on the one hand and the easy availability of credit on the other; astonishing affluence and yet a huge section of society unable to move out of poverty. Perhaps we too are hurtling towards some sort of catastrophe, the effects of which will evoke those of the crash of 1929. After all, as history so often reminds us, there is nothing new under the sun.

This is a subjective survey of the principal events and characters of the time. The Roaring Twenties was an age of iconic events and people, of talismanic names and episodes that have entered our consciousness more like myths – or morality tales – than historical occurrences. This book is my exploration of those icons. From a distance of eighty years, some still glitter while others have grown tarnished, but their fascination endures.

1

'You Cannot Make Your Shimmy Shake on Tea'

IN EARLY 1927, WHEN Chicago's Beer Wars between rival gangs of bootleggers were at their peak, Al Capone invited a group of reporters to his heavily fortified home. Fetchingly attired in a pink apron and bedroom slippers, rather than his usual sharp suit and diamond cuff-links, he dished up a feast of home-made spaghetti and illegally imported Chianti and told his guests that he was getting out of the booze racket. Capone wanted the world – not just the public but the police, the federal authorities and his mob enemies – to believe that he was finished with crime. But despite his public pronouncement, he had no intention of quitting such a profitable business.

At the end of the year, with gangsters still dying in regular shoot-outs on the streets of Chicago, Capone again tried to distance himself from the criminal underworld. Summoning journalists to his suite at the Metropole Hotel, his head-quarters in the centre of the city, he announced his retirement for the second time in a year. He had only been trying, Capone declared, to provide people with what they wanted. 'Public service is my motto,' he insisted. 'Ninety per cent of the people in Chicago drink and gamble. I've tried to serve them decent liquor and square games. But I'm not appreciated. It's no use… Let the worthy citizens of Chicago get their liquor the best way they can. I'm sick of the job. It's a thankless one and full of grief.'

He was no more a criminal than his clients, he argued. 'I violate the prohibition law, sure. Who doesn't? The only difference is I take more chances than the man who drinks a cocktail before dinner and a flock of highballs after it. But he's just as much a violator as I am…' Falsely, he claimed that he and his men had never been involved in serious crime, vice or robbery: 'I don't pose as a plaster saint, but I never killed anyone.'

The worst of it was the suffering that his work – which he implied was practically charity – caused his family. 'I could bear it all if it weren't for the hurt it brings to my mother and my family. They hear so much about what a terrible criminal I am. It's getting too much for them and I'm just sick of it all myself.' Although several of his brothers worked with him, Capone idealized his mother and his wife and son and kept his family life rigidly separate from his professional activities and the late-night perks that went with them of drinking, drugs and girls. It was as if maintaining his family's innocence allowed him to hope that he was not entirely the monster he knew himself to be.

After the press conference Capone headed for Florida. 'I almost feel like sending him and his boys a basket of roses,' said the Chief of Police when he heard the news. The Chicago papers screamed, '"YOU CAN ALL GO THIRSTY" IS AL CAPONE'S ADIEU'.

When Capone made these announcements in 1927 he was at the peak of his power. Just twenty-eight, growing into his role as Chicago's leading gangster, he was becoming ever more confident about engaging with the legitimate world – albeit on his own terms. While on the one hand he was cautious of his safety after the attack of 1925 that had nearly killed his partner, Johnny Torrio, on the other he was increasingly willing to reveal his personality in an effort to win over the public whose approval he craved – and on whose approval, he believed, his continued success depended. This desire for appreciation and attention was what lifted him out of the everyday ranks of mobsters into a class of his own.

His car, a custom-built, steel-plated Cadillac, which weighed seven tonnes and had bullet-proof window glass and a hidden gun compartment, encapsulated the dichotomy between Capone's need for protection and his love of display. Although it was undoubtedly secure it was also instantly recognizable, and became a defining element of the Capone mystique.

Another element of Capone's public image was his distinctive appearance. Even in his twenties Al Capone was a broad man – he stood five foot seven and weighed 255 pounds – but he was capable of grace as well as power. He was softly spoken but immensely charismatic, his air of authority enhanced by an undercurrent of menace. As he was reportedly fond of saying, 'You get a lot further with a smile and a gun than you can with just a smile.'

Capone may have been known for his facial scars (while still in his teens he had complimented a girl in a Coney Island dance-hall on her 'nice ass' and in the fight that ensued her brother had slashed his cheek and neck three times), but he covered his face with thick powder to try to hide them and hated being called Scarface. Among friends the nickname he preferred was Snorky, slang for 'elegant'. His hand-made suits came in ice-cream colours, tangerine, violet, apple-green and primrose, with the right-hand pockets reinforced to hide the bulge of his gun; he wore a marquise-cut diamond pin in his tie to match his cuff-links and an eleven-carat blue-white diamond on the little finger of his left hand, the hand he didn't use for firing a gun. Off duty, he favoured gold-piped royal blue silk pyjamas embroidered with his initials.

Capone wanted to present himself as the acceptable face of crime – a modern entrepreneur rather than a crook. He began playing the role of benevolent public figure, watching baseball games and boxing matches with friends, greeting the aviator Charles Lindbergh when he landed his hydroplane on Lake Michigan in the summer of 1927 following his heroic solo flight from New York to Paris. Celebrities who passed through Chicago were taken to meet him; he was generous with ice-creams for children and racing tips for strangers he met on the street; when buying a newspaper, he'd pay with a five-dollar bill and tell the boy to keep the change.

Golf, a 1920s craze, became a passion – though, as ever, Capone played by his own rules. Wearing baggy grey plus fours held up by a belt with a diamond buckle, pockets bulging with guns and hip-flasks, he and 'Machine Gun' McGurn and 'Killer' Burke played for $500 a hole. They used each other as human tees and wrestled, played leapfrog and turned somersaults on the greens. On one occasion, accused – almost certainly with reason – of cheating, Capone drew a gun on one of his bodyguards. Danger was never far from the surface with Capone, even during a friendly game of golf.

At the same time Capone courted the press, developing close relationships with several journalists. The *Chicago Tribune*'s crime correspondent, James Doherty, found Capone neither entertaining nor articulate, but more than willing to be profiled. He was aware, Doherty wrote, that a positive public image would 'make better business for him'. Another *Tribune* writer, Jake Lingle, a police reporter and, in his spare time, an avid gambler, was well known for his friendship with Capone. But this intimacy with the underworld was dangerous: in 1931 Lingle was shot dead, probably by a rival of Capone's. Subsequent investigations revealed that he had been in Capone's pay.

Perhaps the most useful of Capone's press connections was Harry Read, city editor of the *Chicago Evening American*. In return for exclusive interviews (and generous holidays), Read coached Capone on his image, encouraging him to show his softer side. Read, like Doherty, realized that it was the violence of Capone's world to which the public objected, not his specific crimes. Too many people liked having a flutter on the horses or a stiff drink to condemn Capone for supplying their needs. As Doherty said, Capone 'was giving them a service they wanted. No one minded about them trading booze; it was all the killing that brought about their undoing.'

When the English journalist Claud Cockburn interviewed Capone in 1929, at the Lexington Hotel in Chicago, his new headquarters, he described entering the gloomy, deserted lobby and being stared at by a receptionist with the expression 'of a speakeasy proprietor looking through the grille at a potential detective'.

After being frisked, Cockburn rode the elevator up to Capone's six-room suite on the fourth floor. 'Bulging' henchmen stood idly around; cash was stacked against the wall in padlocked canvas bags; the initials AC were inlaid in the parquet floor. Portraits of Abraham Lincoln and George Washington hung alongside ones of 'Big Bill' Thompson, Chicago's corrupt mayor, and the movie stars 'Fatty' Arbuckle and the Vamp, Theda Bara. Capone's office looked like nothing so much as that of a '"newly arrived" Texas oil millionaire', wrote Cockburn – but for the submachine gun behind the mahogany desk.

Cockburn asked Capone what he might have done if he hadn't 'gone into this racket'. Capone replied that he would 'have been selling newspapers on the street in Brooklyn'. Growing increasingly agitated, distractedly dipping the tips of his fingers in the silver bowls of roses on his desk, he railed against the un-Americanness of the Sicilian mafia (Capone's family came from Naples, but he was always proud to say that he had been born in America), its primitive, unprofessional *mano nero* intimidation tactics. 'This American system of ours, call it Americanism, call it capitalism, call it what you like, gives to each and every one of us a great opportunity if we only seize it with both hands and make the most of it,' he shouted, pushing his chair back and standing up, holding out his dripping hands towards Cockburn.

In January 1920 it became illegal throughout the United States to manufacture, transport, sell or possess – but not to purchase or consume – alcohol. For all the recalcitrance with which Americans greeted it, Prohibition was not foisted upon an entirely unwilling population. When the national law was passed in 1919, thirty-three of the forty-eight states were already dry.

Reformers saw Prohibition as a necessary instrument of social improvement – a way to help the poor and needy help themselves. They associated alcohol with urbanization, with violence, laziness and corruption, and with unwelcome immigrants. Sober men, thought Prohibitionists, would be better Americans. They would stop beating their wives, hold down jobs, go to church (preferably a Protestant church), save their pennies. A sober society would be patriotic, stable, pious and prosperous.

Warren Gamaliel Harding, the Republican President elected in 1920, viewed Prohibition in much the same light as most of his fellow Americans, who were virtuous enough to praise Prohibition but not quite virtuous enough to practise it. Harding may have voted in the Senate to ratify Prohibition but in private he had no intention of abiding by its strictures. He could see nothing wrong with his own fondness for whisky, especially when it was accompanied by a well-chewed cigar and a few poker-playing cronies. Prohibition was a little like an unpleasant-tasting medicine: people recognized its merits and uses, but if they did not think they were sick (and very few did) they were unwilling to swallow it themselves. As a *New York World* satire went, 'Prohibition is an awful flop. / We like it... It don't prohibit worth a dime, / Nevertheless we're for it'.

The reformers had also failed to foresee that once alcohol was illegal it would take on an irresistible glamour. Rather than encouraging people to stop drinking, Prohibition made them want to drink. Writers like Scott Fitzgerald rhapsodized over forbidden cocktails like 'the iridescent exhilaration of absinthe frappé, crystal and pearl in green glasses' or 'gin fizzes [the] colour of green and silver'; the sparkle of champagne suddenly gave drinkers a delightful new sensation of naughtiness; liveried bell-hops rushed up and down hotel staircases bearing soda, buckets of crushed ice and thrillingly discreet brown-paper packages. The popular 1920 song said it all: 'You Cannot Make Your Shimmy Shake on Tea'.

On a visit to the United States in 1928, the English journalist Beverley Nichols observed that 'Prohibition has set a great many dull feet dancing… The disappearance of the "speakeasy" would be an infinite loss to all romanticists,' Nichols continued. 'Who, having slunk down the little flight of stairs into the area, glancing to right and left, in order to make sure that no police are watching, having blinked at the suddenly lighted *grille*, and assured the proprietor, whose face peers through the bars, of his bona fides – who would willingly forfeit these delicious preliminaries? And who, having taken his seat in the shuttered restaurant, having felt all the thrill of the conspirator, having jumped at each fresh ring of the bell, having, perhaps, enjoyed the supreme satisfaction of participating in a real raid – who would prefer, to these excitements, a sedate and legal dinner, even if all the wines of the world were at his disposition?'

Before Prohibition, alcohol had been a cheap high. In 1914, a highball might cost fifteen cents. Six years later a swanky speakeasy could charge $3 – twenty times as much – for a glass of top-quality whisky and even at the bottom of the market that shot would cost about fifty cents (although it was free for the police). But despite the expense and the criminality associated with alcohol after Prohibition came into effect, people were still drinking 'with a frantic desire to get drunk and enjoy themselves'. There were fortunes to be made for those who dared to flout the law.

During the winter, Sam Bronfman ran bootleg whisky on sleds across frozen Lake Erie from Canada into Detroit, where the illegal liquor industry was second only to the motor trade and, by the mid-1920s, was worth an estimated $215 million a year. Bronfman later became head of Seagrams, the world's largest distiller. Rum-runners like Captain Bill McCoy cruised up and down the Atlantic seaboard, playing at pirates as they smuggled Caribbean rum – 'the real McCoy' – into the United States. They were largely controlled by a syndicate headed by Arnold Rothstein, the man said to have fixed the 1919 baseball World Series and the model for Jay Gatsby's shady friend Meyer Wolfsheim, the bootlegger who wore cuff-links made of human molars.

It was still legal for doctors to prescribe liquor for medical problems, jokingly known as thirstitis. Beer was not considered remedial, but in 1921 drugstore owners withdrew over eight million gallons of 'medicinal' whisky from federal warehouses, about twenty times the pre-Prohibition amount.

The final option for thirsty Americans – and the one that carried the greatest risks, less because drinking it might lead to imprisonment than because it might lead to hospital – was moonshine. Throat-burning Yack Yack Bourbon, made in Capone's Chicago, blended burnt sugar and iodine; Panther whisky contained a high concentration of fusel oil, which was thought to trigger paranoia, hallucinations, sexual depravity and murderous impulses; Philadelphia's Soda Pop Moon was blended from 'rubbing alcohol', also used as a disinfectant and in gasoline; Jackass brandy caused internal bleeding. Other poisonous ingredients included soft soap, camphor, embalming fluid and bichloride of mercury, a highly corrosive form of mercury used to treat syphilis and to preserve biological specimens in museums. Most notorious of all was jake, a fluid extract of Jamaican ginger, which caused paralysis and ultimately death.

Distributing bootleg on a large scale required police co-operation as well as a highly organized mob. An investigation in Philadelphia in 1928 revealed that after eight years of Prohibition many police officers there had savings of tens of thousands of dollars, and several of them hundreds of thousands – on average annual salaries of just over $3,000. Of the measly three thousand Prohibition agents covering the country in 1930 (one of whom was Al Capone's brother, inspired by the Wild West and calling himself Richard 'Two Guns' Hart), a tenth had to be sacked for corruption.

Prohibition agents were so well known for their laxity that the most scrupulous and successful agent of the early 1920s became a celebrity. Isadore Einstein, a former postal clerk from New York's Lower East Side whose father had wanted him to be a rabbi, was a short, fat man who looked so unlike an agent that he was forced to protest in his interview that 'there might be some advantage in not looking like a detective'.

Izzy was a performer at heart. Despite his distinctive appearance he appeared unrecognized in bars as a travelling salesman, a judge, a cattle-rancher; perhaps carrying a trombone, covered in coal dust, extravagantly bearded or clad in a swimming costume at Coney Island. Einstein relished his work, utilizing to the full his linguistic gifts (as well as English he spoke German, Hungarian, Yiddish, Polish, French, Italian, Russian and a smattering of Chinese) in a multitude of farcical disguises. He even went to Harlem disguised as a black man, complete with authentic dialect, and once tossed his badge on to the bar of a saloon in New York's Bowery district, demanding (and receiving) a drink for 'a deserving Prohibition agent'. After he had received his drink Izzy would arrest the barman, carefully pouring the alcohol into a special jar hidden in his pocket to produce as evidence in court. As well as being a committed Prohibition agent, Einstein, like Capone, had a talent for self-promotion. Press photographers were often primed to await his duped victims outside the scenes of their arrests.

Along with his straight-man partner, Moe Smith, Einstein smashed hundreds of home-stills, raided 3,000 bars, arrested over 4,300 people and confiscated five million bottles of bootleg liquor. Despite their staggering 95 per cent conviction rate, Einstein and Smith were sacked in 1925, with no explanation given. The most likely reason is that their fame was making it harder for them to escape attention on patrol – they were just as liable to be asked for their autographs as to make an arrest – but they also attracted the resentment of their fellow agents. If they were honest, agents felt that Izzy and Moe's vaudevillian antics were bringing the forces into disrepute; if crooked, that their successes were depriving them of bribe-money.

Einstein reckoned that in most cities it took just half an hour to get a drink – although in Pittsburgh it took only eleven minutes and in New Orleans a matter of seconds. He and Smith had more trouble in Chicago. When they arrived they were recognized immediately and closely followed throughout their stay. Al Capone was taking no chances.

The Capone family had landed in New York from Naples in 1894, five years before Alphonse was born, the fourth of nine children. His father Gabriel worked as a barber and his mother Teresa was a seamstress. Like most immigrants from the more deprived parts of Europe, neither Gabriel nor Teresa could speak English or read and write. The Promised Land, increasingly wary of new arrivals flooding its shores, offered less succour and opportunity than they must have hoped. On average, an Italian-born labourer in New York in 1910 earned about $10 a week – roughly a third less than his 'native-born' American counterpart. Existing home-country ties of family and community assumed even greater importance in this hostile environment.

Al Capone arrived in Chicago from Brooklyn in 1921, aged twenty-two, at the invitation of the racketeer Johnny Torrio. Already marked by vicious scars on the left side of his face, Capone was a rising talent in the underworld. He had been running errands for Torrio and his gangster associates,

Frankie Yale and Lucky Luciano, in Brooklyn since his early teens, finding in the gang mentality of New York a sense of identity and belonging that was painfully absent in the lives of most Southern and Eastern European immigrants. Capone was intelligent and ambitious, but legitimate outlets for his energies and talents did not exist: crime offered him the chance to make it big.

At the hub of a burgeoning railroad network and ideally placed to distribute timber, ice and grain around the country, Chicago in the early 1920s was a town on the make – a Capone of a city – fuelled by brutal, frontier vitality, the scent of freshly made money in the air. Shining new-built skyscrapers soared perhaps twenty storeys heavenwards, steel indicators of the city's lofty ambitions; grimy suburbs, filled with immigrants of all races and colours – Southern blacks, Russian Jews, Italians like Capone himself – sprawled out around the centre, providing the labour on which the city's wealth was built and the markets it would service.

Long before Capone's arrival, Chicago had been home to a flourishing criminal population. Racketeering, gambling and political corruption were commonplace, but vice was Chicago's particular speciality. White slaves – young girls forced into prostitution – were 'broken in', or repeatedly raped, before being sold on to brothels. From 1900 to 1911 the Everleigh Club, run by a pair of stately sisters, Ada and Minna, was the most opulent and expensive bordello in the country. The Levee was so notoriously unruly a district, populated by streetwalkers, that police officers did not dare try to enforce the law on its streets until it was closed down in 1912. Pimps and madams each had their own union-like associations (respectively the Cadets' Protective Association and the Friendly Friends) which raised slush funds with which to pay off the police force. The reign of Big Bill Thompson, the city's crooked mayor since 1915, had only reinforced these traditions.

It was appropriate, therefore, that although Al Capone's business card read 'Second-Hand Furniture Dealer' his first job in Chicago was managing the Four Deuces, Johnny Torrio's headquarters, a whorehouse, saloon and gambling den. In 1924 police seized the Four Deuces' ledgers which revealed Capone's methodical business records – detailed lists of big-spending clients and police and Prohibition agents on the payroll, transport details for smuggled alcohol, itemized income sources – and annual profits of approximately $3 million.

Two years after Capone's arrival in Chicago, Big Bill Thompson had to withdraw from the upcoming mayoral election in the wake of revelations of his corruption. He was replaced by William Dever who campaigned on a pledge of enforcing Prohibition. Torrio and Capone, who had had a good working relationship with Thompson, knew that under Dever they would have to be more circumspect about their activities. They looked to the sleepy suburb of Cicero, which had its own mayor and a police force separate from Chicago's, as their new command centre.

Cicero was one of Chicago's western suburbs, dominated by the Western Electric Company which employed a fifth of its 40,000 inhabitants in making, so the company boasted, most of the world's telephones. It was a quiet, prosperous place, its character determined by the hard-working, old-fashioned and, crucially, beer-loving Czech Bohemians who had settled there. Beer is an easy drink to produce but the most difficult to distribute unobtrusively because breweries and beer-trucks are large and conspicuous; more than any other kind of alcohol, it necessitated large-scale criminal activity.

Johnny Torrio set up Cicero's first brothel in October 1923. At about the same time the Cotton Club, run by Al's brother Ralph, was opened there; police files referred to it as a 'whoopee spot'. Ralph also managed the nearby Stockade which was a sixty-girl brothel as well as a gambling den, weapons dump and hideout. He had received permission for his estab-lishment after rousing the local police chief from his bed in the middle of the night, taking him to the town hall and kicking and beating him over the head with gun butts. Another brother, Frank, was given responsibility for dealing with Cicero's administration, promising Capone support in return for non-interference in their affairs.

It was in this atmosphere, in the autumn of 1923, that an idealistic 21-year-old journalist named Robert St John decided Cicero needed a newspaper that would stand up to the encroaching power of the Capone–Torrio organization. His weekly *Cicero Tribune*, regularly publishing exposés of criminal activity and attacking the alliance between the Capone family and the local political elite, soon had a circulation of ten thousand.

Al Capone responded quickly. He began targeting *Tribune* supporters: an advertiser might find the taxman on his doorstep, requesting old accounts; his usual parking place might be replaced by a fire hydrant; pernickety health inspectors might insist on stringent improvements to his workplace. As if by magic, though, all these restrictions and demands would melt away as soon as local businessmen began subscribing to the Capone-controlled *Cicero Life* instead of the *Tribune*.

Not content with directing the town's illegal activities, Torrio and the Capones set their sights on local government, paying and sponsoring Republican candidates for the primary elections in April 1924, speaking out about their desires to improve Cicero and 'make it a real town'. St John hung on, continuing to defy mob authority while watching his bribed and threatened reporters quit and his advertisers defect to the *Cicero Life*.

On election day Democrat activists and voters were intimidated or beaten by Capone's men; ballot boxes were stolen, one election official was killed and others were kidnapped. Although Chicago had no jurisdiction in Cicero, the recently installed Mayor Dever was persuaded to send a troop of plainclothes policemen in nine unmarked sedan cars to protect the suburb. St John was watching from his office window when the procession of long black cars – identical to the ones used by gangsters – entered Cicero's boundaries. At the same moment as the line of cars stopped abruptly and the plain-clothes men spilled out of them, a neatly dressed man walked out of a house on to the street. St John recognized him as Frank Capone. Turning, Capone reached for the pistol in his rear pocket as the policemen emptied their guns into his body.

Although the inquest found that Frank had lured the police into a gun battle and forced them to shoot him in self-defence, eyewitnesses including St John – not to mention the number of bullets in Frank's body and in his own, unfired, gun – belied these claims. Devastated, Al ordered every speakeasy in town closed as a mark of respect for his elder brother. He wept openly at Frank's lavish funeral which, as the *Cicero Tribune* sardonically observed, would have made a 'distinguished statesman' proud.

Gangster funerals were spectacles of power, sentimentality and hypocrisy. Mourners displayed ardent piety, all the more deeply felt in the knowledge that their own lives were very far from virtuous. At the same time they used elaborately coded rituals to establish their allegiances, their position within the criminal hierarchy and their relationship to the community at large.

In the late 1920s the Illinois Crime Survey reported, 'In great funerals, the presence of the political boss attests the sincerity and the personal character of the friendship for the deceased, and this marks him as an intimate in life and death.' Because the ties between individuals in immigrant communities were based on family and locality, distinctions between legitimate and illegitimate society were blurred. This helps explain why local grandees, businessmen and officials made a point of paying their respects to fallen gangsters. It wasn't necessarily corruption; the dead man might have had roots in a neighbouring Calabrian village or been married to a cousin. These personal links meant far more than an arbitrary legal system.

When 'Big Jim' Colosimo, head of the Italian mafia in Chicago during the 1910s, died in May 1920, five thousand mourners followed his cortège. His more than fifty pall-bearers included judges, aldermen, Congressmen and a state Senator, marching alongside the bootleggers and brothel-keepers who had been his customers and clients. The Church was more scrupulous: Colosimo was refused a Catholic funeral and buried in unconsecrated ground. The Archbishop who had turned him down specified that this was not because of the way he had made his living – but because he had divorced his wife.

Colosimo had been murdered on the orders of Johnny Torrio, his deputy and nephew by marriage. Torrio, who was said to have paid $10,000 to have Colosimo removed, paid all his funeral expenses and wept profusely for his 'brother'. Colosimo had been well known in the business for being anti-Semitic. When Torrio arrived in Chicago to work for him Colosimo had congratulated him on no longer having to work with 'dirty' Jewish hoods like Arnold Rothstein, Bugsy Seigel and Meyer Lansky – hoods who had been Torrio's friends and associates for years. The biggest wreath at his funeral was signed, 'From all the sorrowing Jew boys of New York'.

On the day of Frank's funeral, the Capone family home (one by one, his brothers and sisters and widowed mother had followed Al to Chicago) was hidden by a wall of extravagant flower arrangements, including a lyre created from orchids and lilies and a six-foot heart made of red carnations. His silver-plated, satin-lined coffin was followed by a huge crowd of mourners who, according to Italian custom, had let their beards grow until the day of the funeral. The flowers were supplied by an impish, baby-faced Irishman named Dion O'Banion. As a gangster himself, as well as an orchid connoisseur, he could be relied upon to create floral arrangements appropriate to both the rank of the mourner and the deceased.

Immigrant communities, especially those living outside the law, defined themselves against other immigrant communities. Al Capone was an exception to this rule – like all good employers he valued merit more highly than background – but in the main the Italians hated the Jews, who hated the Irish, and so on. Dion O'Banion controlled the Irish vote in Chicago's northern wards and ran a bootlegging ring from his florist shop opposite Holy Name Cathedral, where as a boy he had served at mass and sung in the choir. In theory, O'Banion worked in alliance with Torrio and Capone; in reality, he was seeking to build up his own power base at their expense.

O'Banion usually wore a lily-of-the-valley buttonhole in the suits he had custom-made with three hidden gun pockets, and his volatile personality was described by a psychiatrist as one of 'sunny brutality'. He was devoted to his wife Viola, but loathed the six swarthy Genna brothers who dominated Chicago's South Side, paying Sicilian families $15 a day to produce corn liquor in their home-stills. When O'Banion started hijacking the Gennas' moonshine deliveries to Torrio, gang warfare began to rage.

After Frank Capone's funeral, apparently throwing in the towel after months of feuding, Dion O'Banion told Torrio and Al that he was getting out of bootlegging and offered to sell them his share in a brewery. The catch was that he knew the police were planning to raid it. Capone missed the assignation, but Torrio was arrested, fined $5,000 and sentenced to nine months in prison.

Capone's organization swung into action. One morning in November 1924, as O'Banion was preparing yet another funeral arrangement, three men walked into his flower shop. O'Banion came towards them, one hand outstretched. Although his assistants later insisted that they didn't recognize the men, O'Banion must have known them for he never shook hands with strangers. In a classic mob assassination, the two outside men grabbed his arms and held him tightly. They fired two bullets into his chest, two into his larynx, preventing him from making a sound, one into his right cheek, and finally, after he fell, one into his head, at such close range that the powder scorched his skin.

Dion's killers were said to have been paid $10,000 apiece

and been given valuable diamond rings, but no witnesses to the crime came forward and no arrests were made. The police – even those who were not on the mob payroll – were content to let the gangsters feud among themselves. As the murder rate on Chicago's streets rose year by year – from 16 in 1924, to 46 in 1925, to 76 in 1926 – in total only six men were brought to trial.

No expense was spared at O'Banion's funeral, which doubled as a victory celebration for Al Capone. Although O'Banion received no religious rites and was buried in unconsecrated ground, a police escort, three bands and ten thousand mourners, Capone among them, followed his bronze-and-silver coffin to the graveyard. Twenty-six vehicles were needed to transport the flowers, which included a large bunch of roses with a card signed 'From Al'.

O'Banion's death only intensified the Beer Wars. His second-in-command continued his vendetta against the Italian gangs, the violence aggravated by both sides' use of the machine gun, or 'Chicago typewriter'. Tommy sub-machine guns, which fired eight hundred rounds a minute, had been designed for use in the Great War but did not go into production until 1921. By the mid-1920s, with their serial numbers filed off, they were available on the black market for as much as $2,000 each.

In early 1925 Johnny Torrio was shot and wounded by O'Banion's men and returned to New York with $30 million in his pocket to work with his old friends, Meyer Lansky and

Lucky Luciano. His departure left Capone in sole – but shaky – charge of Chicago's increasingly divided underworld at the age of twenty-six.

Guarding against another attack, Capone no longer went anywhere without a pair of bodyguards. In public places he always sat at the back of a room, facing the door and near a window he could escape through if the need arose. He preferred not to travel during the day, and his own car always followed one or two smaller scout cars. After one assassination attempt, suspecting his driver of involvement, Capone had him kidnapped, tortured and murdered. The man's mutilated body was found dumped in a water cistern outside the city limits as a warning to other potential traitors.

In the midst of this heightening gang warfare, the young journalist Robert St John was still buzzing around Capone like an impertinent gnat. When a new brothel opened on the out-skirts of Cicero in the spring of 1925, St John sent a journalist to investigate. Nothing was heard from him for two weeks until a registered letter arrived at the *Tribune* office announcing his resignation. The reporter didn't even return to pick up the wages he was owed.

St John took over the assignment himself with, one imag-ines, as much excitement as trepidation. Emptying his pockets of identification – for his name, as he thought, if not his face, would be well known to all Capone's men – he entered the brothel which stood on a deserted road near the race-track. Posing as a customer, he was ushered through the small bar that served as shop-front into a bullet-razed passage closed off at each end by automatic doors. 'Although the place had been open for business only about two weeks, the doors already looked like pieces of Swiss cheese and there were black stains on the floor and walls of the corridor.' From there he entered an ante-room where he paid $5 and waited his turn on a bench.

The clinical mood inside surprised St John. It was, he said, 'the antithesis of pleasure': the girls, dressed in bras and knickers, were 'blasé and businesslike... as if they were selling ninety-eight-cent sweaters in a department-store bargain basement'. When his turn came, St John went upstairs with a girl named Helen and persuaded her to allow him to interview her. After several hours, having extracted 'enough material for a modern-day *Moll Flanders*', he leapt from the window and rushed home to write his story.

When the next edition of the *Cicero Tribune* came out, carrying St John's revelations, the upright burghers of Cicero were finally impelled to protest against the rising tide of sin engulfing their town. Ministers spoke out against Capone and his men; outraged committees and delegations laid siege to City Hall. 'Everywhere they were given promises of action,' wrote St John. 'Yet the weeks went by and nothing happened.' Nothing, that is, until one morning when a professional arsonist, paid $1,000 by the Cicero Citizens' Association, burned down the rickety brothel St John had visited. Care had been taken to ensure that the building was empty when the fire was started.

The fire trail led back to St John, and Capone had no choice but to make an example of him. Murder was risky; St John's outspokenness about the Capones had made him too prominent a victim. Silence was all Capone required. A message was sent to St John: Al and Ralph Capone were angry with him. Recklessly, St John sent a message back. He was angry too, 'angry that the whole lot of them had not yet decided to get out of Cicero'.

Two days later, as St John walked to work, a black car screeched to a halt beside him and four men jumped out. As he dropped to the ground, curling up into a ball with his head buried in his arms, St John recognized Ralph Capone. Using the butt end of a gun, a blackjack and a cake of soap in a woollen sock (a useful mob weapon which, when aimed at the base of the skull, caused maximum damage without leaving a mark), Capone's men beat St John unconscious. Two policemen stood by, watching. When they had finished – leaving St John for dead – the four men got back into their car and drove away.

On the same day, St John's brother Archer, who worked for a newspaper in Berwyn, the town next to Cicero, was kidnapped, held in a remote hotel and later released into woodland. He did not publish the exposé he was planning to run on Capone's designs on Berwyn. 'BOY EDITORS BEATEN; KIDNAPPED' howled the Chicago newspapers. Both the Berwyn and the Cicero police forces issued statements that they were not going to investigate the crimes against the St John brothers.

Robert St John spent a week in hospital recovering from his beating. When he tried to pay his bill, the cashier told him that a dark-complexioned man with a husky voice, very well-dressed and with a diamond stickpin in his tie, had paid the entire amount in cash. 'He didn't give his name. Just said he was a friend of yours.'

Soon afterwards St John asked a friend in the police department to issue warrants for the arrests of Ralph Capone and the three men who had beaten him up. 'Al likes you,' said the friend, demonstrating an intimacy with Capone that surprised St John. 'He likes all newspapermen. But he likes Ralph better. So take it easy, kid!' But St John refused to back down, and eventually the friend told him to come back to his office at nine the following morning to collect the warrants.

Al Capone arrived at the police station at the same time as St John, and they were shown up to the same room. Capone thrust his hand towards St John. 'Glad to meet you,' he said. 'We'll get this over quick.' Disingenuously, Capone explained that he had given orders for St John not to be touched – 'I tell them, "Let the kid alone"' – but that his men had been drunk and 'forgot'. 'Sure I got a racket,' he told St John. 'So's everybody. Name me a guy that ain't got a racket. Most guys hurt people. I don't hurt nobody. Only them that get in my way. I give away a lot of dough. Maybe I don't support no college or build no liberries, but I give it to people that need it, direct.'

This was Al Capone's cherished sentimental side, the side that appealed, as one criminal acquaintance put it, to people's hopes as well as to their fears: buying bicycles for kids on the street; sending flowers to commemorate graduations, weddings or funerals; later, during the early years of the Depression, opening soup kitchens and distributing free milk to poor children. He began peeling bill after bill off a large roll of leaves, slang for hundred-dollar bills. 'Now look, you lost a lotta time from your office… I guess you lost your hat… You had to get your clothes fixed up… I've taken care of the hospital bill, but there was the doctor…' Furious, St John got up and left the room, slamming the door on Capone and his money.

Al Capone may not have been able to charm St John, but he could shut down his mouthpiece. Soon afterwards he bought out the other investors in the *Tribune*, leaving St John in the unhappy position of being employed – at a gallingly generous salary – by the organization he had been risking his life to condemn. With nowhere else to turn, he fled Chicago for a job in Vermont. He became a successful foreign correspondent and never returned to his home town.

With St John out of the way, Capone was able to return his attention to restoring peace to Chicago's streets – but by peace what he really meant was restoring his own authority. 'I told them [his rivals] we're making a shooting gallery out of a great business and nobody's profiting from it,' he recalled later. 'There's plenty of beer business for everybody – why kill each other over it?'

But the violence continued to escalate. In 1928 there were nearly twice as many murders in Chicago as in New York. The city's mob warfare culminated in the notorious St Valentine's Day Massacre of 1929 when in a savagely premeditated attack Capone's men (it is thought), disguised as policemen, machine-gunned down seven rivals. No witnesses could be persuaded to testify and not one of the killers – or his bosses – was brought to trial; to this day there is debate about what actually happened.

Capone, who had stepped deliberately into the spotlight by seeking public admiration and approval, was the most prominent mobster in the United States. Even though he shared responsibility for the rise in crime with other gangsters, they had not courted publicity. People associated Capone with crime, and believed that crime rates would fall if he were removed. Despite his best efforts to convince them of his integrity, Capone's customers – the public – had finally turned against him.

In 1931 he was tried for tax evasion – bizarrely, for not paying taxes on the profits of his illegal activities. Although he had taken the precaution of bribing the entire jury, on the first day of the trial he arrived in court to find that every member had been replaced; he was duly convicted. Al Capone spent the next eleven years in prison, first in Atlanta and then in Alcatraz, California. He died aged forty-eight of tertiary syphilis – the fruit of enthusiastic patronage of his own establishments – at home in Florida in 1947.

2

'The Rhythm of Life'

ONE WINTER NIGHT in 1926, halfway through his set, a terrified Fats Waller found himself being bundled into a car at gunpoint and driven off at high speed. Shortly afterwards the pianist arrived at the Hawthorne Inn in Cicero, where a private party was in full swing. Capone's men had decided to bring Fats as a twenty-seventh birthday present to their jazz-loving boss. For three days champagne flowed, showgirls cavorted and cocaine was almost certainly sniffed; when he was in prison Capone's nasal septum was found to be perforated, a sign of extensive cocaine use. When the party juddered to a halt three days later, an exhausted Waller was sent home, his pockets stuffed with thousands of dollars lavished upon him by a delighted Capone.

Saxophonist Milton 'Mezz' Mezzrow recalled that Al was grinning and good-natured in jazz clubs, always surrounded by seven or eight 'trigger men' having a noisy good time, 'but gunning the whole situation out of the corners of their eyes' and stopping anyone from leaving or entering. Capone's body-guards would pass out tips of $50 or $100 to the hat-check girls, waiters and musicians on his behalf. His favourite songs, as befitted a tough guy, were sentimental numbers.

Al Capone prided himself on making crime into an efficient business, and part of this meant leaving behind the casual racial prejudice that characterized so much of early-twentieth-century American life. Most criminal gangs were strictly segregated by race and religion, but Capone valued loyalty and motivation more highly than the colour of a man's skin. One by-product of Capone's colour-blindness was that during the twenties Chicago became the centre of America's flourishing jazz scene. All the greats of the era – Waller, Louis Armstrong, Duke Ellington, Bessie Smith, Jelly Roll Morton – played in Chicago, often in Capone's clubs with an enthusiastic Capone in the audience.

Fats Waller came to Chicago from New York – he was born and bred in Harlem – but his friend and fellow musician, Louis Armstrong, had followed an established path when in 1922 he left New Orleans, heading north up the Mississippi River. Between 1910 and 1920, 50,000 Southern blacks had emigrated to Chicago to work in the new factories there. Hundreds of thousands more left the farms of the deprived South for Detroit and New York and other northern industrial centres where their labour would help build modern America. Chicago's African-American population more than doubled during the 1920s.

Born at the turn of the century, Louis Armstrong had grown up on the streets of New Orleans, working at various odd jobs like delivering coal to the whores who stood in the draughty doorways of their 'cribs' in skimpy lingerie, beckoning clients in. In his early teens, Armstrong saved fifty cents a week to buy his first blackened horn, 'an old tarnished beat up "B" Flat cornet' that cost $5 from a pawnshop. 'From then on, I was a mess and Tootin' away,' he remembered years later.

New Orleans was a city throbbing with music, where a wealth of vibrant traditions – the mournful energy of the freed slaves' blues; the calypso rhythms of the West Indies; the syncopated beat of plantation banjo music, known as ragtime; the mysticism of Negro spirituals; the lyricism and sophistication of the Creole tradition; and the local love of marching brass bands – fused on the streets into an entirely new type of music.

Young musicians like Armstrong learned and played by ear, constantly listening to and adapting each other's playing, their lyrics reflecting the call-and-response cadences of words and phrases they heard on the street, improvising all the time. Just because they lacked the restrictions of sheet music and scales didn't mean that hard work wasn't important. Playing well was an expression of discipline and dignity as well as an exuberant overflow of natural talent and creativity. It was a complete immersion in the art: the music was inside them, rather than on a page, and they responded to it with a fluidity and instinctive inventiveness that no formal training could ever replicate.

The place where this emerging musical form thrived was

Storyville, the tenderloin district, where in 1902 alongside its two hundred brothels and eight hundred saloons were eighty-five jazz clubs. 'Lights of all colours were glittering and glaring, music was pouring into the streets from every house,' remembered the pianist Jelly Roll Morton. As a mixed-race Creole, he played in brothels in downtown Storyville, stone-built mansions in which white whores wore fine gowns and diamonds in mirror-lined rooms and might make $100 a night. Uptown, where Armstrong played, was the black area, poorer and rougher but full of life, where the girls charged fifty cents. Apart from the prostitutes and their madams, Storyville was populated by men – pimps, crooked policemen, punters and musicians.

Alcohol flowed but if someone wanted cocaine or opium, Chinatown or a lax drugstore was never more than a few blocks away. In 1914 the United States Government banned the non-medical use of cocaine and opiates, and criminalized hard-drug users, but cocaine, heroin and morphine were still relatively easily obtainable, either by prescription or from illegal importers.

Storyville brought musicians like Armstrong and Morton money, respect and autonomy that they could have earned in no other way. When the district was closed down by the police in 1917, as Jelly Roll observed, the madams could find new premises but the jazzmen were forced on to the streets. Most headed for Chicago, where by the mid-1920s there were over ten thousand nightclubs and bars playing music. New York, with its five hundred dance-halls and eight hundred cabarets, many in Harlem, was another target for aspiring black musicians.

Armstrong first left New Orleans in 1919, to play his trumpet on showboats on the Mississippi, returned home in 1921 and left again, this time for good, in 1922. In New Orleans as a boy he had run errands for bandleader Joe 'King' Oliver's wife; now Oliver gave him his first place on a Chicago stage. The quality of the music staggered Armstrong, who had believed New Orleans was the capital of jazz: the musicians around him in Chicago were so inspiring, 'I was scared to go eat because I might miss one of those good notes'. Success came quickly. In 1923 and 1924 Armstrong spent some time in New York, playing in Fletcher Henderson's Orchestra and making his recording debut.

Bessie Smith, 'the Empress of the Blues', also made her first record in 1923. 'Downhearted Blues' sold 780,000 copies in six months. 'She looked like anything but a singer… tall and fat and scared to death,' said Frank Walker, who supervised her first session at Columbia Records. But as soon as he heard her hypnotic voice, utterly original and self-assured, his doubts about her appearance vanished. 'I had never heard anything like the torture and torment she put into the music of her people. It was the blues, and she meant it.'

Smith came from Chattanooga, Tennessee, and at seventeen had begun touring with Fats Chapelle's Rabbit Foot Minstrels, where the great blues singer Ma Rainey took her under her wing. Together they barnstormed through the gin mills, brothels and honky-tonks of the Deep South. By the time she was twenty-four, Bessie had earned her first solo spot in a revue called Liberty Belles.

Her star quality was unmistakable. 'She was the blues from the time she got up in the morning until she went to bed at night.' But it was typical of Smith that she didn't think of her songs or performances as an art form: they were just something she did. When the poet Langston Hughes, meeting Bessie after a show in Baltimore in the mid-1920s, asked her about the artistry of her music, she replied that all she knew was that the blues had put her 'in de money'.

Bessie 'was tall and brown-skinned, with great big dimples creasing her cheeks, dripping good looks – just this side of voluptuous, buxom and massive but stately too, shapely as an hour-glass, with a high-voltage magnet for a personality. When she was in a room her vitality flowed out like a cloud and stuffed the air till the walls bulged', remembered Mezz Mezzrow, who met her in Chicago. 'She *lived* every story she sang; she was just telling you how it happened to her.'

All through the twenties, Bessie was a wanderer, touring with her band, the Harlem Frolics, in her own seventy-eight-foot, two-storey Pullman railroad car. It was like a travelling family circus, with Bessie's brother Clarence and niece Ruby performing alongside her, and her husband Jack Gee sulkily handling their affairs, though Bessie never trusted him to be her manager. Everyone slept in the carriage, which also carried their marquee, sets and instruments and had its own bathroom, complete with flush toilet. In the kitchen-car Southern food like fried pigs' feet and stews were washed down with homemade corn liquor – the type of soul food Smith sang about in 'Gimme a Pigfoot and a Bottle of Beer'.

Themes of travel and transience, of rootlessness and alienation, have been part of musical cultures throughout history and across the world, but for blues and jazz in particular, formed by the experiences of the slave trade, of slavery itself and the Underground Railroad north, they express a profound sense of being uprooted and transplanted, of longing for a home that no longer exists and may never be reached again. Langston Hughes echoed them in 'Blues Fantasy':

> Got a railroad ticket,
> Pack my trunk and ride.
> And when I get on the train
> I'll cast my blues aside.

Another blues refrain is unhappiness in love. Bessie Smith's songs of lust, longing and betrayal were powerful because they were real. In the writer Carl Van Vechten's words, when she sang it was like watching 'a woman cutting her heart open with a knife until it was exposed for us all to see, so that we suffered as she suffered'.

Handsome Jack Gee was jealous of his wife's success and hated her family, but he loved spending Bessie's money. In

1924, when Smith was the best-known and highest-paid black star in the world, earning perhaps $1,500 a week, they were still together but Jack was frustrated by his lack of control over his wife. No matter how often he beat her up Bessie still sought her pleasures where she pleased, slept around, drank voraciously and sometimes disappeared for days at a time.

Bessie's sexual appetite was notorious. Her usual seduction technique was to lavish a member of her team – a handsome young dancer in her chorus, a piano player, her musical director, even a chorus girl – with expensive gifts. Bessie's niece Ruby said, 'She always liked them younger than she was, and it didn't matter if they were men or women, as long as they could show her a good time – like I said, Bessie *loved* a good time.'

Chasing away the blues they played was something of a jazzman's speciality, on stage and off. Most musicians were heavy drinkers. Ruby said Smith never left a party 'until all the liquor was gone'. Her drinking was inseparable from her personality and her performance: 'She was good-hearted and big-hearted, and she liked to juice, and she liked to sing her blues slow,' said the jazz musician Buster Bailey.

Many others were regular pot-smokers, or addicted to cocaine or morphine. 'Tea [marijuana] puts a musician in a real masterly sphere, and that's why so many jazzmen have used it,' wrote Mezzrow. 'You hear everything at once and you hear it right. When you get that feeling of power and sureness, you're in a solid groove.'

The one addiction they all shared was jazz itself. Jelly Roll

Morton observed that although Creoles saw music as a career path, black musicians played in the African tradition – for the sheer joy of it. Something of this passion communicated itself to the audience and back from them to the band in a constantly renewing cycle of energy.

Even when Louis Armstrong was playing shifts at two clubs a night, when he left work he would stay up till morning jamming with friends. On his nights off, Mezzrow loved going to the De Luxe café on Chicago's South Side to watch Alberta Hunter singing, 'He may be your man but he comes to see me sometime'. Hunter thought people only came to see her co-star, Twinkle Davis, because of her wonderful legs, but Mezzrow liked the sly sexiness of her lyrics, a blues hallmark:

Baby, see that spider climbin' on that wall,
Baby, see that spider climbin' on that wall,
He's goin' up there for to get his ashes hauled.

Like crime for Capone, music gave these artists the chance to transform their lives. Doing what they loved brought them undreamt-of rewards: ermine coats, diamond rings, flowing champagne, big shiny cars. Still, despite the sums they earned and the respect they received from their peers, black musicians lived in an almost entirely segregated world. Their ties to the mobsters who owned the clubs in which they worked and often supplied them with the alcohol and drugs on which they depended were inescapable. When Louis Armstrong changed managers halfway through the twenties he was forced to hire bodyguards to protect himself from gang violence.

In 1959 Richard Wright wrote in an introduction to a book about the blues that while its themes may have been negative – experiences of work and transit, bad luck, race, tragic home and family lives, submerged guilt, sexual betrayal, lost love – its message was paradoxically positive. 'The most astonishing aspect of the blues is that, though replete with a sense of defeat and down-heartedness, they are not intrinsically pessimistic; their burden of woe and melancholy is dialectically redeemed through sheer force of sensuality, into an almost exultant affirmation of life, of love, of sex, of movement, of hope. No matter how repressive was the American environment, the Negro never lost faith in or doubted his deeply endemic capacity to live.' Blues and jazz reminded people – especially black people – of their instinct to survive.

Musicians were not the only African-Americans who felt optimistic in the 1920s. Moving to the cities, learning to read and write, buoyed up by having participated in the war effort, becoming conscious of the injustices of racism – all these things stimulated a new sense of self-respect and a determination to create an America in which black men and women could live as equals alongside whites. Activists, historians, philosophers and writers began to believe, in the words of Alain Locke, the first black Rhodes Scholar, that a coming of age beckoned. 'By shedding the old chrysalis of the Negro problem we are achieving something like a spiritual emancipation,' he wrote.

The two great figures of the early civil rights movement were the dapper Harvard scholar W. E. B. Du Bois, one of the founders of the National Association for the Advancement of Colored People (NAACP) and editor of its magazine, *Crisis*, and Marcus Garvey, a bombastic Jamaican immigrant whose United Negro Improvement Association (UNIA) fought to instil 'black pride' in its millions of members.

The middle-class, mixed-race Du Bois was an intellectual, a novelist and a poet as well as a civil rights activist. At the start of his career, he had called for greater tolerance and understanding between the races and worked extensively with whites, believing that their change of attitude was just as important as a shift in black outlook. He hoped that education would be the key to racial equality. 'By every civilized and peaceful method we must strive for the rights which the world accords to men,' he urged, encouraging victims of discrimination to fight prejudice in the law courts instead of on the streets. His aim was an integrated America in which race no longer mattered. But, bitterly disillusioned by the racial hatred he had observed towards black soldiers fighting for America during the Great War, throughout the 1920s Du Bois became increasingly alienated from white America.

Garvey, by contrast, was a separatist from the start. Self-doubt, he said, 'was the cause of the Negro's impotence' and the most debilitating legacy of slavery. He taught black people that their dark skin was not a mark of their inferiority, but 'a glorious symbol of national greatness'. The nation he was referring to, though, was not the United States but Africa. Although Garvey never actually went to Africa, the dream of founding a Negro homeland there was his guiding motivation.

In August 1920, Garvey's UNIA gathered in Harlem for its first international convention. Delegates, including fabulously dressed African tribal chiefs, came from twenty-five countries. On 2 August the UNIA processed through Harlem to the music of brass bands. Black Cross nurses in their starched uniforms marched proudly alongside African Legion soldiers in immaculate navy-blue trousers, swords hanging at their sides. That night, Garvey addressed 25,000 people at Madison Square Garden. 'We do not desire what has belonged to others, though others have always sought to deprive us of that which belonged to us,' he said. 'If Europe is for the Europeans, then Africa shall be for the black peoples of the world.'

This was Garvey's zenith. Despite the passion and sincerity of his message and his inspirational qualities as a visionary and propagandist, Garvey's own ambitions undid him. Having declared himself leader of an as-yet-unformed African nation in 1922, complete with his own personal bodyguard and an aristocracy made up of his followers, the following year he was convicted of fraud and imprisoned. He served his time in an Atlanta prison, was deported back to Jamaica in 1927, and died in London in 1940.

But Garvey's failure to achieve his goals could not diminish the hope his message had engendered in millions of black Americans. This new sense of possibility was fuelled by the flowering of Harlem. The townhouses and apartment blocks of north Manhattan had been built during successive late-nineteenth-century construction booms for a well-off white population which never arrived. From 1904 a black business-man, Philip Payton, began bringing black tenants into this unfashionable neighbourhood.

For its new inhabitants, Harlem represented opportunity – a freedom from old fears and restraints. Anything suddenly seemed possible in a place where black people could live and prosper according to their own rules. As James Weldon Johnson, the historian of what became known as the Harlem Renaissance, said, Harlem was 'a city within a city, the greatest Negro city in the world'. Harlem was a place where black tenants paid rent to black landlords, where black workers were paid not by white masters but by their own bosses, where the goods sold in shops were for black customers, not white ones. Here, black people could flourish by providing services that they needed. Mrs Mary Dean, known as Pigfoot Mary, grew rich from the profits of her fried chicken and pigfoot stand on the corner of Lenox Avenue and 135th Street.

C. J. Walker, whose parents had been slaves, became (according to the *Guinness Book of World Records*) the first female millionaire, black or white, making beauty products aimed at the black market. Her most successful treatments were straighteners and growth stimulants for kinky hair, but she emphatically refused to sell skin-whitening creams. As powerfully as did any of Marcus Garvey's speeches, she taught people to take pride in their blackness. Madame Walker's tall, big-hearted daughter and heiress, A'Lelia, was 'the joy-goddess of Harlem's 1920s'. Wearing a silver turban that showed off her gleaming dark skin, she threw Harlem's best parties in her extravagantly decorated brownstone townhouse.

Writers and artists met in the novelist Jesse Fauset's more modest apartment. Drink flowed more temperately there and the conversation, guided by the plump and gracious Fauset, was of a higher tone than at Miss Walker's — and sometimes conducted in French. Here met the older intellectuals who believed, like Du Bois, Locke and the historian James Weldon Johnson, that high culture would act as a 'bridge across the chasm between the races'. Regardless of their background, they reasoned, artists were less likely to be enchained by prejudice, fear and superstition than ordinary people. This meant that a shared cultural ground might be the starting point for the broader tolerance and emancipation they dreamed of.

And as Locke observed, the very suffering endured through the centuries by black men and women torn from their homeland and living in slavery had given the black artist a unique tragic vision. 'Out of the depths of his group and personal experience, [the Negro artist] has to his hand almost the conditions of a classical art'. Ironically, though, white writers like Eugene O'Neill and Sherwood Anderson were better able to use this motif of the black man as the representative of universal suffering than black writers who were determined not to portrary themselves as victims.

Instead these artists sought out a distinctive 'Negro' culture of which they could be proud — freeing themselves from the tyranny of white, Western ideals of beauty, morality and truth by searching out their own heritage in African art, folk traditions and tribal lore and building a distinguishing racial identity. As one historian of the Harlem Renaissance writes, 'Without distinct Negro character, there could be no Negro genius'. Denying the differences between the races meant denying the past, thought many; it was better to seek out differences and celebrate them.

Music was one area where black artists effortlessly outshone their white counterparts on their own terms. Negro spirituals were recognized as containing not just the self-pity of a craven people, but glimpses of salvation and eternity. Du Bois, who studied them extensively, ascribed to them a mystical force which bound black people together emotionally. Spirituals were, he said, a powerful expression of their collective experiences.

Jazz, blues and popular dance music were another irresistible expression of black pride. Although white musicians tried to imitate black musicians they could not capture their elusive spirit. They 'studied us so hard that you'd think they were in class', said Alberta Hunter. 'And what could *we* do? Only thing we could do was to do those numbers even better — which we did.'

Harlem's first hit of the Jazz Age was 1921's exhilarating revue *Shuffle Along*, which starred Florence Mills and featured a then-unknown Josephine Baker in its chorus, and attracted sell-out audiences of spellbound whites. 'Talk about pep!' wrote one – evidently white – reviewer. 'These people make pep seem something different to the tame thing we known further downtown.' Despite its success with whites, what marked out *Shuffle Along* was that it was written, produced and performed, in Harlem, by black people: for the first time they were creating their own image, rather than reflecting a white view of them.

But the frivolity and indeed the very popularity of shows like *Shuffle Along* made some black intellectuals dismiss the new music as irrelevant to their cause. When the poet Claude McKay reviewed *Shuffle Along* for *The Liberator* magazine he made a point of praising its all-black production because some black radicals 'were always hard on Negro comedy... hating to see themselves as a clowning race'. At best they viewed it as folk art, at worst as something whose sensuality and exuberance demeaned blacks and trapped them in unwelcome stereotypes. High art and literature would unite the races and prove that all were equal, not energetic dances with silly names or mournful songs about lost love.

But a few pioneers did recognize the importance of jazz. 'Originally the nobody's child of the levée and the city slum,' wrote J. A. Rogers in Alain Locke's 1925 anthology, *The New Negro*, jazz was becoming, alongside the dollar and the movie, a symbol of 'modern Americanism', and the only difficulty lay in determining whether it was 'more characteristic of the Negro or of contemporary America' as a whole.

If spirituals and the blues represented the tragedy of black culture, argued Rogers, then jazz was its comedy. 'The true spirit of jazz is a joyous revolt from convention, custom, authority, boredom, even sorrow – from everything that would confine the soul of man and hinder its riding free on the air... It is the revolt of the emotions against repression.'

Rogers recognized the uniquely urban, modern quality of jazz. 'With its cowbells, auto horns, calliopes, rattles, dinner gongs, kitchen utensils, cymbals, screams, crashes, clankings and monotonous rhythm it bears all the marks of a nerve-strung, strident, mechanized civilization. It is a thing of the jungles – modern man-made jungles.'

He emphasized jazz's musical importance, quoting Serge Koussevitsky, the director of the Boston Symphony Orchestra, who described jazz as 'not superficial, [but] fundamental'. Composers Darius Milhaud, Eric Satie and Georges Auric were jazz fans. The conductor Leopold Stokowski summed up its appeal: 'Jazz has come to stay because it is an expression of the times, of the breathless, energetic, superactive times in which we are living, it is useless to fight against it... [Negro musicians] are pathfinders into new realms.'

While Rogers acknowledged that jazz clubs attracted low-life – drinkers, gamblers and prostitutes – on balance he considered that 'those who dance and sing are better off even in their vices than those who do not'. More importantly, jazz served a vital function as a social leveller. It made people more natural with each other, less artificial, and gave hope to those who believed that old restrictions upon society might one day fade away entirely. 'This new spirit of joy and spontaneity may itself play the role of reformer.'

Johnson also took pride in the fact that the black contribution to American cultural and artistic life, in music, dance, the theatre, in literature, had helped 'shape and mold and make America... It is, perhaps, a startling thought that America would not be precisely the America that it is today except for the powerful, if silent, influence the Negro has exerted upon it − both positively and negatively.'

Black artists, he wrote, were 'bringing something fresh and vital into American art, something from the store of their own racial genius: warmth, color, movement, rhythm, and abandon; depth and swiftness of emotion and the beauty of sensuousness'. Johnson acknowledged that some white Americans saw black Americans as a burden. On the contrary, he argued, black people had much to contribute to society as a whole. Johnson believed that the black man 'is an active and important force in American life; that he is a creator as well as a creature; that he has given as well as received; that he is the potential giver of larger and richer contributions.'

The greatest poet of black America in the 1920s was Langston Hughes, although he would have hated to have been described as a 'black' artist: he wanted recognition for his talent, not his skin colour. Hughes rejected the idealized image of Africa as a salve for his dissatisfaction with his place in the world. 'I did not feel the rhythms of the primitive surging through me,' he wrote. 'I was only an American Negro – who had loved the surface of Africa and the rhythms of Africa – but I was not Africa. I was Chicago and Kansas City and Broadway and Harlem.'

Instead he found in the cadences of jazz and slang a vocabulary that reflected his American heritage, rather than harking back to a lost Africanness or trying to imitate the western canon. Hughes's first volume of poetry, published in 1926, was called *The Weary Blues* and was inspired by the themes of the music he loved and the Harlem streets where he heard it played. As he wrote in 'Lenox Avenue: Midnight':

> The rhythm of life
> Is a jazz rhythm,
> Honey.

Hughes identified less with Western poets than with black jazzmen, whom he saw as wandering troubadours like himself. He understood that it was their music, as much as his poetry, that would transform American society.

'Let the blare of Negro jazz bands and the bellowing voice of Bessie Smith singing Blues penetrate the closed ears of the colored near-intellectuals until they listen and perhaps understand,' he wrote. 'Let Paul Robeson singing "Water Boy" and

Rudolph Fisher writing about the streets of Harlem, and Jean Toomer holding the heart of Georgia in his hands, and Aaron Douglas drawing strange black fantasies cause the smug Negro middle class to turn from their white, respectable, ordinary books and papers to catch a glimmer of their own beauty. We younger Negro artists who create now intend to express our individual dark-skinned selves without fear or shame. If white people are pleased we are glad. If they are not, it doesn't matter. We know we are beautiful. And ugly too. The tom-tom cries and the tom-tom laughs. If colored people are pleased we are glad. If they are not, their displeasure doesn't matter either. We build our temples for tomorrow, strong as we know how, and we stand on top of the mountain, free within ourselves.'

Black pride and growing demands for equality and respect were threatening to many whites who preferred America's black population to be cowed and submissive. The arch-conservative senator Henry Cabot Lodge had Claude McKay's defiant poem, 'If we must die, let it not be like hogs' read out to the Congressional Record as evidence of the unsettling new spirit rising up among American blacks.

Pseudo-scientific works like Lothrop Stoddard's *The Rising Tide of Color* of 1920 warned that America was being swamped by 'colored' races. It was Stoddard whom Tom Buchanan, in *The Great Gatsby*, misremembered as 'this fellow Goddard': 'The idea is if we don't look out the white race will be – will be utterly submerged. It's all scientific stuff; it's been proved.'

Stoddard quoted the scholarly Du Bois as an example of the threat posed to whites by blacks. 'These nations and races, composing as they do a vast majority of humanity, are going to endure this treatment just as long as they must and not a moment longer. Then they are going to fight, and the War of the Color Line will outdo in savage inhumanity any war this world has yet seen. For colored folk have much to remember and they will not forget.'

Madison Grant, chairman of the New York Zoological Society and a trustee of the Museum of Natural History, wrote the foreword to Stoddard's book, using spurious scientific and historical claims to back up Stoddard's racial prejudices and prophesy disaster if white men did not safeguard their position of racial dominance. Allowing the races to mingle, or even permitting 'brown, yellow, black or red men' to share in Western European democratic ideals, said Grant, would be 'suicide pure and simple, and the first victim of this amazing folly will be the white man himself'. 'Oh,' wrote Claude McKay, 'I must keep my heart inviolate / Against the potent poison of your hate!'

But despite the racism still deeply entrenched in American society, changes had started to take place. The work of anthropologists and sociologists studying foreign and 'primitive' cultures discredited eugenicist literature that sought to demonstrate the inherent inferiority of blacks and other unwanted immigrants. President Harding – for whom Duke Ellington's father worked in the White House as butler – urged educational and economic support for blacks, proposed an interracial committee to find ways to improve race relations and, in a brave speech in Birmingham, Alabama, in October 1921, was the first President to call for an end to lynching.

Harding supported a bill that would have made lynching illegal by federal rather than state law, although this move was rejected in 1922 by a block of Southern senators. But gradually the South grew ashamed of its violence and, while eighty-three people were lynched in 1919, by 1928 that number had fallen to eleven. Harding's efforts on behalf of blacks were especially poignant because rumours of his having unacknowledged black ancestors had threatened his presidential chances during his campaign of 1920.

And yet, even while one section of the nation was seeking fresh ways to stamp down what they saw as the threat represented by a newly confident black population, another group found itself strongly drawn to black culture. Bohemian white Americans found themselves envying their black countrymen's spontaneity, vitality and sexual liberation. The art of Picasso and Modigliani exalted the purity and innocence of African primitivism; the theories of Freud told people that they were unhappy because they were repressed. To be black, and thus (so the theory went) less restrained by social artifice and civilization, was to be somehow more purely human, more elemental.

The easy physicality and emotional intensity of black culture both attracted white audiences and terrified them. An early account of the rise of jazz in New York began, 'One touch of jazz makes savages of us all.' Doctors warned that jazz 'intoxicates like whisky and releases stronger animal passions'. The *Ladies' Home Journal* launched an anti-jazz crusade, condemning the decadence and immorality that jazz and modern dancing (with its 'wriggling movement and sensuous stimulation') were breeding in the young.

But the young didn't care. Jazz was their music too. 'If... we give up jazz we shall be sacrificing nearly all there is of gaiety and liveliness and rhythmic power in our lives,' wrote the white critic Gilbert Seldes proprietorially. Jazz expressed his generation's 'independence, our carelessness, our frankness, our gaiety'. Well-bred, well-off New Yorkers began coming to Harlem in their thousands to hear real jazz – and taste real life. If Puritanism was what had ruined American society, then Harlem, 'a cultural enclave that had magically survived [Puritanism's] psychic fetters' was just a cab ride away.

In this sense, according to the historian Nathan Huggins, the 'creation of Harlem as a place of exotic culture was as much a service to white need as it was to black', and its black inhabitants recognized this and resented it. Claude McKay called Harlem an 'all-white picnic ground'; Langston Hughes said Harlem merely accepted 'the role forced on it – that of bookie, bootlegger and bordello to white downtown'.

'It was a period when local and visiting royalty were not at all uncommon in Harlem,' wrote Hughes. 'It was a period when Harold Jackman, a handsome young Harlem schoolteacher of modest means, calmly announced one day that he was sailing for the Riviera for a fortnight, to attend Princess Murat's yachting party. It was a period when Charleston preachers opened up shouting churches as sideshows for white tourists. It was a period when at least one charming colored chorus girl, amber enough to pass for a Latin American, was living in a penthouse, with all her bills paid by a gentleman whose name was banker's magic on Wall Street... It was the period when the Negro was in vogue.'

The most expensive and theatrical nightclubs in Harlem catered almost exclusively for white clients. Most of these speakeasies were little more than pastiches of a world still inaccessible to whites. In the real Harlem clubs like Lincoln Gardens, liquorice-tasting gin cost $2 a pint and, when King Oliver and Louis Armstrong played, the 'whole joint was rocking, tables, chairs, walls, people moved with the rhythm'. The Lincoln Gardens' clientele had no need for the professional dancers provided by the touristy clubs to guide the uninitiated through the abandoned and demanding steps of the Cakewalk, the Black Bottom or the Monkey Glide.

White visitors went instead to what Hughes called 'Jim Crow clubs' like the Plantation Club, with its interiors based on an ante-bellum Southern plantation complete with a white picket fence round the dance floor and a real 'black mammy' cooking waffles in a miniature log cabin at the end of the evening, or the Cotton Club, where revellers ate fried chicken and barbecued ribs against a backdrop of African sculpture, jungly vegetation and bongo drums. This was how Harlem sold itself to the white tourists from downtown: as a place of exotic, primitive sensuality and abandon – with reassuringly racist undertones.

Harlem's inhabitants hated the flocks of white people swarming through their streets in the evenings, staring at them as if they were 'amusing animals in a zoo. The Negroes said, "We can't go downtown and sit and stare at you in your clubs. You won't even let us in your clubs." But they didn't say it out loud – for Negroes are practically never rude to white people,' wrote Hughes. 'So thousands of whites came to Harlem night after night, thinking the Negroes loved to have them there, and firmly believing that all Harlemites left their houses at sundown to sing and dance in cabarets, because most of the whites saw nothing but the cabarets, not the houses.'

The most prominent and influential white promoter of black culture was Carl Van Vechten, a collector and connoisseur of the new and the exotic. In the early 1920s Van Vechten became friends with James Weldon Johnson, an expert on Negro spirituals, and captivated the party-loving heiress A'Lelia Walker. He championed the blues as a serious art form in *Vanity Fair*; he worked to bring talented black writers into the literary mainstream.

Langston Hughes met Van Vechten properly in 1926. In less than three weeks, Van Vechten had secured him deals with *Vanity Fair* magazine and the publisher Alfred A. Knopf, and went on to write the glowing introduction to Hughes's first volume of poems. Van Vechten 'never talks grandiloquently about democracy or Americanism. Nor makes a fetish of those qualities,' observed Hughes with gratitude. 'But he lives them with sincerity – and humour.'

Harlem became Van Vechten's passion, but Harlem was ambivalent about Van Vechten. Du Bois and his future son-in-law, the poet Countee Cullen, found him subtly patronizing while Claude McKay 'was eager to meet a white man who bothered to be subtle in his patronizing'.

Though she usually avoided the white world, as a favour to a friend, Bessie Smith agreed to attend one of Van Vechten's parties downtown. When she arrived, Van Vechten archly offered her 'a lovely dry martini'. Deliberately abrasive, Smith replied that she didn't know about dry martinis, or wet ones either – she wanted a large whisky. She downed the first drink she was given in one and immediately demanded another.

Then she sang, in the voice Van Vechten described as being 'full of shouting and moaning and praying and suffering, a wild, rough, Ethiopian voice, harsh and volcanic, but seductive and sensuous too... the powerfully magnetic personality of this elemental conjure [sic] woman with her plangent African voice, quivering with passion and pain, sounding as if it had been developed at the source of the Nile'.

Finally, drunk, Bessie took her leave. When bird-like Mrs Van Vechten tried to kiss her goodbye, she screamed, 'Get the fuck away from me!' and stalked out of the apartment, with Van Vechten's congratulations on her magnificent performance floating unnoticed and uncared-about in her wake.

Although his 1926 novel *Nigger Heaven* sought to portray blacks without prejudice or stereotype, Van Vechten was derided for arguing that blacks 'civilized' themselves at their own spiritual cost. 'We are, for the most part, pagans, natural pagans,' declared one character. But when Johnson reviewed *Nigger Heaven* in *Opportunity* magazine, he argued that his friend's understanding of black culture was authentic and valuable. 'If the book has a thesis it is: Negroes are people, they have the same emotions, the same passions, the same short-comings, the same aspirations, the same graduations of social strata as other people,' he wrote. Johnson was only too aware that this in itself would be a revelation to many white Americans.

Regardless of the merits or demerits of Van Vechten's liter-ary take on Harlem, no one who knew him denied that he sincerely respected black culture – but even with Van Vechten there was a sense that Harlem provided him with an outlet for dark desires that he could not reveal in his normal life. Van Vechten threw most of the parties for which he was celebrated at the downtown apartment he shared with his wife, but he also kept a second apartment in Harlem of which she knew nothing. Here, in black-painted rooms lit by red lights, Van Vechten surrendered himself to his fantasies, entertaining strapping young men on red velvet cushions.

Other white tourists slumming in Harlem were fascinated by the ease with which social and sexual taboos were flouted there. Drugs as well as moonshine were freely available on Harlem's streets. Certain clubs were frequented by exquisitely beautiful transvestites – 'some women wished they could look so good,' remembered Ruby Smith. Beverley Nichols, the visiting English journalist, was taken to a shabby Harlem speakeasy where no one thought it remarkable that four white boys and two black boys, all dressed as girls, all drunk, sat flirting and preening and powdering their noses at one table, while nearby a group of debutantes drank champagne and women dressed as men danced cheek-to-cheek on the smoky dance floor. This louche atmosphere was what his friend Van Vechten had enticingly described to Nichols as 'shi-shi with an undercurrent of murder'.

Ironically, although the white writer Scott Fitzgerald coined the phrase the Jazz Age, the people and places he described were only dimly related to the mysterious rhythms of Bessie Smith or the poetry of Langston Hughes. This colonization of jazz and the blues by white, collegiate, prosperous America was in some ways a betrayal of its original spirit and the new confidence of black culture, but it also represented jazz's irresistible allure to American youth of all backgrounds. Modern, liberated, open-minded, sophisticated, urban – jazz was a symbol of the changes sweeping through America during the 1920s. As Mezz Mezzrow put it, 'A creative musician is an anarchist with a horn, and you can't put any shackles on him... Freedom and jazz are synonymous.'

3

Femme Fatale

JAZZ WAS A MUSICAL REVOLUTION and the people moving to its rhythms were an entirely new breed. The girl who jumped on to a table at a Harlem nightclub and started swinging her arms wildly above her head as the charleston played was a type of woman America had never seen before. The word 'flapper' described a chick desperately flapping her wings as she tried to fly, although she had not yet grown adult feathers; it had come to mean a precocious young woman whose modern appearance, attitudes, values and behaviour utterly mystified her parents' generation.

Zelda Fitzgerald, immortalized as the heroine of the Jazz Age in story after story by her husband, epitomized the Flapper – in all her worst, as well as her best, qualities. She was the flesh-and-blood incarnation of the generic woman to whom the novelist Warner Fabian dedicated his 1923 bestseller, *Flaming Youth*: 'restless, seductive, greedy, discontented, craving sensation, unrestrained, a little morbid, more than a little selfish, intelligent, uneducated, sybaritic, following blind instincts and perverse fancies, slack of mind as she is trim of body, neurotic and vigorous, a worshipper of tinsel gods at perfumed altars, fit mate for the hurried, reckless and cynical man of the age'.

Born in 1900, Zelda was the adored youngest child of a respectable and respected judge of Montgomery, Alabama, and his artistic wife. Their golden-haired baby grew up indulged and fearless, 'without a thought for anyone else'. The fairies at her christening, said the literary critic Edmund Wilson, had squandered choice gifts on Zelda 'with a minimum of stabilizing qualities'.

When the aspiring writer Scott Fitzgerald arrived at an army training camp in Montgomery, eighteen-year-old Zelda was the most sought-after beauty in the state, as alluring and unpredictable as she was unattainable. She smoked and drank and danced too close and dived off the top board of the local swimming pool in a costume made of flesh-coloured fabric that made her look naked. 'She, she told herself,' wrote Zelda years later of her youthful self, 'would move brightly along high places and stop to trespass and admire, and if the fine was a heavy one – well, there was no good in saving up beforehand to pay it… Relentlessly she convinced herself that the only thing of any significance was to take what she wanted when she could.'

Less sure of himself than Zelda, Scott was captivated by her self-absorbedness and her absolute confidence in pursuit of what she wanted. Zelda 'took all the things of life for hers to choose from and apportion, as though she were continually picking out presents for herself from an inexhaustible counter,' he wrote. After two years of resisting Scott's proposals – she loved him, but wanted to marry a rich man – Zelda's arrival in New York to become Mrs Fitzgerald coincided with the publication of his first novel, *This Side of Paradise*, which would make both of them stars.

People often commented when they met the Fitzgeralds that they were the most beautiful couple they had ever seen. Carl Van Vechten, almost as fascinated by Zelda and Scott as he was by Harlem, made them the protagonists of his 1930 novel, *Parties*, as Rilda and David Westlake. The writer Dorothy Parker first saw them riding on a taxi, Zelda on the bonnet, Scott on the roof. She knew their behaviour was intended to shock, but she couldn't help thinking that they looked 'as if they had both stepped out of the sun'. They were a dazzling pair: Scott with his promise and grace, his ability to make everyone around him feel as if something exciting was just about to happen; Zelda, 'caresser of her own dreams', brave and tragic like a 'barbarian princess', her eyes 'full of cool secrets' – all this counterposed by the impression she gave of wearing nothing beneath her dress.

Their celebrity and the fact that their public manners and physical appearance so perfectly matched the fascinating, wanton images projected in Scott's stories made it natural for the Fitzgeralds' joint portrait to be used on the cover of his second novel, *The Beautiful and Damned*, and for them both to be offered starring roles in its movie adaptation and that of *This Side of Paradise* (which was never made). Just as the Gibson Girl had personified the 1890s, so Scott, and especially Zelda, became the living embodiment of the generation he described and defined. As their actress friend Lillian Gish said, 'They didn't make the twenties; they *were* the twenties.'

New York was outraged and delighted by them in equal measure. Sober, they jumped into the fountain in front of the Plaza Hotel; Zelda got Scott into fights in Harlem's rough Jungle Club; she danced with Scott's friends and said things like, 'My hips are going wild – you don't mind, do you?'; they were found at parties curled up like kittens, peacefully asleep in each another's arms. Soon after they were married Scott and their friend Alec McKaig 'argued with Zelda about the notoriety they are getting through being so publicly and spectacularly drunk'.

If one of the social revolutions brought about by Prohibition was the inextricable association of booze and crime, another was the introduction of women (and the young) to drinking in public. No respectable female would have entered a saloon before 1914 – the very word conjured up images of sawdust, whisky and uncouth masculine behaviour – and she would have been highly unlikely to drink anywhere else. After 1920 the culture changed: illicit drinking was seen as exciting. Speakeasies stimulated a new kind of informal socializing. The *New York Times* in 1922 said clubs were not 'considered a real success unless there is a care-free tendency among the guests to toss remarks to each other from table to table'. The most glamorous college co-eds carried silver flasks tucked into their rolled stocking-tops.

Cocktails became fashionable because bootleg liquor needed to be sweet and highly flavoured to mask its venomous ingredients; they appealed just as much to women as to men. Orange Blossoms – gin, orange juice and sugar syrup – were a Fitzgerald favourite; another was the Pink Lady, 'a disastrous concoction of bathtub gin, applejack, grenadine and egg white served in fancy, long-stemmed glasses'. By the end of the decade, a poll taken at Yale confirmed that Prohibition was almost completely ignored by America's young Establishment. Seventy-one per cent of its students (and presumably their female companions) admitted to drinking.

This was true of smoking, too. A woman could be arrested for smoking in public in the early 1900s; in 1929 the restrictions against women smoking in railway dining cars were finally lifted. Promoters of Lucky Strike cigarettes deliberately linked smoking with female emancipation, sending photographers to capture attractive young models lighting up what they called 'Torches of Liberty' at New York suffragist parades.

Unrestricted and boyish, twenties fashions were another expression of the new freedoms the Flapper was determined to enjoy. It was estimated that between 1913 and 1928 the amount of fabric used to dress a woman fell from 19 1/4 yards to 7: just a thin frock over a brassiere, a pair of knickers and silk stockings.

Before the war women were arrested for not wearing corsets; in the 1920s, girls refused to wear them, protesting, 'the men won't dance with you if you wear a corset'. Bloomers and thick, itchy black stockings were exchanged for loose silk cami-knickers, or step-ins, and translucent stockings rolled beneath the knee. For a time Zelda wore men's silk jersey underwear.

Flesh-coloured feather-light silk and newly developed artificial fabrics like rayon replaced whalebone, heavy wool and starched cotton. Chests were flat – often bound – waist-bands and heels low, skirts soared to the knee, fitted cloche hats imitated the cropped hair they covered. Bangles and long strings of beads clattered wildly on the dance-floor.

The most daring accessory was a tiny gold spoon or box containing cocaine worn dangling from a thin necklace. In Noel Coward's 1924 play, *The Vortex*, references are made to the dissolute Nicky's 'small gold box'. Caresse Crosby, part of the fast set in Paris, voiced the prevailing view of different drugs: cocaine 'sniffers' were 'dirty and unkempt, sly and evasive. It gets into one's clothes, under one's nails, down one's back.' Caresse believed that opium was 'not habit forming' and was therefore harmless and that hashish, as tried by her and her husband Harry in North Africa, was 'wicked'.

Smoking was promoted as a healthful slimming aid, and advertisements showing female smokers featured in women's magazines for the first time in 1927. Constance Talmadge, the actress Scott Fitzgerald called the 'flapper de luxe', appeared in Lucky Strike ads urging women to 'Reach for a Lucky instead of a sweet' to keep their figures fashionably slender. The campaign was so successful that sales increased by 300 per cent in its first year.

Youthful, androgynous figures were achieved by strict dieting and exercise as well as by drugs and nicotine. Girls struggled to become what one doctor called 'pathologically thin', starving themselves on diets of orange juice, tomatoes and spinach, newly available throughout the country year-round thanks to improvements in refrigeration and food transportation. The waif-like Lillian Gish knew she had to 'keep fit for my pictures' and described her regime as 'very Spartan'. She swam in the sea every morning, 'went once or twice a week to exercise classes, and I watched carefully what I ate and drank'. Zelda Fitzgerald was equally body-conscious, probably at times to the point of anorexia. Alabama Beggs, her fictional self-portrait, 'was gladly, savagely proud of... [her jutting hip bones], convex as boats in a wood carving. The complete control of her body freed her from all fetid consciousness of it.'

Pregnancy was an unflattering indignity. 'I value my body because you think it's beautiful,' said the heroine of *The Beautiful and Damned* when she found out she was having a baby. 'And this body of mine – of yours – to have it grow ugly and shapeless? It's simply intolerable.' Birth control – and illegal abortions, which killed 50,000 women a year and left many more barren; Zelda is thought to have had one – helped to keep the Flapper unencumbered.

The activist Margaret Sanger introduced American women to the diaphragm from 1916 onwards, illegally importing them from Germany and Holland until she helped fund the first US manufacturer in 1925. After 1919, sales of vastly improved latex condoms, thinner and seamless unlike those previously made from rubber cement, soared throughout the decade. Because the 1873 Comstock Act banned the sale and advertising of contraceptive devices as well as pornographic material, these products still had to be procured behind a veil of euphemism. Women bought ambiguous items labelled 'feminine hygiene'; men asked their doctors to prescribe condoms for their health.

This growing awareness of contraceptive methods freed women in a multitude of ways. In the first place, it allowed the very daring to experiment with sex before marriage without fear of an unwanted pregnancy. One of Scott's principal insecurities about Zelda was that she had made love to other men before she married him. The flip side of this was that marriage was no longer seen as the price men paid for sex, and that women, as well as men, began to view sexual desire as an essential element of a fulfilled relationship.

Within marriage, contraception meant women had fewer children, and having fewer children transformed a woman's role from that of primarily mother, to that of primarily wife – or even allowed her to feel like an individual in her own right. Women with one or two children, as opposed to five or six, could have lives of their own, perhaps even jobs; their family's standard of living tended to be higher; they could indulge their own needs – for an independent social life, to remain youthful and attractive – as well as those of their children and husband.

Smaller families also helped change how parents brought up their children. Ideas derived from the new science of psychology – especially those of Sigmund Freud and John Watson, whose 1913 article on what he called 'Behaviourism' was hugely influential in the 1920s – prompted parents to be more demonstrative and permissive with their offspring. Children were given more attention and affection and were encouraged to express their personalities. Increasingly, independence was valued more highly than obedience. But children, when they came, were no less a hindrance than pregnancy to the true Flapper. In Paris in 1924, when their three-year-old daughter Scottie wouldn't sleep, Zelda fed her a mixture of gin and sugar-water so that she and Scott could leave her at the hotel while they went to a party.

Dyed hair and make-up, like smoking and drinking, no longer marked out the fallen woman – or perhaps women no longer cared about flaunting their descent from respectability. Being deliberately provocative was the height of chic. Scott described Zelda as Gloria, heroine of *The Beautiful and Damned*, earnestly explaining that she had worn a fur-trimmed grey suit on her first date with Anthony Patch, 'because with grey you *have* to wear a lot of paint'.

When cosmetics began to be seen as an 'affordable indulgence', beauty became a multimillion-dollar industry. In 1920 there were only 750 beauty salons in New York; that number had risen to 3,000 in 1925, and by 1930 there were 40,000 nationwide. Madame C. J. Walker had made a fortune with her hair 'de-kinker' in Harlem; downtown, Elizabeth Arden and Helena Rubinstein were launching flourishing business empires capitalizing on the Flapper's obsession with her looks. Far from liberating women, bobbed and bleached hair necessitated frequent visits to the coiffeur; nail varnish was considered delightfully daring; lipstick, rouge and powder had become everyday essentials.

A powder compact hidden in a shoe-buckle was aimed at the modern party girl, dancing too uninhibitedly to carry a handbag. Movie stars and society beauties appeared in aspirational advertisements promoting face creams, soap and make-up. The message was that women were constantly on display — and it was their responsibility to make the best of themselves by using the best products they could afford. The beauty industry had invested $1.5 million a year in advertising in 1915; by 1930, it was spending over ten times that amount.

Successful advertising campaigns of the twenties capitalized on popular worries about fat, body odour, constipation and bad breath as well as the desire to be beautiful, using new techniques based on psychology. The idea of consumer sovereignty had been vanquished by research that established that human beings were motivated less by reason than by instinctive drives — vanity, fear, sex, the desires to conform and impress. Increasingly buyers were seen by advertisers as a manipulable mass: admen had realized that selling was no longer about need, but about choice. A 1917 article in *Harper's* declared that the advertisers' object was to 'make each reader dissatisfied with himself, until he follows your suggestion'.

'I'm going to make a list of all the things I've got to get,' cries Myrtle Wilson, Tom Buchanan's overblown mistress, in *The Great Gatsby*. 'A massage and a wave, and a collar for the dog, and one of those cute little ash-trays where you touch a spring, and a wreath with a black silk bow that'll last all summer for mother's grave. I got to write down a list so I won't forget all the things I got to do.'

Recklessness, frivolity and self-indulgence were the Flapper's watchwords. 'I can't be bothered resisting things I want,' declared Zelda, as Gloria Patch. Adoring being the centre of attention, she thought nothing of seizing the limelight by tossing her knickers into somebody's lap at dinner or stripping off at a party. She boasted of being unfit for anything but 'useless pleasure-giving pursuits'. The scriptwriter Anita Loos, bored by her antics, commented tartly that although her face was extraordinary 'she really should have kept her bosom under wraps'.

Flaunting herself, as Loos said, because she thought she was 'delectable', was intended as invitation. Zelda drove Scott mad, especially at the start of their marriage, by making passes at his friends (none known to have been successful), kissing them, bursting into their bathrooms and demanding to be given a bath, all the while telling Scott that sleeping with other men wouldn't affect her feelings for him. Fidelity was just a sign of puritanical repression.

Flappers and their college-boy consorts were the first generation to be on easy terms with the ideas of Sigmund Freud. The psychiatrist had delivered a series of lectures outlining his theories at Clark University in Massachusetts in 1909 and they were published in the United States the following year. A decade later words like repression, taboo and the unconscious rolled casually off co-eds' lips. All over the country, commented the writer Malcolm Cowley, young women 'were reading Freud and attempting to lose their inhibitions'.

It was typical of the younger generation's impulsiveness, though, that their understanding of Freud's work was largely superficial. As the commentator Frederick Allen remembered, Freudianism was simply taken to mean, 'If you want to be well and happy, you must obey your libido.' Psychology seemed to provide a scientific reason why social convention and personal inhibition ought to be challenged and why self-gratification was the ultimate human endeavour.

Social anthropology, another rapidly developing discipline, provided a further incentive to rebel against the constraints of 'civilized' society. In 1925 the young anthropologist Margaret Mead spent several months studying teenage girls in Samoa whom she found to be sexually experimental and unrestrained by Western morals and inhibitions (her research has since been partially discredited). She believed that concepts of celibacy, monogamy and fidelity were 'meaningless' to Samoans and had been largely created by modern society.

The conclusion of Mead's best-selling book of 1928, *Coming of Age in Samoa*, was that man is shaped more by society than by biology. Implicit in her work was a critique of the repressive tendencies of American society – against which Mead herself would struggle in order to live out the sexually liberated life she desired. Contemporaries interpreted her book to mean that the troubles American teenagers endured on their path to adulthood were related to the inhibitions society inflicted upon them. Freeing oneself from civilization's constraints was thus the route to happiness. The Flapper, with her devil-may-care attitude, epitomized this defiance of convention and consequence.

Literature reinforced science's arguments. In 1920, the poet Edna St Vincent Millay famously summed up her appetite for life and adventure in 'A Few Figs from Thistles':

> My candle burns at both ends;
> It will not last the night;
> But ah, my foes, and oh, my friends –
> It gives a lovely light.

Millay's hedonistic philosophy was an imperative for the young in the twenties: living in the present, as intensely as possible, was all that mattered.

Like Millay and Fitzgerald, the heroines of best-selling

twenties novels were untamed and unsentimental. Yvonne, the flame-haired beauty in Kay Brush's *Glitter*, says that if she were a man she would be a racing-driver and announces her intention of living – and dying – 'sensationally'. In *The Sheik* by Edith Hull, spoiled Diana Mayo declares with some pride that she hasn't a heart. Their code was Zelda's: 'Not to be sorry, not to loose one cry of regret, to live according to a clear code of honour toward each other, and to seek the moment's happiness as fervently and persistently as possible.'

Partly because of Scott's portrayals of Zelda as the 1920s ideal, being called fast became almost a compliment, rather than a slur on a girl's character. Journalists wrote in shocked tones about the prevalence of 'petting parties'. It was well-known that cars provided unchaperoned young couples with a boudoir on wheels. Magazines featured 'sex adventure stories' called 'Indolent Kisses' or 'Watch Your Step-Ins'; movies advertised 'things you've always wanted to do and never DARED'.

Although the Flapper was the product primarily of a youth movement, middle-aged women were also attracted by the lure of abandoned pleasure-seeking. Evalyn McLean, a generation older than Zelda, described the new morals to her friend Florence Harding, the First Lady, from a holiday in Florida in 1923. One was nobody there without a beau, she said: 'You must never be seen with your husband, and never go to bed until morning!' According to Malcolm Cowley, the bohemian spirit of Greenwich Village had died by the late 1920s 'because women smoked cigarettes on the streets of the Bronx, drank gin cocktails in Omaha and had perfectly swell parties in Seattle and Middletown'* – in other words, because every woman in America had become a Flapper.

It was not so easy for the prototype. The Fitzgeralds' friends had long predicted that disaster would be the result of their excessive lifestyle. Soon after they were married Alec McKaig lamented Zelda's desire 'to live the life of an "extravagant". No thought of what the world will think or of the future. I told them they were headed for catastrophe if they kept up at present rate.' Even Fitzgerald recognized that increasingly their hedonism was just 'despair turned inside out'.

As the years wore on, Zelda found her life with Scott frustrating and meaningless, despite the glamour she had longed for as a girl. While other women of her generation had taken real advantage of the new freedoms available to them, she felt she had never been able to create an identity for herself as anything other than Scott's wife – the outrageous and desirable Flapper incarnate. By her late twenties she was desperate to use her talents, to have something of her own, not to be merely what she called a 'complementary intelligence'. She 'felt excluded by her lack of accomplishment... she felt she had nothing to give to the world and no way to dispose of what she took away'.

---

* An average, medium-sized, middle-American town (later revealed to be Muncie, Indiana) studied by the sociologists Robert and Helen Lynd in the mid-1920s. Their findings were published in 1928 in *Middletown: A Study in Modern American Culture*.

Lacking the career which both advertised Scott's worth and provided his retreat from the world, in her late twenties Zelda rejected their past intemperance and took up ballet, her childhood ambition. She became consumed by the dream of becoming a professional dancer even though, aged twenty-seven when she began, her chances of success were virtually non-existent. But she refused to be persuaded, practising up to eight agonizing hours a day for over two years, relishing discipline for the first time in her life, pushing herself harder and harder to achieve the impossible.

Zelda's furious obsession with ballet was not just a desire for order, it was also a futile attempt to stop time. She and Scott had always held that youth and beauty were the altars on which any considerations of the future must be sacrificed. Fear of losing the looks and attitude which had set her apart haunted Zelda. Like Nicky in Noel Coward's *The Vortex*, she was straining 'every nerve to keep young'.

More and more in the late 1920s there was the sense with Zelda that something wasn't right. The novelist John Dos Passos said that looking into her eyes during this period was 'like peering into a dark abyss'. In the spring of 1930 Zelda had her first breakdown and that summer was institutionalized and later diagnosed with schizophrenia.

In 1932, during a six-week period of feverish lucidity, Zelda wrote *Save Me the Waltz*, a barely-fictionalized account of her relationship with Scott, her brief affair with another man and her failing struggle against mental illness set against their shared backdrop of literary life in New York and as prosperous Americans in Europe. Hardly coincidentally, much of it was similar to *Tender Is the Night*, the novel Scott was working on at the same time. Knowing this, Zelda deliberately provoked Scott's fury by sending her manuscript to his editor without showing it to him first. This was her account of the shared experiences that had made them both rich, famous, envied and unhappy – her defence against being made into just another flawed character in one of her husband's books – and she was determined to tell it to the world.

During their life together Zelda had provided Scott with inspiration and living material for his female characters – he had lifted long passages straight from her diary for *The Beautiful and Damned* – and written occasional articles and short stories which they had published either jointly or under Scott's name. 'I am so outrageously clever that I believe I could be a whole world to myself if I didn't like living in Daddy's better,' says Zelda's self-portrait, Alabama, to her daughter. Since Scott was the literary celebrity, it made sense to capitalize on his fame; Zelda writing alone could command a fraction of the sum a Scott Fitzgerald piece might bring in. Reading her book, it is hard not to feel that at last – and too late – Zelda had decided that her life was her own material, not her husband's.

Zelda spent her remaining years, on and off, in asylums, still fuelled by the urge to create. She had always had a striking and highly unusual visual sense, but when her schizophrenia set in it became ever more hallucinatory and intense. 'There was a new significance to everything,' she wrote in *Save Me the Waltz*. 'Stations and streets and façades of buildings – colors were infinite, part of the air, and not restricted by the lines that encompassed them and lines were free of the masses they held.' During her last years she painted these strange visions.

As a girl, Zelda had identified with the heroine of Owen Johnson's best-selling novel and movie of the 1910s, *The Salamander*, its title taken from the lizard thought in classical times to be able to pass untouched through fire: 'I am in the world to do something unusual, extraordinary. I'm not like every other little woman.' Looking back on her life, Zelda sadly acknowledged that her 'story is the fault of nobody but me. I believed I was a Salamander and it seems I am nothing but an impediment.' In 1948 a fire razed her sanatorium to the ground and she died in the blaze – no salamander, after all. She was forty-eight years old.

For most women of Zelda's generation, being a Flapper was a stage rather than a Faustian pact. Even in literature and the movies, however wildly they danced or however many cigarettes they smoked, most Flappers ended up choosing love and conventional marriages – they wanted happy endings, not tragic ones. The heroine of *The Sheik*, independent Diana Mayo, discovers that she loves the macho Bedouin who has kidnapped her and meekly submits to his will; *Glitter*'s glamorous but fallen heroine, Yvonne, forces herself to abandon her lover to ensure that he marries a 'nice' girl; the British romantic novelist Elinor Glyn's smoking, cocktail-drinking Flapper insists she's only marrying for the alimony, to cover up the shameful fact that she's in love. The defeat of romance and morality was only ever temporary.

A more enduring social change can be seen in twenties women's attitudes to work. On one hand, the technological advances of the period freed women from heavy housework. Electric stoves, dishwashers, vacuum cleaners, refrigerators and washing machines appeared; new houses were built with central heating, running water and modern plumbing. Clothes could be bought ready-made, laundry sent out, bread and ice-cream brought home from the shops. As standards of living rose, the time a woman needed to devote to keeping house fell.

But these modern conveniences did not come cheap, and the desire to contribute to the household income and give their family the best start in life led many women, married as well as single, to take up jobs outside the home. The twenties were a time when social and financial aspirations seemed achievable. 'I've always wanted my girls to do something other than house-work,' said one working-class Middletown mother. 'I don't want them to be house drudges like me!'

Part of this new attitude was the legacy of the Great War. While men were away training or at the front, women had taken their places in offices and factories. Despite being paid dramatically lower wages than their male counterparts, many found that they did not want to give up their newly discovered salaries and independence when peace was declared.

In Middletown in 1924, 89 per cent of girls in the last three years of high school said that they planned to get jobs after they graduated – although most would give them up when they married. Women may have been willing to work, but many men were ambivalent about permitting them to do so. A 1923 poll showed that 90 per cent of students from Vassar College were prepared to put marriage before a career. Still, by 1928, five times as many women had jobs as in 1918.

Increasingly, these jobs were white collar, rather than in factories or as domestic servants. Women became librarians, teachers, nurses, clerks, telephone operators, secretaries, stenographers, shop assistants. A few women blazed trails in areas hitherto dominated by men, as journalists, artists, advertising copywriters or scriptwriters, social workers, sociologists, photographers, doctors and lawyers.

Film was one of the first industries in which women competed on roughly equal terms with men, directing, producing and writing as well as acting. Like many best-selling authors of her day, Elinor Glyn was offered handsome terms to come to Hollywood to write and develop film scenarios. She arrived in 1920 to take up an offer of $10,000 per picture and ended up staying seven years, both writing and directing. 'I wanted,' she wrote later of her time in Los Angeles, 'to stir up in the cold hearts of the thousands of little fluffy, gold-digging American girls a desire for greater joy in love than is to be found in candy-boxes and car rides and fur coats'. Glyn named perhaps the most enduring marketing concept in movie history: 'It', or sex appeal, as embodied by Clara Bow in the 1926 film of the same name. When asked what 'It' was, a bemused Bow is said to have replied, 'I ain't real sure.'

Anita Loos, author of *Gentlemen Prefer Blondes*, was another female writer who helped shape early Hollywood. A child actor, she knew the industry inside out by the time she started writing for the director D. W. Griffith in 1912, aged twenty-four; Mary Pickford, the greatest female star of the silent movie era, starred in her first screenplay. Loos would write over two hundred movies and claimed that her scripts made Douglas Fairbanks famous. Petite, determined, talented and self-reliant, Loos was the opposite of her most famous creation, the statuesque gold-digger Lorelei Lee − although she shared with her a taste for serious frocks. 'I've had my best times when trailing a Mainbocher evening gown across a sawdust floor,' Loos once said, in true Flapper style. 'I've always loved high style in low company.'

Scott Fitzgerald's favourite actress, the ethereal Lillian Gish, was another protégée of D. W. Griffith's and star of the first modern blockbuster, *The Birth of a Nation* of 1915. Griffith offered her the chance to direct *Remodelling Her Husband* in 1920, but Gish was unimpressed by the experience. She told reporters afterwards that directing was a man's job.

Gish had been introduced to Griffith by Mary Pickford. Perennially typecast as an innocent girl because of her ringlets and childlike body, she was known as America's Sweetheart but behind the scenes wielded immense influence in 1920s Hollywood and was the first actress to earn over a million dollars a year. In 1919, she, Chaplin, her lover Douglas Fairbanks and D.W. Griffith set up United Artists, which would allow artists for the first time to produce and distribute their own work, and to be properly credited for their role in creating it. 'The lunatics have taken over the asylum,' quipped one of their former bosses; but their success confounded the doubters.

The gravest threat to Mary Pickford's hold on American hearts came not from another actress, but from her personal life. Unhappily married to an alcoholic actor, Owen Moore, who was jealous of her fame, when she met swashbuckling Douglas Fairbanks in 1916 the attraction between them was immediate. Fairbanks wanted to divorce his wife and marry Pickford, but she was terrified of the damage a scandal would do to her wholesome reputation and hard-won career. Being a Catholic, she was also reluctant to divorce on religious grounds.

As women became more emancipated, divorce became more common and more socially acceptable. There were 100,000 divorces in 1914 and 205,000 in 1929. Once they could support themselves, fewer women were willing to remain in unhappy marriages. 'The reason there are more divorces is that people are demanding more of life than they used to,' a female journalist from Middletown explained.

A divorced woman used to be disgraced, but now, 'We see that no good purpose is achieved by keeping together two people who have come to hate each other.'

Fairbanks and Pickford married in March 1920 – two years after his divorce and just a month after hers. At first Mary was pilloried by the scandal-sheets of the day, but public opinion swung to her defence when the abuse she had suffered at the hands of Owen Moore was revealed. The fairy-tale nature of her match with Fairbanks – America's Sweetheart married to its most dashing screen idol – was another factor that contributed to her rehabilitation, although conservatives continued to frown upon the Pickford–Fairbanks match for making divorce acceptable for 'respectable' people.

Mary Pickford knew that her plucky, childlike screen persona was the key to her success and, apart from her divorce, she was reluctant to jeopardize her image. Not until 1929 did she dare to cut off the golden curls that had made her name. 'I am a servant of the public,' she once said. 'I've never forgotten that.' But although she continued to make successful movies and held on tightly to her position as uncrowned queen of Hollywood, as the twenties wore on, Pickford – who was twenty-eight in 1920 – was gradually eclipsed by younger and more daring actresses whose Flapperish reputations were more in keeping with the mood of the age.

For a time Zelda Fitzgerald hoped that a movie director would discover her and make her a star, but her beauty was not unusual in Hollywood and there were plenty of eager starlets hoping to embody the Flapper on the silver screen. Some had the right attitude, but lacked focus. Constance Talmadge, known as Dutch, was the ultimate party girl, a 'sparkling blond clown' who was always getting engaged 'but never to less than two men at the same time'. For Dutch, fun was the main aim in life; she looked on her film career as a means to an end – a way out of poverty. Having made her money and secured her future, she retired in 1929 aged just thirty-two.

Gloria Swanson possessed none of Talmadge's reticence or Pickford's innocence: she was hungry for fame and all the delights success would bring her. Her big break came in 1919 when Cecil B. deMille cast her as his heroine in *Don't Change Your Husband*. Soon afterwards, the twenty-year-old Gloria gave an interview to *Motion Picture Magazine*, cementing her image as a modern sophisticate. 'I not only believe in divorce, but I sometimes think I don't believe in marriage at all,' she declared, and would prove her sincerity by going on to divorce five husbands. In 1923, fearing scandal would affect her popularity, Paramount forced Swanson to settle her second divorce out of court because her estranged husband was accusing her of committing adultery with fourteen men. Her popularity was unaffected, or perhaps enhanced, by these allegations. In the same year, she was receiving ten thousand fan letters a week.

Glamour and extravagance were essential parts of her persona. On screen, Swanson was usually shown in magnificent gowns, often with trains, wearing turbans or feathered headdresses, draped in fur and jewellery. She deliberately cultivated her image as a magnetic, mysterious star. In her hands a cigarette holder became the most dramatic of accessories. As deMille said, 'She knew how to lean against a door.'

Mary Pickford may have been the first woman to have made a million in Hollywood, but (so the saying went) Gloria Swanson was the first to spend it. *Photoplay* reported that her annual expenditure in 1924 included nearly $10,000 on silk stockings, $6,000 on perfume, $50,000 on dresses… and an unspecified amount on jewels. 'In those days they wanted us to live like kings and queens… so we did,' Swanson remembered. 'And why not? We were in love with life. We were making more money than we ever dreamed existed, and there was no reason to believe that it would ever stop.'

Like Pickford, Swanson had ambitions as a businesswoman. If she was to be packaged as a commodity, she wanted to reap the rewards herself. In early 1928, having made a disastrous attempt to set up her own production company under the aegis of United Artists, her lover Joseph Kennedy helped her form Gloria Productions (still in association with United Artists). Kennedy was one of the major forces behind the transition to sound in movies. Swanson was nominated for a Best Actress Oscar (her second) for her role in the first talkie they produced together, *The Trespasser*, but the end of her affair with Kennedy and the financial strain of producing her own films took their toll on her career in the 1930s.

Swanson's great rival in the femme fatale stakes was Pola Negri, billed by her studio as a 'wildcat'. Negri adored the trappings of celebrity and played up to her image as an exotic bird of paradise whom men could not resist. Each day the floor of her dressing room was strewn with orchid petals. She wore only black or white, always with scarlet nails. Chinchilla was her fur of choice. She could often be seen on Sunset Boulevard taking her pet tiger for a walk, or being driven around flanked by two white wolfhounds. At the funeral of her lover, Rudolph Valentino, in 1926 Negri appeared heavily veiled and fainted several times over his coffin.

Like Swanson, Negri made a virtue out of being single. 'I do not believe in marriage. It is not for me. I am selfish, no, not selfish, for I have sacrificed everything for love. I am independent. Freedom comes before anything. I am a gypsy...' This brand of intensely independent, highly sexualized glamour looked to many women like emancipation. With their gaze fixed on the immense profits to be made, Hollywood studio bosses were only too glad to sell women liberation and modernity for the price of a movie ticket.

4

'Five and Ten Cent Lusts and Dreams'

NEITHER POLA NEGRI NOR Gloria Swanson could claim to be the first true screen siren; that prize is reserved for Al Capone's favourite actress, Theda Bara, who became a star uttering the immortal words, 'Kiss me, my fool'. Bara's nickname, the Vamp, came from her role in *A Fool There Was* as a vampire who uses her sexuality to enslave and devour respectable middle-aged men. The publicity photographs for the film, released in 1915, show her posed above the discarded skeletons of her victims.

Promotional photos for her other movies (only six of the forty she made between 1914 and 1926 survive) are equally suggestive: Bara was always shown in the most fiercely come-hither of poses and the most darkly revealing of outfits. Her studio let it be known that she came from Arabia and was escorted everywhere by Nubian footmen. But this exotic, man-eating image was entirely fabricated – in fact the happily married Theda came from Cincinnati, Ohio, and no whiff of scandal was ever attached to her private life. Although she came to resent being typecast, for over a decade Bara thrilled audiences as Cleopatra and Salome and in titles like *The Serpent*, *The Vixen* and *The She-Devil*.

By glamorizing seduction and excitement, stars like Bara, Swanson and Negri helped change public views on morality. Mary Pickford might have been horrified at the thought of her fans seeing her as a divorcee, but the 1924 movie *Alimony* was promoted with irresistible images of 'brilliant men, beautiful jazz babies, champagne baths, midnight revels, petting parties in the purple dawn, all ending in one terrific climax that makes you gasp'. Scriptwriter and director Elinor Glyn said that the aim of her movies was 'to spread the ideals and the atmosphere of romance and glamor into the humblest home'; it was she who taught the heart-throb Rudolph Valentino to kiss not the back, but the palm of a lady's hand.

No wonder that half of the older girls at Middletown High School, tutored by weekly movies, told the sociologists Robert and Helen Lynd that 'nine out of every ten boys and girls of high school age have "petting parties"'. In 1933, a University of Chicago survey studied the effects of movies on teenage girls and found that 40 per cent wanted a man to make love to them after seeing a romantic film – and that 14 per cent were inspired by the movies to become 'gold-diggers'.

In an increasingly secular age, movie theatres had become the focus of an almost spiritual yearning for beauty and glamour and people flocked to them as they had once flocked to the austere clapboard churches of New England. Lavishly comfortable, exotically decorated as Egyptian temples or rococo palaces, often air-conditioned, in 1925 there were 20,000 cinemas across the United States, selling 100 million tickets a week. The Lynds estimated that the 35,000 inhabitants of Middletown went to one of its nine theatres on average more than once a week.

The fact that the same films were shown across the country at roughly the same time had a powerfully unifying impact on American society: popular films became shared and defining American experiences. But while movies, like radio and national newspapers and magazines, brought the United States together as a cohesive cultural whole, their practical effect on family values (moral content aside) was subversive. Families seldom attended a movie together, as they would once have gone ice-skating or to a church picnic. More often teenagers went with friends or on dates, generally driving themselves in cars they had borrowed from their parents, free from the chaperones who would once have been observing and monitoring their behaviour.

Investment in films soared from $78 million in 1921 to $850 million in 1930 and huge advances were made in film technology during this period leading up to the development of cartoons and the tentative introduction of sound in *The Jazz Singer* of 1927. Cutting, editing, music recording and sound mixing and dubbing became increasingly sophisticated. Different studios honed their specialities: between 1912 and

1917 the Keystone Film Company under Mack Sennett produced slapstick comedy; Metro-Goldwyn-Mayer made spectacular musicals from its foundation in 1924; Warner Brothers, established in 1918, was celebrated for its thrillers. Profit was always the bottom line. Hollywood was, as John Dos Passos put it, a 'bargain sale of five and ten cent lusts and dreams'. The British novelist J. B. Priestley, writing for the movies in the 1930s, quipped that Hollywood was 'run by businessmen pretending to be artists and artists pretending to be businessmen'.

Like its sister industry, advertising, Hollywood drew customers in by persuading them that their normal lives were bereft of value. 'All the adventure, all the romance, all the excitement you lack in your daily life are in – Pictures,' declared one mid-1920s advertisement. 'They take you completely out of yourself into a wonderful new world... Out of the cage of everyday existence! If only for an afternoon or an evening – escape!' A film like *The Sheik* set an entire generation of young men pomading their hair and learning to tango in the hope of capturing some of Valentino's allure.

A new type of journalism sprang up to feed the public's hunger for information about movies and their stars. The first tabloid, the *New York Daily News*, came out in 1919; William Randolph Hearst's even more lurid *Daily Mirror* followed it on to the newsstands five years later. These papers pioneered 'keyhole journalism' – intrusive, usually sensationalized (and often entirely fabricated) accounts of celebrity lives. Well aware of how tabloid exposés fuelled public interest in their stars, studios encouraged an almost parasitical relationship between actors and gossip columnists.

Gloria Swanson listed the inane questions reporters fired at her: 'They wanted to know whether I liked tall men or short men, how often I ate dessert, what my favourite breed of dog was, if I dyed my hair, what my favourite color was, if I got depressed on rainy days, what my favourite flower was, if I considered myself stuck-up, if I thought So-and-so was a nice dresser, if I ever obeyed silly impulses.'

In 1924 the starlet Ruby Miller 'sensationally' revealed to the *Los Angeles Times*, her tongue firmly in her cheek, how she made her love scenes so convincing. 'I must have time to know my hero and always insist that my love scenes come last of all... I'm always a sympathetic listener. He... thinks me brilliant when I permit him to explain, by the hour, how he would have "holed" in two if only that d— caddie had kept his eye on the ball... Then dawns the day of the big love scenes. I appear in a beautiful gown. By this time the hero is so crazy to kiss me that it requires no effort upon my part. His natural fervor awakening my own – and hence the perfect love scene. I am told that my method is very dangerous and liable to wreck the homes of my heroes. My reply is, "I am first, last and all time an artist – and if my love scenes are destined to thrill millions, why worry about wrecking a few thousand homes?"'

Contemporary moralists were concerned that the movies' obsession with sex appeal was destroying traditional American values, but in an essay of 1927 John Peale Bishop argued that, on the contrary, the most popular and enduring actors were innocent rather than sexualized. No other stars were adored like Charlie Chaplin and Mary Pickford, whose appeal lay in their childlike naïveté rather than in high-voltage glamour.

Directors didn't need to be sophisticated to appeal to moviegoers, either. D. W. Griffith's views on race, sex and morality were reactionary in their simplicity. Although Cecil B. deMille admired the Flapper as a 'maligned and plucky little person. Youth always revolts; it wouldn't be worth its salt if it didn't', he described himself as essentially conservative. Even when film heroines dressed provocatively, drank cocktails or allowed themselves to be kissed, most still viewed love and marriage as their ultimate aim. America may have been spellbound by 'sex, sin and sensation', but it was not ready to abandon its values altogether.

In many ways, what the movie industry was apotheosizing was not a new and debauched code of ethics, but the glamorous background against which the debate over those ethics was played out. Both on screen and off, Hollywood fetishized conspicuous consumption, reflecting back to this most materialistic of ages its own aspirational image of itself. Beautiful women, elegant clothes, fabulous houses, custom-built cars: in a movie theatre, Hollywood promised its eager audiences: all this could be yours.

Although Mary Pickford played ingénue roles, as perhaps the most commercially minded actor of her generation she was acutely aware of how closely her fans identified with her and how passionately they wanted to feel they knew her. Like many of them – and like many of her fellow actors – she had come from a desperately poor immigrant background. As she told Anita Loos, one of her favourite scriptwriters, her family was 'shanty Irish': 'Ma looked like a washerwoman.' Hard work and determination, as much as looks or talent, had raised her out of the circumstances into which she was born.

Her alcoholic father had abandoned the family (then living in Toronto) when Mary, the eldest, was three and to support her children their mother worked as a seamstress and took in boarders. It was through one of them that Mary got her first acting job, and that inspired the entire family – Mary, her mother and her younger brother and sister – to seek their fortunes on the stage. For six years they toured the United States by rail, working in shabby melodramas. Finally they reached Broadway where in 1909 Mary was given a screen test by D.W. Griffith. Griffith was so impressed by what a later reviewer called her 'luminous tenderness in a steel band of gutter ferocity' that he promised to pay her double the usual rate for movie actors, $10 a day. By 1913, Mary had moved into feature films and was earning $500 a week. Two years later she was on $2,000 a week, plus half the profits of her films. 'I hated being poor,' she told *Motion Picture Magazine* in 1920.

She also hated not being in charge. In 1916, aged twenty-four, Pickford asked for and received permission from her studio, Adrian Zukor's Famous Players, to form her own production unit, the Pickford Film Corporation. Although she was not Hollywood's first female film producer, she was its first female mogul, using her company to ensure control over her roles, directors, scripts and finances (she installed her mother as the Pickford Film Corporation's treasurer). Mary oversaw every detail of the films her company made, from hiring the crews, to editing the scripts, to shooting, to final release and promotion. In the Pickford Film Corporation's first two years she earned a guaranteed million-dollar salary.

When Pickford, Griffith, Fairbanks and Chaplin founded United Artists in 1919, Hollywood studios were vertically integrated, owning the movie theatres as well as producing the movies they showed in them. United Artists was different because it was solely a distribution company – and therefore the producers and actors it used were, for the first time, independent from 'the bankers, the distributors and the sales executives'. From 1920, Pickford and Fairbanks made their own films at their shared studio on Santa Monica Boulevard.

Mary described her career as 'planned, painful, purposeful' and her extraordinary achievements attest to that. The most important element of her success was her dedication to what her fans wanted of her. 'We love Mary Pickford because she loves us,' said *Motion Picture Magazine* in 1918. As her worries over her divorce and remarriage show, Pickford knew that her off-screen life was just as important to her public persona as her on-screen roles and she deliberately cultivated a dignified, almost matronly image. The Fairbanks's Beverly Hills mansion, Pickfair, was as sumptuously decorated as her fans might have hoped, with the first private swimming pool in Los Angeles, but the atmosphere was relatively staid for Hollywood in the 1920s.

Before dinners at Pickfair, Fairbanks would take their male guests for a Turkish bath at the studio. Evening entertainment was often a movie; Douglas's little mongrel might perform tricks. Despite its extravagance – Pickfair introduced Hollywood to 'a land of vintage wine and caviar in iced swan boats, glittering jewels and French chefs, aviaries and peacocks in formal gardens' – there was very little drinking and no 'jazzing'. 'You couldn't take off your shoes and dance' there, said one friend. Mary herself danced sedately only with her husband who was notoriously jealous. After their marriage he said firmly that, from now on, America's Sweetheart would just be *his* sweetheart.

Douglas Fairbanks was unusual in Hollywood in that his family background was middle-class although, like Mary, his father had abandoned his mother when he was a small child. After more than a decade acting on Broadway Fairbanks moved to Hollywood in 1915 where, working with the writer-director team of Anita Loos and her future husband John Emerson, he quickly became a star. Like Pickford he was an astute operator, making it his business to understand movies inside out. On screen Fairbanks gave off an almost tangible physical radiance that was a projection more of his genuine exuberance and virility than of any acquired acting skills. Tall, strong, athletic, darkly tanned, glowing with health, Fairbanks always appeared decent and honourable, and never took himself too seriously.

United, Pickford and Fairbanks were an even bigger draw than they had been as individual stars. When they travelled to New York and Europe in the months following their wedding, vast and uncontrollable crowds formed at their public appearances. In Paris, two butchers saved Pickford from being crushed by the mob at the market of Les Halles by locking her into a meat cage until the gendarmerie arrived to escort her to safety. Even English aristocrats were in thrall to their glamour: the leaders of the rich bohemian set, the Earl and Countess of Milford Haven and their younger brother and sister-in-law, Lord and Lady Louis Mountbatten, who honeymooned at Pickfair, wooed the Fairbankses on their visits to London. Their friend Charlie Chaplin said their manner with the 'exalted' was wonderful.

In Hollywood their status was assured: Mary and Douglas were 'Hollywood royalty'. People instinctively stood up when Pickford entered the room. As the film actress Joan Crawford put it, although the newspaper magnate W.R. Hearst was richer than the Fairbankses and his California estate, San Simeon, far larger and more opulent than Pickfair, Marion Davies (Hearst's mistress) 'was always just one of the gals, and Hearst put the catsup bottle on the table, but Mary was a queen and everyone knew it'.

But despite the majestic image she projected, the reality of Mary Pickford's life was far from serene. Her mother had a decided weakness for whisky; her sister Lottie (whose great friend was Dutch Talmadge) was a party girl who dabbled in cocaine and eventually married four times; her brother Jack was a charming boozer. Once her marriage with Fairbanks broke down in the early 1930s, following revelations of his affair with a British model and actress, Sylvia Ashley, Mary finally surrendered to her genetic inheritance; she would struggle with alcoholism for the rest of her life. This contrast between a carefully controlled public image and a chaotic private life was far from rare in twenties Hollywood.

Behind the Zenith-like façade of respectability cultivated by Pickford and Fairbanks, Hollywood was alive with easy money, sex, bootleg liquor and drugs. In many ways Los Angeles was still a frontier town. Charlie Chaplin remembered hearing coyotes howl at night in Beverly Hills when he first arrived there in the mid-1910s. Violence was commonplace. Screenwriter Elinor Glyn was shocked to hear isolated shots and cries ringing out in the balmy night air. After dinners at Pickfair (in the wilds of Beverly Hills) a second car would follow her back to her hotel in case she was held up en route.

Far more than New York or Chicago, Los Angeles was a modern Babylon, an explosive concentration of new wealth, ambition and the easy accessibility of anything one could dream of. 'Money was abundant,' remembered Lillian Gish. 'Luxury was everywhere. Shoeshine boys and cab drivers played the stock market... indigent young actors were getting used to travelling in limousines.'

But as the *Photoplay* columnist Adela Rogers said, 'Low education and high income don't mix.' Most Hollywood actors in the early 1920s came from poverty to find themselves lavished with popular adoration and, at relatively young ages, with more money than they had ever imagined. Few had stable family backgrounds or much education. It was hardly surprising that they spent their silly money like water, had affairs with everyone they could, drank heavily and took drugs.

This was one aspect of what Elinor Glyn described as the 'Hollywood disease' – to which she confessed she also succumbed, although (in her sixties) perhaps not to the same extremes as some. It started almost on one's arrival, Glyn wrote, producing 'a sense of exaggerated self-importance and self-centredness, which naturally alienates all old friends. Next comes a great desire for and belief in the importance of money above all else, a loss of the normal sense of humour and of proportion, and finally, in extreme cases, the abandonment of all previous standards of moral value'.

The one star more beloved than Mary Pickford was Charlie Chaplin, who had come to Hollywood in late 1913 from the English music-hall stage, after three years touring America in vaudeville shows. Like Pickford, his youth in and out of workhouses and paupers' schools in south London had been marked by desperate poverty and deprivation. Chaplin never forgot the fear and isolation of his childhood, and even – or perhaps especially – his most comedic work was indelibly marked by his early experiences. As a friend said, he was 'one of the loneliest souls that ever walked this earth'.

Chaplin described finding New York a frightening and unfriendly place when he arrived there in 1910 at the age of twenty-one. While others swaggered on the streets Charlie looked and felt 'lone and isolated'. These feelings never left him. Three years later, with his first decent pay-cheque in his pocket, Chaplin booked himself into an expensive hotel for the first time. He said he wanted to weep when he saw his well-appointed room and sat by the bath turning the hot and cold taps off and on, thinking, 'How bountiful and reassuring is luxury!' Years later he would say that the saddest thing he could 'imagine is to get used to luxury'.

It was in his third film for Keystone, released in February 1914, that Chaplin introduced the Tramp. His defining character came into being almost by accident. 'On the way to the wardrobe I thought I would dress in baggy pants, big shoes, a cane and a derby hat. I wanted everything to be a contradiction: the pants baggy, the coat tight, the hat small and the shoes large. I was undecided whether to look old or young, but remembering [Mack] Sennett had expected me to be a much older man, I added a small moustache, which I reasoned, would add age without hiding my expression. I had no idea of the character. But the moment I was dressed, the clothes and the makeup made me feel the person he was. I began to know him, and by the time I walked on stage [set] he was fully born.'

'You know this fellow is many-sided, a tramp, a gentleman,

a poet, a dreamer, a lonely fellow, always hopeful of romance and adventure,' said Chaplin elsewhere. 'He would have you believe he is a scientist, a musician, a duke, a polo player. However, he is not above picking up cigarette butts or robbing a baby of its candy. And, of course, if the situation warrants it, he will kick a lady in the rear – but only in extreme anger.'

As the humble, noble, hopeful Tramp, in film after film, Chaplin had found a way of communicating the naïve bewilderment felt by modern man as he confronted a world which seemed determined to rob him of his dignity. His own experiences were a fundamental part of his astonishing appeal; as he said, the Tramp was never a character constructed to appeal to audiences, but 'myself... something within me that I must express'. 'There is no tragedy of life's seamy side which Charlie Chaplin does not know,' wrote the journalist Beverly Nichols, 'not only because he has a great heart, but because he has shared the tragedy himself.'

This intense vulnerability was the secret of Chaplin's universal appeal. He encapsulated the nameless sense of longing felt by so many Americans during this period, from Zelda Fitzgerald to the compulsive womanizer President Harding. Even Sinclair Lewis's fictional George Babbitt, the Midwestern estate agent whose name became a synonym for middle-class conformity and complacency, was not immune to these yearnings. Lewis describes his most unromantic of heroes tucked up in his sleeping-porch (the *dernier cri* of modern suburban house design) but 'restless again, discontented about nothing and everything, ashamed of his discontentment' and dreaming of a 'fairy girl' who waited for him in mysterious, magical groves. Only Charlie Chaplin could have understood this side of George Babbitt. As the critic Gilbert Seldes said, Chaplin corresponded to all 'our secret desires'.

Charlie existed outside space and time, wrote Seldes, in a world that he had created and where he became an 'eternal figure of lightness and of the wisdom which knows that the earth was made to dance on. It was a green earth, excited by its own abundance and fruitfulness, and he possessed it entirely... As it spins under his feet he dances silently and with infinite grace upon it.'

By the late 1910s and throughout the 1920s, critics like Seldes were competing to see who could praise Chaplin the most highly. *Harper's* decided his vulgarity was an essential element of his art, in the tradition of Aristophanes, Cervantes and Swift; the *New Republic* praised the democratic breadth of his appeal. Chaplin was all things to all men: the social commentator Waldo Frank commended him for creating 'a viable alternative to the materialism of American culture' while the literary critic Edmund Wilson marvelled at his reactions, 'as fresh, as authentically personal, as those of a poet'.

The Gold Rush, Chaplin's masterpiece, was released in 1925. It grossed over $4 million dollars, earning United Artists $1 million and its star $2 million. The cartoonist and comic writer Robert Sherwood (who himself sported a Chaplinesque moustache) summarized what he called Chaplin's 'symbolical autobiography' for *Vanity Fair*: 'It is the story of a stampede in the Klondike, with an enormous mob of eager prospectors storming the heights of Chinook Pass in a wild scramble for gold. With the procession, and yet utterly detached from it, is a lonely figure in a derby hat and a burlap Inverness cape, who carries a bamboo cane to aid him in his perilous climb up the icy slopes. He would like to mix with the others, but they will have none of him; they are too busy, too anxious to get down to business to bother with him. So he must go his way alone. He finds the gold, but the dance-hall girl of his heart jilts him – and he is compelled to return home with nothing but vast wealth to show for his efforts.'

Chaplin's gold-mine was the movie industry and, like the Tramp, although he found immense wealth there true love was more elusive. Comedy was his only release, the only way he could stop being overwhelmed, as he put it, 'by the apparent seriousness of life'. 'Charlie Chaplin's secret is that he has created for himself a mask in which all this gamut [from comedian to sensualist, from sentimentalist to ironist] lives,' wrote Waldo Frank in an early edition of the *New Yorker* the year *The Gold Rush* came out. 'What a strange mask it is: a bit of a moustache, a bit of a cane, baggy trousers, flapping shoes. Yet it has satisfied the world, from China to Paris. It has failed him in but a single way – a cruel one: for it has failed to satisfy its maker.'

In 1920, Chaplin had spotted a young extra named Lillita MacMurray while directing *The Kid*. Struck by the twelve-year-old's precocious allure, he asked her to play the provocative angel-temptress in the film's dream sequence. Four years later (having not seen her in the interim) he cast her as the Tramp's love interest in *The Gold Rush*, but by the time filming had started several months later Lita Grey (the stage-name Chaplin had chosen for her) was pregnant. Her role was filled by another actress and, because she was still only sixteen and refused to have an abortion, she and Chaplin were secretly married in Mexico.

Although she and Chaplin had two sons in the next two years, the marriage was miserable from the start. In December 1926 Grey left Chaplin and filed for divorce, accusing him of neglect and cruelty and demanding $1.25 million in alimony. Hollywood may have turned a blind eye to Chaplin's taste for young girls, but the nation was aghast at the revelations of the Little Tramp's 'immorality' and 'degeneracy'. The exposure of his marriage to a minor and his negligent and abusive treatment of her nearly destroyed him. Grey's suit included claims that Chaplin had tried to force her to abort both of her babies, demanded oral sex (considered utterly reprehensible at the time) and asked other women to join them in bed, and she threatened to name five prominent women with whom Chaplin was said to have been involved during their marriage. Across the country appalled wives and mothers formed groups petitioning for Chaplin's films to be banned and raising money to help feed his abandoned children.

The divorce, which awarded Grey over $600,000 (the largest settlement made up to that time) and each of her sons trusts of $100,000, and cost Chaplin almost a million dollars in legal fees, was finalized in August 1927. But somehow Chaplin's appeal was undimmed. Out of a series of scandals that shook Hollywood to its foundations during the 1920s, he was the only survivor.

One evening in the mid-1920s Chaplin, Elinor Glyn and Marion Davies saw a murder being committed outside the door of Glyn's suite at the Ambassador Hotel in Los Angeles. When Glyn enquired what had happened, the following day, the hotel denied all knowledge of a crime; only the much-scrubbed bloodstain on the carpet remained as evidence of what Glyn and her friends had witnessed. This was Hollywood's initial approach to the scandals that threatened to destroy it: if the evidence could be concealed, then no one would be the wiser. The real problems started when the scandals happened so regularly that the truth could no longer be suppressed.

In September 1920, Mary Pickford's appealing but wayward brother Jack and his exquisite starlet wife, Olive Thomas, returned to the Ritz in Paris after an evening slumming at a seedy Montmartre bar, Le Café du Rat Mort. As the Pickfords went through the lobby witnesses observed that they looked 'unsteady, but not drunk'. That night Olive took mercury tablets and died after five days of excruciating suffering. Despite the verdict of accidental death it is unclear whether she took the pills by accident, thinking they were sleeping pills, or whether she intended to kill herself perhaps because of her husband's infidelities and the syphilis he had given her, or because of her own addiction to morphine or cocaine.

A year later, the comedian Roscoe 'Fatty' Arbuckle was charged with the murder of a young actress named Virginia Rappe. Arbuckle was a brilliant physical comedian who was the first actor to be contracted for a million dollars a year. Banners advertising his movies read, 'He's worth his weight in laughs'; reviewers hailed his success as proof 'that everybody loves a fat comedian'. But Arbuckle resented being called Fatty and hated the fact that his stardom was linked to his size. In 1917 he complained to *Photoplay* that 'if Joe Schenck [his producer] didn't harbor the hallucination that fat is my fortune, I'd be a contender for Doug Fairbanks's athletic honours in the movies. [But] my fat is my fortune.' Arbuckle feared that his bulk prevented him from being taken seriously as an actor and looked jealously on as his contemporaries – Chaplin, Pickford and Fairbanks – attracted critical acclaim on top of popular applause and huge salaries.

As well as torturing him professionally, Arbuckle's size made him insecure in more private ways. His success invited the attentions of the usual gaggle of ambitious young ladies, but Arbuckle was afraid that they would find him wanting sexually. His wife, the comic actress Minta Durfee (from whom he was living separately by 1920), said that 'He was smart enough to know that women weren't attracted to him because of his good looks or his physical beauty. Sometimes women on the lot in the powder room would whisper intimate questions about

Roscoe: Is he big all over…? Does he crush you when…? Does he hurt you when…? How often…? But I never answered them.'

Minta said that, perhaps because of his size, Arbuckle was frequently impotent. He was also a heavy drinker and a regular user of morphine, which he had begun taking following an inflamed and infected mosquito bite which had nearly lost him his leg. Drugs were a constant theme in these years. The California State Board of Pharmacy listed five hundred actors as drug addicts. Morphine was freely prescribed without proper consideration of its side-effects because it was the only effective painkiller of the day. In 1923 Wallace Reid, a dazzlingly handsome, well-respected, happily married matinee idol, died aged thirty-one following an illness caused by his drug addiction. It emerged that his studio had essentially created his dependence by giving him morphine injections following an injury sustained during filming so that they could continue with their tight shooting schedule.

In early September 1921, Arbuckle had gone to San Francisco for a long weekend with two male friends. On their arrival at the St Francis Hotel, they had ordered buckets of ice and ginger ale to be sent up to their suite to accompany their bootleg gin and whisky, and invited over some friends who happened to be in San Francisco at the same time. The actors' agent Al Semnacher came up to the suite at about half past ten on the morning of Monday 5 September with Maude Delmont, a model, and her friend Virginia Rappe.

Throughout the day everyone except Arbuckle danced to the records played on the portable phonograph; he sat beside it, watching the others, clad only in pyjama bottoms. By the afternoon the girls were very drunk and Virginia, complaining of being unable to breathe, began to take off her clothes. She went into the bathroom adjoining Arbuckle's bedroom and he followed her in. They were alone for about fifteen minutes and then Arbuckle came out of his room to report that a semi-clad, semi-conscious Rappe was writhing in pain on his bed. The hotel doctor examined her and said that her symptoms were caused by intoxication; the party broke up and Rappe was left to sleep off her hangover in another room.

Two days later, after Arbuckle had returned to Los Angeles, Maude Delmont came back to the hotel to see her friend and found her still in great pain and calling out for Arbuckle. On Thursday Virginia was taken to a hospital where she was diagnosed as having alcohol poisoning, a relatively common complaint in the days of contaminated bootleg liquor. She died there the following day; the cause of death was given as peritonitis resulting from a ruptured bladder apparently brought on by 'external force', and bruises and fingermarks were found on her body. Delmont said Rappe had told her that Arbuckle had raped and beaten her. He was charged with her murder.

What had really happened is unclear. Arbuckle always insisted that he had found Virginia unconscious in his bathroom and simply carried her to the bed (thus causing her bruises). Delmont, whose reliability was later called into question when she was found to be a bigamist, testified that she had heard Arbuckle say to Rappe, 'I've been trying to get you for five years,' before locking the bedroom door behind them. One theory was that Arbuckle had crushed Rappe while making love to her or, frustrated at his impotence, had damaged her internally by penetrating her with a bottle. Another girl who was present in the suite at first backed up Delmont's accusations but later insisted that Rappe had gone into Arbuckle's bedroom 'because she wanted to'.

Revelations about Virginia Rappe did not clarify the situation. It transpired that she had a bit of a reputation in Hollywood: the journalist Adela St Johns said she was more an 'amateur call-girl' and 'studio hanger-on' than an aspiring actress, 'who used to get drunk at parties and start to tear her clothes off' before accusing men of attacking her; she was said to have spread syphilis throughout one studio. According to some, Arbuckle had long been infatuated with Rappe after hearing stories of her exploits, and had specifically invited her to the St Francis. It was also rumoured that the reason she was in San Francisco on the weekend she died was that she had had her fifth illegal abortion the day before Arbuckle's party — which may have accounted for her internal injuries.

Arbuckle was cleared in April 1922 after three trials. The deciding factor was the defence's courtroom display of Virginia Rappe's ruptured bladder in a jar, intended to prove that the damage to her internal organs was the long-standing result of numerous abortions. Despite his acquittal, Fatty's career had been destroyed. His friends, his peers and his audience were as divided as his juries had been as to his involvement in Rappe's death. His wife told the press that he was nothing more than 'a big, overgrown baby who couldn't handle his own success'; Charlie Chaplin believed him 'a genial, easy-going type who would not harm a fly'; Adela St Johns thought him simply naïve, 'a lovable, fat innocent'. Perhaps Gloria Swanson's scepticism was more widely spread. 'Maybe three trials couldn't prove that Arbuckle was guilty,' she said later, 'but nobody in town ever thought he was all that innocent… I know Arbuckle was acquitted, and I know that Al Capone's only crime was tax evasion.'

Although his greatest friend, Buster Keaton, tried to find writing and directing work for Arbuckle, it was not until the early 1930s that he began acting in short films again. Arbuckle died of heart failure in 1933, aged forty-six, on the evening of the day he had signed a contract with Warner Brothers to make his first feature film since his disgrace.

Another mysterious death occurred in February 1922 when the director William Desmond Taylor was found shot in his apartment. It appears likely that the mother of one of the young actresses he worked with, Mary Miles Minton, murdered him – possibly because she was infatuated with Taylor too. The investigation was never concluded but rumours of Taylor's secret homosexuality, and ones connecting Minton and another actress friend of Taylor's, Mabel Normand (Charlie Chaplin's first regular co-star in the mid-1910s and a huge star in her own right), to known drug-dealers, were hard to dispel. Minton's and Normand's careers were ruined.

Two years later the eccentric newspaper magnate William Randolph Hearst took a group of friends on a yacht trip between Los Angeles and San Diego to celebrate his sixty-first birthday. Hearst was obsessively jealous of his young mistress, Marion Davies, and with some reason. During this period she was said to have been having an affair with Charlie Chaplin, thought to have been one of the other guests on the yacht; her name was on Lita Grey's list of Chaplin's mistresses. Also present was the producer Thomas Ince who had pioneered the movie western. Rumour held that Ince was shot on board, either because Hearst found him embracing Davies or because he found Davies embracing Chaplin, threatened him, and Ince got in the way.

In his autobiography Chaplin said that the man who made the greatest impression on him during his early years in Hollywood was Hearst – ruthless, childish, mercurial, shrewd Hearst, who 'spent millions as nonchalantly as though it were weekly pocket money'. Hearst lived in extravagant style at his ranch in San Simeon, where the dining room was a replica of the nave of Westminster Abbey and the indoor swimming pool was lined with 10-carat-gold mosaic tiles imported from Venice.

Hearst had wooed Marion Davies, then a Ziegfeld girl, by pressing diamond wrist-watches into her hands when they met. Despite succumbing to this method of courtship, Davies was utterly unpretentious, funny, warm and generous – the kind of woman whose diamond-and-onyx cigarette case was held together by a rubber band. Hearst, who was becoming obsessed by the movies, fell in love with her and insisted on promoting her film career even though she protested, stuttering charmingly, that she had no talent for acting; in fact she was a gifted comedienne. Hearst's Catholic wife would not agree to a divorce, but Davies didn't mind not being able to marry WR, or Pops, as she called him. 'Love doesn't need a wedding ring... Why should I run after a streetcar when I was already aboard?' She would prove her devotion to Hearst by saving him from financial ruin in the late 1930s.

Weekend house parties at San Simeon were as famous as dinners at Pickfair. As many as fifty guests spent their days playing tennis, swimming, riding around the estate or admiring WR's private zoo. Hearst was an old-fashioned host. When Jean Harlow came down to dinner in a dress Hearst considered too revealing, he asked Marion to tell her to change. Harlow returned to the dining room pointedly wearing her coat.

As a teetotaller, Hearst frowned on excessive drinking. The first cocktails of the day were served at 6 p.m., and although Marion gathered friends in her rooms for surreptitious drinks, people who made the mistake of bringing their own flasks would find them emptied by the butler who unpacked their bags. Each guest at San Simeon was permitted two cocktails, no more.

For all his stuffiness, Hearst could be endearingly childlike. One night his feelings were hurt because he hadn't been included in a game of charades. 'Well,' said the actor Jack Gilbert, 'we'll play a charade on our own, and act out the word "pill-box" — I'll be the box and you can be the pill.' WR rushed out of the room, slamming the door: 'I don't want to play your old charades.' On other, happier occasions he would get up and tap-dance with the most 'charming gaucheness'.

Hearst was powerful enough — and his friends were loyal enough — to suppress the Ince affair when news of his death became public. Some years later Elinor Glyn insisted that all the rumours were lies, and that Ince had left the boat and died of heart problems following acute indigestion which he had refused to have treated because he was a Christian Scientist. Chaplin said that he had not attended the boating party at which the death was alleged to have occurred, but that Glyn had told him Ince had died of a heart attack. To this day no one knows what really happened because the only witness who might have spoken out, the gossip columnist Louella Parsons, accepted a lucrative job from Hearst when she stepped ashore and never spoke of the incident again. The matter was not investigated by the police.

At last even Washington found it impossible to ignore scandals of this magnitude. Fears about Hollywood's corruption of America and American values were compounded by the knowledge that the film industry was created and run principally by ambitious, innovative Jewish and Catholic immigrants including (to name producers and directors alone) the Polish Warner brothers, Louis Mayer, Irving Thalberg, Adrian Zukor and Sam Goldwyn. In this xenophobic era, nothing could have made Hollywood seem more threatening.

In 1922 the US president Warren Harding's staunchly Presbyterian former campaign manager, Will Hays, was created first president of the Motion Picture Producers and Distributors of America (at an annual salary of $100,000) and charged with imposing codes of morality both on movies that were made and on the stars performing in them. His recommendations, designed to safeguard 'American' family values and the sanctity of marriage and the home, were approved in 1930 and enforced from 1934. The first dictat read, 'No picture shall be produced that will lower the moral standards of those who see it.' Heated love scenes — like those for which Pola Negri had been celebrated — and references to 'impure love' were banned, in case they aroused improper passions; virtue and morality were to triumph by decree; the clergy were not to be ridiculed and gangsters were not to be portrayed as sympathetic. But, for Hollywood hotshots as for Washington politicians, the appearance of morality remained far more important than the practice of it.

5

'My God! How the Money Rolls In'

WILL HAYS'S CONNECTION WITH Hollywood dated back to two years before he was appointed president of the Motion Picture Producers and Distributors of America. In August 1920, the 'Harding-Coolidge Theatrical League' arrived in Warren Harding's home town of Marion, Ohio, to give their support to Harding's presidential campaign which Hays was master-minding. Newly married Mary Pickford and Douglas Fairbanks led a group of actors and entertainers pledging their support for Harding in the upcoming election.

Hollywood loved Harding for his easy good nature, his sociability, his sincerity – and perhaps above all for his nobly presidential looks. Lillian Gish described him as 'a Roman statue carved out of marble' and was charmed by the way he held his arms out to her and her sister, Dorothy, when they were invited to the White House for a screening of one of their movies, calling them both 'Darling!'

Fellow politicians found him less impressive. Harding won

the Republican nomination by default: delegates and fixers agreed that the times didn't require a 'First-Rater' but that Harding, politically conservative (as a senator he had always voted with the party) and with immense popular appeal, would be as malleable as he was electable. Harding was no less realistic about his attributes. After receiving his party's nomination he said he felt 'like a man who goes in with a pair of eights and comes out with aces full'.

His campaign confirmed expectations. 'America's present need is not heroics, but healing; not nostrums, but normalcy; not revolution, but restoration; not agitation, but adjustment; not surgery, but serenity; not the dramatic, but the dispassionate; not experiment, but equipoise; not submergence in internationality, but sustainment in triumphant nationality...' he declared, without running out of breath. Somehow Harding's bungled language and overblown rhetoric convinced voters that he stood for a return to what he called 'normalcy' after the turbulent war years.

Even the man who became Harding's Secretary of Commerce, Herbert Hoover, commented on his preference for 'three-dollar words'. William McAdoo, one of the failed Democratic contenders for candidate, said Harding's speeches 'leave the impression of an army of pompous phrases moving over the landscape in search of an idea; sometimes these meandering words would actually capture a straggling thought and bear it triumphantly, a prisoner in their midst, until it died of servitude and overwork'.

The journalist William Allen White, who liked Harding, agreed that he was 'densely ignorant. At best he was a poor dub who had made his reputation running with the political machine in Ohio, making Memorial Day addresses for the Elks, addressing service clubs – the Rotarians, Kiwanians, or the Lions – uttering resounding platitudes and saying nothing because he knew nothing'. Harding may have looked like a president, but he wasn't equal to the challenges of the job. Yet Harding's simple, well-intentioned affability struck a chord with millions of American voters. His election win was less a landslide than an earthquake, the most sweeping presidential victory ever; he came to office in early 1921 on a national wave of buoyant optimism. 'The populace is on a broad grin,' reported one newspaperman.

Despite his astonishing majority – Harding won 61 per cent of the popular vote and thirty-seven of forty-eight states – his campaign team must have heaved a sigh of relief. For months they had been struggling to prevent Harding's many affairs being made public. In return for signed affidavits denying their involvement with Harding, and the passionate letters and erotic poetry Harding had written to them (often on blue Senate writing paper), his mistresses had been paid off out of a secret account funded by the National Republican Committee. One woman demanded and received $20,000. But Harding's craving for romance was hard to suppress. Even on the night before his inauguration the President-elect had to be prevented from sneaking out of his room in the middle of the night for an assignation.

People joked that anyone who had to live with Florence Harding deserved extra-curricular activities, but despite his infidelities Warren (or 'W'rr'n', as Florence called him) seemed to dote upon his determined, heavily-marcelled wife. Certainly he always deferred to the woman he called the 'Duchess' and trusted her implicitly; she was the one person he knew for sure had his interests at heart.

Seven years her husband's senior, Florence Harding was the most emancipated First Lady America had known. When the Belgian queen, Elizabeth, had visited Washington in 1919, Mrs Harding (then a senator's wife) had met her not with a curtsy but with a 'level eye [and]... an outstretched hand'. A declared suffragist, she was the first president's wife to have voted for her husband, following legislation that granted women the vote in 1920. 'If Warren G. Harding is elected there will be two P— well, *personalities* in the White House,' wrote a journalist during the campaign. 'For Mrs Harding is no mere gentle shadow flitting in the background of her husband's greatness.'

Florence had made her own living as a single mother before meeting Harding and then helped him make a success of his newspaper, the *Marion Star*. Domestic life didn't interest her. 'I'd rather go hungry than broil steak and boil potatoes,' she said. 'I love business.' She refused to pretend that she wasn't interested in the running of her husband's administration. Having bossed W'rr'n around for years, she had no compunction about pressing for appointments, reviewing budgets, writing his speeches, attending government conferences and lobbying on behalf of her many interests, which included all-female prisons, Girl Scouts and animal welfare. She and Warren were childless but they both loved animals; their Airedale, Laddie Boy, was familiarly known as the 'Publicity Hound'.

Mrs Harding brought a breath of fresh air and modernity to her role as First Lady and to the White House, throwing open its doors to visitors (and often leading tours herself), screening movies in the East Room and playing jazz at presidential functions. She was the first First Lady to fly in an aeroplane (with a woman pilot), the first to hold her own press conferences for female reporters, the first to welcome divorcees to the White House, and she made a point of entertaining black schoolchildren as well as white at White House receptions. Her unabashed prominence meant that she was popularly thought to be the power behind the throne. When John Anderson, a Swedish immigrant taking the US citizenship test in the early 1920s, was asked who would assume the president's duties if he should die in office and replied Mrs Harding, the judge, smiling, let him pass.

After a crisis in 1911, when Florence discovered letters from her best friend to Harding revealing the affair they had been having for more than five years (and would continue for almost a decade), an impasse was reached. Florence decided to stay with the man she still adored and turn a blind eye to his infidelities, as long as they were contained enough to

Cosying up to the law: sharp-suited gangster Al Capone (left) with
Henry Laubenheimer, US Marshall for Illinois, at the height of Capone's attempts
to present himself as a legitimate businessman,1928

Prohibition agents Izzy Epstein and Moe Smith as themselves, top,
and disguised to ensnare bootleggers, bottom

Blues legend Bessie Smith photographed by
Harlem-phile Carl Van Vechten in 1936

Langston Hughes, the greatest poet of the
Harlem Renaissance, in the 1920s. Jazz and
the blues were stronger influences upon him
than the literary canon

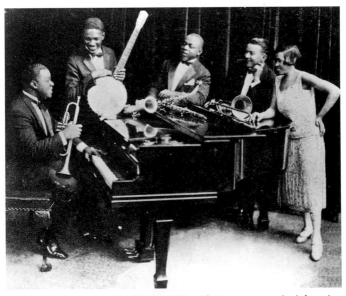

The Louis Armstrong Hot Five in 1925, with Armstrong on the left and
his wife, the pianist Lil Hardin, on the right. Despite Hardin's
classical training, the quintet played without sheet music

Scott and Zelda Fitzgerald drove through the Deep South in the early 1920s.
They had matching knickerbocker suits made for the journey

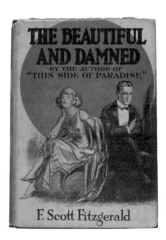

The original cover for Scott's 1922 novel
The Beautiful and Damned featuring
Scott and Zelda as the models for his hero
and heroine Anthony and Glora Patch

Scott, Zelda and their daughter Scottie in
Paris, Christmas 1925

The actress Gloria Swanson in her heyday. Note the admiring glances from the men behind her

The Vamp: Theda Bara at her most darkly seductive as *Cleopatra* (1917). Al Capone had a photograph of Bara in his office

Marion Davies in 1926. Her talents as a comedienne were outshone by her off-screen role as newspaper magnate W. R. Hearst's mistress

jeopardize neither her pride nor his career. The price she paid was isolation. Afraid of making female friends because she suspected that they would try to ensnare Warren, she devoted herself to his interests. 'I have only one real hobby,' she said. 'My husband.'

This willingness to put Harding's needs before her own was evident in the public sphere. Friendly, easy-going Harding never put anyone's back up or said no to anyone – his razor-sharp wife decisively did it for him. As bold as she was abrasive, Florence relished political battles. Her secretary described Warren looking on with admiring pride as she took on opponents like Henry Cabot Lodge.

But while Florence's tenacity and drive in part compensated for her husband's weaknesses, like him she was a poor judge of character. They were no match for the band of unscrupulous cynics who saw in the laid-back President an unparalleled opportunity to get rich quick. When the Hardings moved into the White House, wrote the popular historian Frederick Allen in his 1931 review of the 1920s, 'blowsy gentlemen with cigars stuck into their cheeks and rolls of very useful hundred-dollar bills in their pockets began to infest the Washington hotels... [and] the oil-men licked their chops.'

For all his skirt-chasing, Warren Harding was a man's man, a member of fraternal and civic societies, a lover of cards and golf, whisky and women, and his administration reflected his interests. He created, said Alice Roosevelt Longworth (daughter of former President Theodore Roosevelt and a prominent Washington hostess), 'a general atmosphere of waistcoat unbuttoned, feet on the desk, and the spittoon alongside' – and, with his 'girlies', as Longworth said he called them, 'put the White House closets to a whole new range of uses'.

Harding's informal, guileless style made his intellectual inadequacies hard to disguise. The year he took office, he confessed to a journalist that he was having trouble coming to terms with the complexities of his new duties. '"I don't know what to do or where to turn in this taxation matter. Somewhere there must be a book that tells all about it, where I could go to straighten it out in my mind. But I don't know where the book is, and maybe I couldn't read it if I found it. And there must be a man in the country somewhere who could weigh both sides and know the truth. Probably he is in some college or other. But I don't know where to find him. I don't know who he is and I don't know how to get him. My God, but this is a hell of a place for a man like me to be!" He put his hand to his head, smiled at his own discomfiture, turned and walked heavily away.'

Harding's initial response was to form a cabinet to compensate for his deficiencies. He was persuaded to give the State Department to the respected lawyer Charles Evans Hughes, the Republican presidential candidate for 1916; he brought in the efficient and progressive Herbert Hoover, who had served under Woodrow Wilson during the war, as Secretary of Commerce; his commitment to business interests was underlined by his choice of Andrew Mellon, the aluminium magnate, as

Treasury Secretary. These men were experienced and reliable.

Less popular was Harding's decision to appoint to the Attorney-General's office his closest political ally, Harry Daugherty, as a reward for his long-standing support. Under his aegis the Justice Department became known as the Department of Easy Virtue. Daugherty was the most prominent member of what came to be known as the Ohio Gang, a group of trusted friends (many from Ohio days) with whom Harding played whisky-soaked poker sessions through the night in the private rooms of the White House with the Duchess beadily serving the drinks.

Harry Daugherty and his sidekick, Jess Smith, lived in a house two blocks from the White House on H Street (overlooking Lafayette Square, a notorious gay cruising ground) from where Daugherty conducted most of his Department of Justice business. Both men were devoted to Daugherty's invalid wife, Lucie, who had remained in Ohio. Harry loathed Jess's ex-wife, Roxie, although Jess remained close to her. They were, said one friend, 'partners if ever two men were'. Daugherty declared Smith was 'indispensable to my personal comfort'; Smith worshipped Daugherty (according to one of Daugherty's agents) 'with a dog-like devotion'.

Snappily dressed, shifty-eyed Jess Smith was a tall, plump, lazy mama's boy who always wore a large diamond-and-ruby ring. He took care of Daugherty's informal business, keeping house and keeping his fingers in all the pies in town, humming his favourite popular song with its catchy chorus:

My sister sells snow [cocaine] to the snow-birds
My father sells bootlegger gin
My grandma does back-street abortions
My God! How the money rolls in!

My brother's a poor missionary
He saves fallen women from sin
He'll save you a blonde for five dollars
My God! How the money rolls in!

Smith sold useful introductions to shady businessmen, pardons and paroles for criminals, and impounded booze and licences to sell liquor from drugstores out of a small green-stone house on K Street. An Ohio lawyer-turned-bootlegger, George Remus, paid Daugherty and Smith $350,000 a year for government licences to sell medicinal alcohol, making $40 million in three years. When the regime changed he was caught and imprisoned.

Harding's attitude towards Prohibition was emblematic of his administration's self-serving hypocrisy and his own eagerness to ignore unpleasant facts if they interfered with his pleasures or peace of mind. 'Though President Harding likes to drink as much as I do, he is prepared to stand or fall by the enforcement of Prohibition on the ground that it is the law and must be enforced,' one of his former Cabinet ministers commented in 1923. Alice Roosevelt Longworth said that throughout the twenties, 'the Cabinet member who did not take a drink when it was offered to him was an exception'.

Although Longworth herself later became what was called a 'constitutional dry' (supporting and practising Prohibition because it was the law), when Prohibition first came into effect she had a home-still from which her butler concocted 'a very passable gin from oranges'.

One of Daugherty's Department of Justice agents, Gaston Means, later claimed that it was in 'the little green house in K Street' that, between 1921 and 1923, he had turned over $7 million to Smith from bootleggers. Means had started work at the Justice Department on a weekly salary of $90 but, thanks to Jess Smith, and Means's own rapid grasp of his job requirements ("I was to do as I was told and ask no questions"), he was soon living in a fully-staffed house with a monthly rental of $1,000 and being driven around Washington in a chauffeured Cadillac. His house contained an arsenal of weapons and had a buried safe in its garden.

Smith held notorious parties where showgirls were shipped in from New York at weekends to dance on the tables. Pornographic films, 'featuring a couple of dolls who later put on clothes, changed their names and became famous in Hollywood, were shown nightly', remembered one journalist acquaintance. One evening things went too far. A 'dope fiend' call-girl was either accidentally hit on the temple by someone throwing bottles or had a glass smashed in her throat by another girl, and died. Harding, who was present, was hustled away; when the dead girl's brother tried to blackmail the President he was hastily put behind bars.

Daugherty and Smith's H Street house, known as the Love Nest because Harding used it for assignations with his 'lulla-paloozas', was owned by Evalyn and Ned McLean. Wealthy, feckless Ned McLean was proprietor of the *Washington Post*, known during Harding's administration as the 'Court Journal'. He shared Harding's passions for drinking, gambling and womanizing; his mistress, Rose Davies, was the sister of Marion Davies, W. H. Hearst's lover. It was McLean, aided by Gaston Means and Jess Smith, who had been entrusted with paying off Harding's girlfriends in the run-up to the election. McLean even moonlighted as a spy: Daugherty appointed him a Special Agent of the Bureau of Investigation (which a former private eye, William Burns, ran for him as a personal protection racket) with a nominal salary of a dollar a year.

Mrs McLean was the indulged only daughter of an imm-ensely rich gold prospector. She had grown up, as she put it, in a home where the cost of things never influenced decisions. On their honeymoon she and Ned had driven round Europe in a vast, pale yellow Mercedes filled with whisky, with Evalyn in a chinchilla coat 'decked with fifty marks' worth of violets'. Stopping in Paris on the way home, the jewel-obsessed heiress went shopping for a wedding present and bought the cursed 92½-carat diamond the Star of the East for $120,000, declar-ing confidently that bad luck for other people would be good luck for her.

Ever since she first stole what she called 'fluid emerald' (*crème de menthe*) from her parents' drinks cupboard in her early teens Evalyn had been an alcoholic. When her brother died at a tragically young age, grief helped turn her into a morphine addict. 'In those days a woman, diamond laden, could buy laudanum by the quart if she would simply pay the druggist what he asked,' she wrote, describing the animal cunning with which she would hide caches of the drug under her bedroom carpets or in the stuffing of furniture.

Her extravagance was legendary. Alice Roosevelt Longworth cattily declared that she loved going to the McLeans's parties because they were 'so endearing in [their] vulgarity'. Evalyn, she said, 'could be very likeable with her queer loud voice and great generosity' although Longworth, who despised the Hardings, had dropped her when she became friends with Florence in about 1915.

Perhaps because she showed no interest in sleeping with Warren, or perhaps because they both had notoriously unfaithful husbands, Evalyn became Florence Harding's only trusted female friend. She found Warren 'a stunning man... full of life and eagerness to enjoy the world of riches that had been opened to him by politics' — although she added that while he had the charm necessary to succeed, it was his wife who possessed the ambition.

Unlike most of the hyenas circling the President, Ned and Evalyn McLean seem to have had nothing to gain from their intimacy with the Hardings except the cachet of being known to be their closest friends. According to Lillian Gish, their home was 'said to be the unofficial White House'. They provided an escape from the pressures of official life in the form of their estate outside Washington, Friendship (which, incongruously, had once been a monastery), where Evalyn's pet monkey and llama ran wild and Harding did the rounds of the 18-hole golf course. Jess Smith called Friendship 'a damn swell layout'. It was on the lawn there during Harding's presidential campaign that the McLeans burned the entire print-run of *The Illustrated Life of President Warren G. Harding*, a book exposing Harding's mistresses and alleging that he was descended from runaway slaves and that Florence had Jewish blood.

Other Harding cronies were greedier. A character in John Dos Passos's 1925 novel *Manhattan Transfer* justified graft like this: 'a live man, nowadays, wants more money, needs more money than he can honestly make in public life. Naturally the best men turn to other channels.' By this definition corruption was only natural – a form of survival of the fittest and evidence more of a man's ambition than of immorality or criminality. This philosophy seems to have characterized the men with whom Harding surrounded himself and to whom he felt such a misplaced sense of loyalty.

When he became President, Harding had wanted to make Albert Fall, his former seat-mate in the Senate, Secretary of State, but Republican elders dissuaded him. Fall contented himself with the Department of the Interior. William Allen White thought the six-shooter-carrying Fall looked like a 'patent medicine vendor' selling Wizard Oil out of the back of a wagon. Evalyn McLean also found Fall menacing. He customarily wore a black cape and big hat and 'the cigar that stuck forward from his angular jaw was about the size of a lead pencil and as poisonous as a cobra'.

Harding had none of White and McLean's scruples about his friend, but his faith in him was grievously misplaced. A confidential Bureau of Investigation file recorded that Albert Fall, a one-time district judge, had borrowed money to buy his seat in the Senate, and had colluded in the murder of one man and his six-year-old son and tried another man for murder knowing that he was innocent. Having made (and spent) a fortune prospecting in the wild Southwest, Fall was an arch anti-conservationist determined, as Secretary of the Interior, to exploit the nation's rich resources of oil, timber and coal. By the time he took the job he was also dangerously short of ready cash.

It was Fall who introduced the Hardings to Harry Sinclair. Sinco, as he was known, was a self-made oilman designed to appeal to Warren. He knew Daugherty, had contributed to Harding's campaign fund, was a keen poker-player and, as part-owner of a baseball team and owner of a Kentucky Derby winner, had attractive connections to the sporting world. When Fall asked Harding to approve the lease to Sinco of oil-rich naval land at Teapot Dome, Wyoming, Harding was only too pleased to sign. As a mark of gratitude, Sinclair's company gave Fall's son-in-law $233,000 in bonds, $85,000 in cash and a herd of pedigree cattle.

Sinclair was not the only oilman to benefit from his ties

to Fall. In return for a black bag containing $100,000 in cash Edward Doheny, head of Pan-American Petroleum, was granted the lease of naval property at Elk Hills, California, also on extremely favourable terms. Like Sinclair, Doheny had supported Harding's presidential campaign, donating $25,000 to pay for publicity photos of Harding with his parents to counteract rumours of Harding's black ancestors.

The Hardings had befriended the ingratiating Charles Forbes and his wife when they were holidaying in Hawaii in 1915 and Forbes was supervising the construction of the new naval base at Pearl Harbor. Six years later, despite having almost no relevant experience, Forbes was placed at the head of the new Veterans' Bureau with a $450 million budget at his disposal. The gallant wounded veterans of the Great War were the official cause closest to Florence Harding's heart. Genuinely moved by their plight, she fund-raised on their behalf, nursed them in hospital and tirelessly pursued individual cases brought to her attention. Utterly taken in by Forbes's boastful affability, she had urged her husband to appoint him to what she considered the most important of roles.

In just two years, Forbes sucked the Veterans' Bureau dry. He reported medical and hospital supplies damaged and then sold them, pocketing the profit, and bought replacements from the companies that paid him; he inflated the price of government land sold for hospitals in return for a share of the profit from the sale; he awarded hospital construction contracts to firms who gave him a cut. One of these firms belonged to the husband of one of his mistresses – who just happened to be Warren Harding's sister; a second mistress was the wife of another rich building contractor to whom he also gave access to his rivals' bids. He took friends and girlfriends on lavish, bootleg-fuelled junkets across the country, ostensibly on Veteran's Bureau business. In all, it is estimated that in two years he cost the Government $200 million – of which he personally appropriated perhaps $36 million.

These unprincipled men recognized that Florence Harding needed to be flattered and cajoled into bestowing her support upon them. Both Fall and Edwin Denby, the Secretary of the Navy implicated in Fall's leasing of naval land, wrote to the First Lady assuring her that they would do all they could 'to do as you desire'. Daugherty himself wrote, almost in apology for having seen the President without her, 'Of course you know it – you know everything which he or I do or think… I am loyal to him – that is as loyal to him as I can be considering that I always give your instructions preference over his'. Only Forbes – perhaps the closest socially to Florence – paid little attention to her demands that he investigate the cases of specific veterans with whom she was concerned. But finally Mrs Harding's suspicions as to Warren's friends' true activities and motives were awakened.

By the summer of 1922, less than eighteen months after he had taken office, the pressures of his position were wearing on Warren Galamiel Harding. He began to drink whisky at official meetings. The appalled president of the Rail Workers Union described Harding as being too drunk to negotiate during talks at the White House. Harding confessed to a friend that he had no appetite for the exercise of power and would rather be a diplomat than president – although he added, pathetically, 'probably I should be a very poor ambassador'.

Florence was also affected by the strained atmosphere. Her health, which had been fragile for many years, declined rapidly in September 1922 and she relied ever more heavily on the quackish and eccentric homeopath 'Doc' Sawyer whom she and Warren had brought with them to Washington from Marion. While she was convalescing she summoned the popular psychologist Emile Coué to the White House and daily repeated his mantra: 'Every day, in every way, I am getting better and better.'

The First Lady also requisitioned the Department of Justice agent Gaston Means to act as her spy and messenger. Bemoaning Harding's blindness 'to the faults of his friends', she said that her role was to shield and guard him. Means said that she asked him to investigate Attorney-General Harry Daugherty, Secretary of the Interior Albert Fall, Secretary of War John Weeks – and Nan Britton, a young woman from Marion whose childhood crush on Harding had developed into a passionate adult affair.

Means thought little of his new employer, calling the First Lady paranoid, desperate, deluded and – perhaps most cuttingly of all, for the rigidly elegant Florence – overdressed. He said she was increasingly dependent on the advice of a string of astrologers and psychics; the secret duties she required of him included retrieving indiscreet letters she had written to a fortune-teller he called Madame X. Means ridiculed Florence's faith in Madame X's declaration that she was a 'child of destiny'.

Before Harding accepted the Republican candidacy another spiritualist, Madame Marcia, had predicted disaster and sudden death if he became President, and Florence was determined that she would protect her husband from this fate. It was typical of what William Allen White described as Harding's 'courtier thieves, Rasputins, drunkards, [and] harem favourites' that Madame Marcia also gave advice to Roxie Smith, Jess Smith's estranged wife; that Gaston Means's direct boss was Harry Daugherty – whom Mrs Harding had asked Means to investigate; and that Florence's links to both had been established through Evalyn McLean.

Charlie Forbes's transgressions were the first to be made public. In February 1923 the Senate voted to investigate the 'waste, extravagance, irregularities and mismanagement' at the Veterans' Bureau. Harding refused to believe that his friend had betrayed his trust until Florence convinced him it was true. Then he summoned Forbes to the White House and almost throttled him, screaming, 'You yellow rat! You double-crossing bastard!'

By the time the investigation began, Forbes had fled the country. His probably innocent legal adviser, Charles Cramer, shot himself in the head in his bathroom, either horrified at the crimes Forbes had committed or racked with guilt at his own complicity. The suicide note Cramer had left for the President disappeared; no investigation was ever made into his death. Forbes was fined $10,000 and imprisoned in a penitentiary for two years.

In May, attention turned to happy-go-lucky Jess Smith. He was excluded from the cosy poker evenings he had once so enjoyed in the White House and ordered to change his ways. Herbert Hoover thought Daugherty had warned Smith that he was on the point of being arrested. On 30 May, Smith was found with a bullet in his head at the home he shared with Daugherty. Although his death was presented as suicide, many people, including Gaston Means and Evalyn McLean, believed he had been silenced. Conveniently, none of his papers were discovered.

The following month the Hardings set off on an official tour of the Rockies, Alaska and the West Coast. For once, the McLeans were not invited to attend them. Earlier that spring, Alice Roosevelt Longworth had told Florence about what she called Evalyn's kindness in allowing the President to use Friendship to entertain 'women friends from Marion'; by this she meant Nan Britton. Evalyn's betrayal wounded Florence deeply just at the time she most needed a friend.

Throughout the trip, both Warren and Florence were ill and seriously worried about the escalating allegations of misconduct. Death and bad luck seemed to hang in the air: three journalists died when their car crashed into a canyon; a tram collision was narrowly avoided; their train engineer was killed in a landslide. Harding was only able to muster up his customary energy and good spirits when pretty girls were around. To calm his nerves he played bridge day and night with exhausted aides. 'My God! This is a hell of a job!' he said to the journalist William Allen White. 'I have no trouble with my enemies… But my damned friends, my God-damn friends, White, they're the ones that keep me walking the floor at night.'

One afternoon Harding asked Herbert Hoover, who was with them on board their ship travelling south from Alaska, to join him in his cabin. 'If you knew of a great scandal in our administration, would you for the good of the country and the party expose it publicly or would you bury it?' he asked. Hoover replied, 'Publish it, and at least get credit for integrity on your side.' Harding 'remarked that this method might be politically dangerous. I asked for more particulars. He said that he had received some rumours of irregularities, centring around [Jess] Smith, in connection with cases in the Department of Justice. Harding gave me no information about what Smith had been up to. I asked what Daugherty's relation to the affair was. He abruptly dried up and never raised the question again.'

Harding came down with a bad attack of food poisoning as the presidential entourage continued southwards. By the time they had reached San Francisco it had developed into pneumonia and he died, either of a heart attack or a stroke, on the evening of 2 August. He was fifty-seven. Florence, utterly dependent – as she had been for years – on the unreliable advice of their quackish personal physician, 'Doc' Sawyer, refused to permit an autopsy. This led to wild speculation that she had poisoned her husband to prevent him being implicated in the scandals swirling around him. Perhaps Hoover's assessment was closest to the truth. 'People do not die from a broken heart,' he wrote of Harding's death, 'but people with bad hearts may reach the end much sooner from great worries.'

One consolation for Harding would have been that he was never implicated in the corruption of his so-called friends – his only crime seems to have been that he was too loyal to them to suspect what they were up to – and that when he died and was buried it was as one of America's best-loved presidents. Millions of bareheaded mourners queued alongside the train tracks as his coffin thundered back across the country towards the capital, quietly singing his favourite hymns.

Granite-like, Florence Harding returned to Washington with her husband's body. After his funeral, having made her peace with Evalyn McLean, she went to stay at Friendship. There the two women burned all the Hardings' private papers. Over the bonfires, Florence said to Evalyn, 'Now that it is all over I am beginning to think it was all for the best.' Within a few months, the kidney disease that had plagued her for fifteen years persuaded her to return to her home town of Marion. She died there just over a year after Warren in November 1924.

Revelations of the corruption of Forbes, Smith, Daugherty, Fall and Sinclair, among others, continued throughout the 1920s. In 1924 Daugherty managed to avoid cross-examination by a Senate committee on the grounds that his personal relations with the Hardings made it impossible for him to give evidence – either by using them as a shield or trying to implicate them in his own corruption. Coolidge, Harding's succ-essor, stepped in and forced Daugherty to resign, but he was never tried for any crime.

Albert Fall loudly protested his innocence, claiming that the large sum of cash he admitted having received came not from Edward Doheny or Harry Sinclair but was a loan from Ned McLean. He had not, he swore, been given 'one cent on any account of any oil lease or upon any other account whatsoever'. But McLean, although he was willing to write Fall a predated cheque to cover the money, could not be prevailed upon to testify on his behalf in court. Pleading ill-health, he refused to come to Washington from Florida, where he was spending the winter, and finally confessed that he was lying. Fall was convicted of conspiracy and bribery and sentenced to a year in prison – the first Cabinet officer in US history to be jailed.

Sinclair was acquitted of bribery charges but served a double term in 1929 for contempt of the Senate (he had refused to answer the investigating committee's questions) and for contempt of court (he had offered at least one member of his jury a car 'as long as this block' if he voted to acquit him). In 1924 Will Hays was asked by the Senate investigating committee how much Sinclair had given the Republican Party and replied $75,000; four years later, asked again, he revealed that there had also been a loan of $185,000 which he had not disclosed because he had not been asked about 'bonds'.

Further unpleasant disclosures continued to emerge. Having failed to persuade Harding's family to pay her a $50,000 settlement, in 1927 Nan Britton revealed in *The President's Daughter* not only that Harding was the father of her eight-year-old daughter, but that the child had been conceived in Harding's Senate office. In *The Strange Death of President Harding*, published three years later, Gaston Means claimed that Jess Smith had been murdered and that Florence Harding, pushed to the edge by Warren's womanizing, had killed her husband. Others put forward theories about Harding having committed suicide.

Evalyn McLean saw the political scandals of Harding's administration as being on an epic scale, with herself and her husband as its protagonists. 'What happened to us all was just about as tragic as if each one, instead of only I, had worn a talisman of evil,' she wrote many years later, referring to the Star of the East. 'Some died, one probably was killed [Jess Smith], one is blind, some went to jail; I suffered humiliation, and Ned lives on, a fancied fugitive, in an asylum where he pretends, with characteristic slyness, that he is someone else who does not know McLean.' In the early 1930s one of Ned's fellow inmates was Zelda Fitzgerald, with whom he reportedly used to dance the hokey-kokey.

It was a sign of the moral lethargy of the times that the public was more hostile towards the men who scrutinized the Harding scandals than towards the perpetrators of them. The senators investigating the oil scandals and the Department of Justice under Daugherty were labelled 'assassins of character', 'mud-gunners' and, worst of all, unpatriotic. People muttered darkly about a socialist conspiracy to bring down America.

Nothing could challenge the national sense that the Republicans were the only party fit to govern. As their collectively apathetic attitude to Prohibition showed, many Americans were only too happy not to probe too deeply into difficult truths that would interfere with their complacent enjoyment of 1920s prosperity. What they were really interested in was not politics but 'motion pictures, baseball, prize fights, automobiles, dress, murder and divorce'. Harding's taciturn Vice-President, Calvin Coolidge – conveniently free from any whiff of implication in his predecessor's shortcomings – was re-elected in another Republican landslide in 1924. His supporters sang,

> When we get to Washington, home, sweet home,
> We won't give a darn for the Teapot Dome!

6

'The Business of America is Business'

DESPITE THE CORRUPTION OF many of the men with whom
Harding had surrounded himself, Calvin Coolidge's typically
succinct 1924 campaign slogan, 'Coolidge or Chaos', still appeared to reflect the political reality. All through the 1920s
the Democratic Party, torn apart by bitter internal divisions,
seemed out of touch and unelectable, competing against a
party that spoke for middle America's hopes and aspirations.
The Republican Party were seen to be making America
prosper – and against that argument, the Democrats had no
response.

Warren Harding (President from 1920–23), Calvin Coolidge
(1923–28) and Herbert Hoover (1929–32) were all elected by
vast majorities. All three believed in small, non-interventionist government; all three believed that the interests of big
business were synonymous with the national interest – and
therefore that business ought to be given what Coolidge called
a 'free hand'. It was the age, wrote Malcolm Cowley, 'when

directors' meetings were more important than Cabinet meetings and when the national destiny was being decided by middle-aged bankers and corporation executives'.

'What we need in America is less government in business and more business in government,' declared Harding when appointing as his Treasury Secretary the austere banker and industrialist Andrew Mellon, the third-richest man in the United States after John D. Rockefeller and Henry Ford. Mellon, heir to those nineteenth-century capitalists who believed that the rich were uniquely suited to arrange the affairs of the rest of mankind, resigned from fifty-one directorships to take up his government post. He served at the Treasury until Franklin D. Roosevelt took office in 1932, pursuing two objectives: to reduce public debt and to lower taxes. In both of these he was successful.

Immediately after the Great War, an economic downturn brought with it industrial action and striking workers, but business, supported by the government, stood firm. Supreme Court decisions in the late 1910s and early 1920s upheld the rights of industry over the rights of child workers and women, declaring it unconstitutional for the Government to regulate labour conditions, and illegal for unionization or picketing to be mandatory. Trade unions were systematically undermined. In 1920 the president of Bethlehem Steel (an industry which had gone on strike across the nation the previous year) announced that he would not recognize a union even if 95 per cent of his workers belonged to one. He was backed up by

Harry Daugherty, the Attorney-General, who said that he would do all he could 'to prevent the labor unions of the country from destroying the Open Shop'.

Replacing unions, altruistic companies – it was thought – would look after their workers, providing them with health insurance, baseball teams and glee clubs. Successful businesses would share their profits with workers in the form of high wages. The worker could then encourage industry by spending and, if he were clever, could even buy his own share in it by investing in the stock market.

Each successive administration continued to develop this idea of 'welfare capitalism'. Easy-going Harding simply wanted to see everyone prosper; Coolidge believed that government functioned best as a 'businessman's government'; Hoover, a former head of the Department of Commerce, campaigned on the message that the United States would thrive if business thrived. 'Wealth creation', the pursuit of money for its own sake, was lauded as natural, even noble. Coolidge said, 'Brains are wealth and wealth is the chief aim of man.'

Businessmen were seen (and saw themselves) as creative, daring and public-spirited. Even Al Capone tried to promote an image of himself as an entrepreneurial benefactor rather than a hood. The American businessman had replaced 'the statesman, the priest, the philosopher, as the creator of standards of ethics and behaviour'. By 1928, one-time progressives like the journalist Walter Lippmann had been converted to the new dogma. Businessmen, Lippmann declared, are 'for once more novel, more daring, and in general more revolutionary than the theories of the revolutionaries'.

Many flourished under this regime, but some groups were thrown into unrelieved poverty. Farmers, who had enjoyed 16 per cent of the national income during the war years, by 1929 found themselves with a share of less than 9 per cent. New methods of transporting, processing and storing food meant that wheat and corn prices dropped. Modern women in thrall to silk stockings and nylon no longer wanted to wear cotton and wool. Instead of raising profits, the increasing mechanization of farming created worldwide markets – and worldwide competition. The value of farmland dropped by nearly a quarter over the twenties, while the value of town land doubled; bankruptcies and suicide rates among farmers rose. Feeling excluded from the country's new urban and industrial wealth, rural Americans bitterly resented the Republican single-interest Government. 'Farmers have never been rich,' said Coolidge flatly. 'I don't believe one can do much about it.'

Apart from in farming areas, from 1921 onwards the economy – and the parallel exaltation of business over the interests of workers – rose steadily. By the mid-1920s Robert and Helen Lynd recorded that in Middletown, which they described as 'an aggressive industrial city' dominated by glass, metal and automobile factories, public opinion no longer sided with organized labour, and trade unions had all but disappeared.

Perhaps because industry was expanding rapidly, the workplace had become increasingly impersonal. Bosses took less time to get to know their workers individually and manual workers especially derived scant satisfaction from their labours. President Coolidge saw factory work differently. 'Those who build a factory build a temple of worship,' he intoned. 'Those who work in a factory, worship there.'

This glorification of 'business methods' and the pursuit of 'success' became almost a religion. Government and society reflected back at each other their rapacious zeal for making money. Clubs like the Rotarians, founded in 1905, and the Kiwanis, founded in 1915, promoted this aggressively optimistic idea of collective achievement, encouraging men to 'sell themselves', to be 'boosters not knockers', as a patriotic and spiritual duty. Women founded their own clubs with mottoes like 'Progress', as often devoted to the improvement of their towns as their own social lives. In 1929 there were 1,800 Kiwanis clubs nationwide; 150,000 men worldwide were Rotarians by 1930. Even God was commandeered into promoting the new gospel. Jesus was said to have been 'the first Rotarian'. Henry Ford called machinery 'the new Messiah'.

Adman Bruce Barton's self-help book, *The Man Nobody Knows*, depicted Jesus as the 'founder of modern business' and became the best-selling title in the United States in 1925 and 1926. Barton, a minister's son, made Jerusalem sound like Sinclair Lewis's Zenith and Jesus a latter-day George Babbitt. Not only was Jesus a 'go-getter' and 'the most popular dinner guest in Jerusalem' (no doubt because of his ability to turn water into wine) but he was also a great executive who had 'picked twelve men from the bottom ranks of business and forged them into an organization that conquered the world'.

Selling in particular was seen as a distinctively American trait, a unifying characteristic in a country still searching for a sense of its destiny in the wider world. The journalist Mark Sullivan called 'the passion to sell... the impelling power in American life'. An apocryphal story of the times told of a company said to give an annual banquet for its salesmen. Every year, the best performer would sit down to a lavish feast; the second-best achiever would be served the same dinner, but without oysters; and so on down the line to the least effective man, who dined on beans and crackers.

Salesmen were the 'angels and evangels' of Coolidge prosperity, persuading people not simply to buy what they needed – but what they hadn't yet dreamed they wanted. 'Consumption is a new necessity,' wrote the Lynds of mid-1920s Middletown. Shoppers, whose disposable incomes rose by nearly a third in this period, found they had extra money to spend on fashionable factory-made clothes, cigarettes and lighters, make-up and wristwatches. Even children were given pocket money.

Everywhere there were what the Lynds described as 'new urgent occasions for spending money'. No one owned a radio in 1920; a decade later, 40 per cent of all households had one. President Harding installed the first radio in the White House in February 1922. Over four million sets, at a cost of about $100 each, were sold between 1922 and 1925.

Instalment-buying and new methods of providing credit removed the stigma from debt and allowed people to spend well beyond their incomes. By the second half of the 1920s, an estimated 15 per cent of all retail sales were on credit. Half of household appliances and three-quarters of cars were sold on hire purchase in 1929. Accessible mortgages fuelled a housing boom.

As well as more money, Americans had more leisure time. It was becoming more common to have Saturday afternoon as well as Sunday off, and many workers began to enjoy an annual two-week paid holiday. More and more people were working in offices in towns, rather than in factories or on farms, and their hours were determined by electricity rather than daylight. Between 1902 and 1929 the electric light and power industry expanded nineteen times.

The gap between people's basic physical needs – food, shelter, clothing – and what they did to make a living grew ever wider. After a packaged breakfast cereal a typical American drove into town from his suburban home to begin work at a desk at eight-thirty rather than outside at sunrise. Families or groups of friends could now spend their electric-lit evenings playing mah-jong (the craze of 1922), dancing to music on the radio or the gramophone, or going to the movies – all of which created a sense of belonging to a single American culture.

Following fads like mah-jong, using new slang words or

knowing the latest dance song 'are absolutely necessary if one wishes to be like everyone else', explained a college newspaper. Changes in fashion were making it harder to tell the social classes apart. Increasingly, the rich liked to look casual and approachable while the aspiring poor were spending as much as they could afford on clothing to demonstrate their social mobility.

This was a culture of extravagant consumerism as well as conformity: mass production, mass consumption, mass culture. A French professor, visiting the United States in Alexis de Tocqueville's footsteps in 1927, observed that, 'In its pursuit of wealth and power, America has abandoned the ideal of liberty to follow that of prosperity.'

In *The Theory of the Leisure Class* (1899), the sociologist Thorstein Veblen had explored human acquisitive and emulative instincts, arguing that expenditure and leisure are the ways men gain and display status. Conspicuous consumption (a phrase Veblen coined) was the wasteful use of resources or money to impress others; conspicuous leisure (another Veblen phrase) the wasteful use of time to demonstrate wealth. According to Veblen's ideas, aspiration and acquisition were unavoidable elements of the human make-up, and they were actively encouraged by the structure and ethos of 1920s society. 'Everyone lives on a slope from any point of which desirable things belonging to people all the way to the top are in view,' observed the Lynds of Middletown.

Advertisers, studying the work of academics like Veblen,

began educating the poorer classes to imitate the buying patterns of the richer, appealing to Americans' newly discovered desires to be glamorous and envied. One Middletown girl stopped going to school altogether because her parents couldn't afford what she thought were the right clothes – without which she claimed she would have been neglected by the boys and scorned by the other girls. It was typical of the period that her parents apparently accepted her argument and allowed her to drop out.

Stanley Resor, president of the New York advertising agency J. Walter Thompson, was much influenced by the work of the psychologist John Watson in analysing buying patterns. In blindfold tests Watson showed that smokers could not tell cigarette brands apart – so that although they bought one brand and had brand loyalty, other factors than the taste of the tobacco (despite what they may have thought) were influencing their choice. Advertisers soon learned how to capitalize on these other factors.

Creating and playing on consumer insecurities, advertisers told potential buyers that one key to maintaining beauty, youth, energy and attractiveness was health and personal hygiene. The actress Constance Talmadge, promoting cigarettes, declared, 'There's real health in Lucky Strike... For years this has been no secret to those men who keep fit and trim. They know that Luckies steady their nerves and do not harm their physical condition. They know that Lucky Strike is the favourite cigarette of many prominent athletes, who must keep in good shape.' Advertisers' success in manipulating the gullible buying public became an article of faith. An essay of 1922 on the subject opened with the words, 'Do I understand you to say that you do not believe in advertising? Indeed! Soon you will be telling me that you do not believe in God.'

In the early 1920s Listerine, variously used in the nineteenth century as a surgical antiseptic, a cure for venereal disease and a floor-cleaner, was transformed by advertising into a magical product which would free its user from the dreadful, life-ruining scourge of halitosis – a faux-medical term for bad breath invented by the marketing men. Their advertisements showed a downcast girl holding her friend's bridal bouquet above the caption, 'Often a bridesmaid, but never a bride'. The cause of her loneliness was 'chronic halitosis' – which, happily, Listerine (rebranded as a mouthwash) promised to cure. Listerine's profits soared from $115,000 to $8 million in just seven years.

Advertisers promoted an obsession with cleanliness and good hygiene because it would sell their products; as the historian Stephen Fox puts it, it also 'projected a WASP [white Anglo-Saxon Protestant] vision of a tasteless, colourless, odourless, sweatless world' that chimed with the rampant nativism of American politics. The unspoken message was that immigrants could become better Americans by swilling away their garlic breath with Listerine or covering up their spicy body odour with deodorant. The growth of national advertising (and the prosperity that fuelled it) fostered a very specific sense of Americanness and patriotism – wholesome, moral, aspirational and conformist – a sliced-white-bread and apple-pie view of the world. Those who did not fit into this mould, or could not afford to, were branded as outcasts.

Many industries boomed in the 1920s, but one stands tall above the rest: the automotive business. 'Why on earth do you need to study what's changing this country?' asked one of the Lynds' interviewees in Middletown. 'I can tell you what's happening in just four letters: A–U–T–O!' In 1920 there were 7.5 million cars in the United States; a decade later that number had soared more than three times to 27 million, or one car for every five people. In mid-1920s Middletown, owning a car had become by 1924 'an accepted essential of normal living', just as owning a telephone had been at the turn of the century. Half of Middletown's working-class families owned cars, almost all paid for by instalment – although, of that group, a third did not yet have a bathtub.

Cars and the network of roads and suburbs that sprang up in their wake transformed America physically and psychologically. Distances shrank. For the first time people could travel more than five miles to work or school; trips of a hundred miles or more suddenly became a regular occurrence. In 1920 each car would travel 55,000 miles in its lifetime; by 1930 that number had jumped to 200,000 miles. Three million miles of government-co-ordinated asphalted highways criss-crossed America by 1927, including a transcontinental road that allowed motorists to drive directly across the country from coast to coast. Filling stations, perhaps the archetypal image of twentieth-century America, were built by the sides of these new roads in their thousands; traffic lights and parking regulations were gradually introduced in towns.

Traditional patterns of living were also transformed by the introduction of the car. Rural communities were no longer isolated islands surrounded by empty prairies. Children who did not live in towns could go to school, and thus had the chance to create lives different from their parents'. Work patterns changed. Teenagers borrowed their parents' cars to meet their friends on their own; families went for a drive instead of going to church on Sunday. Social commentators attributed the breakdown of family values and piety as much to the negative influence of cars as to the movies.

Auto-related industries like rubber, oil, steel, petroleum and glass – and the cities they were based in – boomed. Detroit expanded by 126 per cent between 1910 and 1920; Akron, Ohio, the tyre capital, grew 173 per cent in the same period; the wealth and population of oil-producing cities like Houston and Los Angeles ballooned.

With fuel prices reaching record highs in the early 1920s, oil companies aggressively pursued potential new fields in the Middle East, especially in Iraq and Iran, between them dividing regions into the provinces of individual companies and exploiting them ruthlessly. The Government's non-interventionist policies allowed them to integrate vertically, controlling every aspect of oil production and distribution from refineries to petrol stations.

By 1930 the car industry accounted for a tenth of America's manufacturing wages and more than a tenth of all its manufactured goods. An English visitor to the States wrote, 'As I caught my first glimpse of Detroit, I felt as I imagine a seventeenth-century traveller must have felt when he approached Versailles.' The age of steam had been vanquished by the age of petrol.

The self-made pioneers of the motor trade – the Dodge brothers, Billy Durant, John Jakob Raskob, the Fisher brothers, and Walter Chrysler – were hailed as modern-day buccaneers and their work was called 'our greatest industry': 'Business has become the last great heroism... a conflict of the hard-muscled and strong-willed, for only they will survive'.

One man in particular was credited with developing this uniquely American industry: that irascible, eccentric genius, Henry Ford. Ford had invented the self-starting car in 1912, perfected the assembly-line production method at his Highland Park plant near Detroit two years later, and by 1924 controlled over half the motor industry. *Vanity Fair* hailed him as a member of their annual Hall of Fame the following year: 'Because he has changed the whole rural life of America by lowering the price of motors cars; because he has made some of the most ludicrous statements ever conceived by a public man; and finally because the benevolent paternalism prevailing in his factories is enormously applauded and admired by everyone except his employees.'

Henry Ford's revolutionary idea was to provide farmers with a cheap, practical car that would replace their horse. The first Model Ts – fondly known as Flivvers or Tin Lizzies – were sold in 1909 for about $850 (by the mid-1920s falling to less than $300), as compared to several thousand for other, more sophisticated marks. His main problem was keeping up with demand. In the year that his assembly-line system was installed at Highland Park, which allowed his workers to put together a car every ninety-three minutes, he produced more cars than every other manufacturer combined. By the time the Ford plant produced its ten-millionth vehicle, nine out of every ten cars on the road worldwide were Fords.

What was later called mass production was the key to Ford's success. 'The way to make automobiles is to make one automobile like another automobile, to make them all alike... just as one pin is like another pin, when it comes from the pin factory,' he said. Making individual parts – and thus whole cars – exactly identical and interchangeable was as important for repairing existing cars as for manufacturing new ones.

Despite (or perhaps because of) the fact that the machine he had made available to millions of Americans was changing society irretrievably – hastening the march of the urbanization and new codes of morality he deplored – Ford was incurably romantic about the simple pastoral America into which he had been born. He held on tightly to the populist values of a late-nineteenth-century Midwestern farmer throughout his life.

At his birthplace of Dearborn, Ford constructed a replica

nineteenth-century farming community, supported a back-to-the-soil movement, collected Americana and encouraged old-fashioned folk dancing. He himself was an enthusiastic and energetic dancer. In 1918, Ford bought his local newspaper, the *Dearborn Independent*, which he intended to use as the mouthpiece for his homespun philosophy. 'Mr Ford's Own Page' – which he did not write – discussed homilies like 'Opportunity will not overlook you because you wear overalls'.

But there was a darker side to Ford's nostalgia for a lost rural heartland. For two years, between 1920 and 1922, the *Dearborn Independent* took on an overtly anti-Semitic tone. The 'International Jew' was described as 'the world's foremost problem' and blamed for the high rents, low morals, short skirts, gambling and drunkenness that Ford believed were destroying America. His outspoken views earned him an interesting fan: Adolf Hitler was said to have had Ford's picture on the wall by his desk in Munich in 1922 and copies of his books scattered around his office. The flow of anti-Semitic articles stopped as suddenly as they had started, probably because Ford was thinking of running for president and realized that a hate campaign would not serve his interests. Lawsuits had been threatened.

It was typical of Ford's contrariness that although he openly expressed his anti-Semitic views, he also had a number of Jewish friends. In 1927 Ford shut down the *Dearborn Independent* altogether, running a long apology for everything he had written against Jews in past issues; this did not stop him accepting the Grand Cross of the German Eagle from the German consul in 1938 on his seventy-fifth birthday.

With his distrust of foreigners, bigoted views and pride in his limited education, Ford represented the successful side of political fundamentalism. 'Facts mess up my mind,' he said; one might add that abstract thought seems to have done the same. Despite his hypocritical contempt for 'big business', he was a single-minded businessman with the morals of a robber baron, who spared scant consideration for the workers who made him rich. To him, they were simply cogs in the machine. His factory was an altar to capitalism, 'a vast, satanic cathedral of private enterprise'.

There were some ways in which Ford was a good boss. One book he had read was Ralph Waldo Emerson's essays, which inspired him with a strong sense of social justice. As long as they could do the job required of them, he was happy to hire black workers, women, the disabled, immigrants (including Jews) and ex-convicts. A sociological department at Highland Park urged Ford's workers to be clean, healthy and family-minded, rather than spending all their money in speakeasies; foreigners were encouraged to learn English. Ford also paid his workers generously – a previously unheard-of $5 a day for factory work – because, he said, he wanted them to be able to afford the cars they were making. Ford's paternalistic philosophy epitomized the idea of 'welfare capitalism' that 1920s politicians hoped would arise out of a business-dominated society.

But Ford expected an awful lot for his $5: he was known for raising 'the pain threshold of capitalism'. Obsessively high standards of workmanship, as well as of behaviour, were insisted upon. Philanthropic innovations were intended less to please his workers than to make them more efficient. From Ford's point of view, the most important advantage of the high wages he offered was that however much he demanded from his workers, there would always be others waiting to replace them if they could not keep up.

By the early 1920s Ford was motor manufacturing's Colossus. The Tin Lizzie had proved so dominant that between 1917 and 1923 Ford hadn't even needed to advertise her merits. As the industry liked to say, 'If you could deliver automobiles you could sell them.' Production was the only issue. Slowly, though, other motor manufacturers were beginning to think of ways to weaken Ford's ascendancy, grasping in a way that he did not that cars needed to be sold, not merely distributed.

In 1924 the single-colour, single-model Model T was knocked off her pedestal. General Motors had started to offer rainbow-coloured cars in a variety of styles, including enclosed bodies and self-starting motors – realizing that the next challenge to the automotive industry was not how to get people to buy a car (most of those who could afford it already had one) but how to get them to buy another, and then another.

As the market became more competitive, cars became more sophisticated and the range of people they were targeted towards broadened. Improved engine technology and fuel made driving smoother, quieter and easier. Crank shafts were replaced by electric starter motors. New developments in lacquers that dried in twenty-four hours rather than up to thirty days allowed customers to buy a car in Liberty Blue, Versailles Violet or Apache Red rather than black.

At first Ford refused to accept that the common man didn't want to remain the 'common' man – that he aspired to something greater and more elusive than cheap and efficient uniformity. His market troubles were compounded by conflict with his son, Edsel, who had been president of Ford Motors since 1918, over the direction the business should take. Finally convinced by arguments that he needed to adapt to this strange new desire for choice, Ford shut down his plant and modernized it, sacking all his workers. Since his was the only factory in town it was almost impossible for them to find new jobs without leaving their homes. When he was ready, Ford hired them back – at the same rate they had received before they were fired, $5 a day, and without any compensation for the $50 million they had collectively lost in missed wages.

Although it was the conglomerate General Motors who had ousted Ford from his position as market leader, the most interesting car manufacturer of the 1920s was Walter Chrysler. He had started out as a railway engineer before joining Buick (part of General Motors) as works manager in 1912, where he was described by one of his team as the 'greatest production man in the industry', and quickly rose to become company president. While Ford was developing his assembly line, Chrysler was innovating in other directions. The introduction of electric lights and starter motors made him think for the first time that the new breed of emancipated women might be potential car buyers.

Chrysler left Buick in January 1920. At his farewell dinner he was lavished with the highest possible praise, lauded as 'a real American and one who understands Americanism and keeps things in the main current of American life'. He took over Maxwell Motors which began selling the first Chrysler cars in 1924 and became the Chrysler Corporation the following year.

While Ford was (both to its advantage and its detriment) a one-man band, and while General Motors, an amalgamation of various smaller companies like Buick, depended on its organizational capacity, the Chrysler Corporation's success was founded on Walter Chrysler's extraordinary management skills. Chrysler himself personified 'traditional American qualities of initiative, courage, leadership and resourcefulness'. He believed 'in the dignity of work'. Not only was he unfailingly energetic and driven, but he was 'absolutely fair to his people, square with his customers, and faithful to his stockholders'. Most importantly of all, he created an atmosphere in which his workers were encouraged to be inventive, dynamic and responsive.

His engineering team, in particular, flourished under Chrysler's guidance. The first Chrysler car they created was a tribute to his high standards and commitment to the consumer's needs. It was stylish, luxurious, quiet, smooth-driving and easy to handle – but although reasonably priced it was still in the mid-range bracket as too few could be produced each year.

Chrysler was determined to capture the low-price market dominated by General Motors and Ford, while giving the customer a high-quality car. 'The person who prefers to drive a small car is entitled to every consideration that can be given him,' he said, 'comfort, roominess, easy riding and long life.' To this end he brought out the affordable Plymouth in 1928. Hoping for it to appeal to women as well as men, Chrysler invited the aviator Amelia Earhart to launch it in Madison Square Garden.

The name Plymouth was chosen to evoke the 'endurance and strength, the rugged honesty, the enterprise, the determination of achievement and the freedom from old limitations of that Pilgrim band who were the first American colonists'. To underline the message, Chrysler salesmen were sent Pilgrim costumes in which to promote the new car.

As manufacturers like Chrysler realized, advertising and marketing were crucial elements of retailing success. Entranced customers were sold freedom, speed, glamour and romance along with their motors. Perhaps the most famous car advertisement of the 1920s was for the Jordan Motor Company. It showed a girl in an open Jordan racing a cowboy through wilderness, her scarf flying out behind her. 'Somewhere west of Laramie', read the tagline, 'there's a bronco-busting, steer-roping girl who knows what I'm talking about. She can tell what a sassy pony, that's a cross between greased lightning and the place where it hits, can do with eleven hundred pounds of steel and action when he's going high, wide and handsome. The truth is – the Jordan Playboy was built for her.'

Celebrity endorsements also attracted valuable consumer attention. Cadillac was famous for the bullet-proof limousine it built for Al Capone. Movie stars commissioned custom-built cars in striking colours and finishes. Pola Negri liked to be driven around Hollywood in her white velvet-upholstered white Rolls-Royce, complete with white-liveried driver – except when it rained, when he wore black.

In January 1928, Walter Chrysler made a public declaration explicitly linking car-owning and road-building to prosperity and progress – to the march of civilization itself. 'My associates and I have looked ahead and we failed to see any reason for change [in current levels of growth]. We could find no economic justification for cycles of depression. All the indicators we could see were that times were good and would continue good.' It looked as though the pro-business attitudes of the US Government, and indeed of the country as a whole, had triumphantly succeeded in creating an economy that could not fail.

But even in the years of what felt like unbridled prosperity, cracks were beginning to show. Partly because cars made possible the development of the suburbs, reached by newly built roads, property was another booming industry, funded by new methods of financing. Florida, made newly habitable by air-conditioning and refrigeration, was its epicentre; holiday-makers and investors rushed to purchase property there. Developers began converting Florida's salt-water swamps into a web of streets and houses. Addison Mizner, creator of Boca Raton, built ever more extravagant houses in a style that came to be known as 'Bastard-Spanish-Moorish-Roman-esque-Gothic-Renaissance-Big-Bull-Market-and-Damn-the-Expense'. There were 30,000 people living in Miami in 1920. Five years later that number had soared to 75,000 – of whom it was said that a third were estate agents.

Stories of the money that could be made abounded. One man had bought a building lot near Miami for $25 in 1896 (when Miami had only had sixty inhabitants) and sold it in 1925 for $150,000; another cursed himself as he watched land he had sold for $12 an acre being successively sold on for $17, then $30, then $60. An evangelizing estate agent lectured prospective buyers on the property market's three cardinal sins: fear, caution and delay. 'If Jesus Christ were alive today,' he declared, 'he'd buy a lot right here!'

The frenzied speculation came to a halt in September 1926 when a violent hurricane laid waste to the state of Florida. Four hundred people were killed; 40,000 were left homeless; tankers were beached on Miami's streets. The man who had watched his property value rise from $12 to $60 an acre found that the entire string of payments was in default and he couldn't even lay hands on his original sale price – he was forced to take the land back himself in lieu of payment.

Somehow America's faith in its inexorable good fortune remained undampened. 'The Florida boom was the first indication of the mood of the twenties and the conviction that God intended the American middle class to be rich,' wrote the economist John Kenneth Galbraith thirty years later. 'But that this mood survived the Florida collapse is still more remarkable.'

In 1926 Andrew Mellon's Revenue Act passed into law, lowering taxes for everyone – but especially the rich. Before the new laws, a man with an income of a million dollars had paid $600,000 in tax; afterwards he paid just $200,000. Three-quarters of one percent of the population paid 94 per cent of the Government's tax revenue – but then again, the top 5 per cent of the population earned a third of the nation's income.

Mellon could argue that with the passage of his tax package he had accomplished his aims. Government spending had been reduced by nearly a half, government debt was down by $6 billion, taxes were minimal and the economy was booming. By the time Mellon's new tax system came into effect in 1927 a few people were starting to worry about the effects of over-speculation and the over-extension of credit, but neither Mellon nor Coolidge would countenance an interest-rate rise; they believed the market should be self-regulating. This would have grave implications in the coming years.

Perhaps more serious still was the general acceptance of a

two-tier society in which, despite America's escalating wealth, discrepancies in income were growing ever wider. America's vast new national wealth was deceptive. Its burgeoning prosperity was distributed unevenly and depended either on high levels of business investment or astronomical luxury spending or both. In 1929, 71 per cent of American families lived on annual incomes of less than $2,500, which was the generally accepted minimum standard for decent living; of these, 42 per cent survived on less than $1,500. Immigrants in particular were the victims of this gross economic inequality.

7

Fear of the Foreign

IN THE MID-1910s, an Italian immigrant called Bartolomeo Vanzetti was living in Plymouth, Massachusetts, and working for the local cordage company which dominated the town. Factory conditions across the United States were harsh — twelve- or fourteen-hour days, six- or seven-day weeks, heavy, dangerous labour, desperately poor pay, fetid, filthy conditions — and Plymouth was no exception. To add insult to injury, foreign factory workers were often paid as much as a third less than their American-born colleagues, reflecting the popular assumption that, being of different 'racial stock', they were less intelligent and less capable.

When in 1916 the cordage workers decided to strike for better conditions, Vanzetti (who was no longer working for the factory) led the protest. He had lived in America for eight years, doing one wretched job after another. Over the years he had absorbed the radical ideas of men like Giuseppe Mazzini and Karl Marx who spoke of a time when all men would have decent jobs, roofs over their heads and food on their tables. As Vanzetti would later write, 'I sought my liberty in the liberty of all; my happiness in the happiness of all. I realized that the equity of deeds, of rights and of duties, is the only moral basis upon which could be erected a just human society.' When he stood on a soapbox and told his fellow workers that they deserved better, they believed him. The company grudgingly raised their wages by a dollar. Afterwards Vanzetti was the only person who was explicitly barred from ever working for the factory again.

From this point onwards, Vanzetti worked for himself, selling fish from a hand-pulled cart and, when money was tighter than usual, building roads, cutting ice or shovelling snow for the Board of Public Works – earning his bread in the open air and, as he put it, 'by the honest sweat of my brow'. His interest in radical politics and activism continued. Knowing he could not pursue his intellectual and social interests in a conventional job, he preferred to work for himself. Later he would say that he disdained business because it was a form of speculation using human lives.

During the cordage strike, Vanzetti had met one of his communist-anarchist heroes, Luigi Galleani, a passionate advocate of violent revolution, who came to Plymouth to encourage the protesters. For several years Vanzetti had been a subscriber and contributor to Galleani's Italian-language journal, the *Subversive Chronicle*, which plotted the overthrow of the capitalist regime and argued in favour of terrorism and political assassination. The *Chronicle* had also published the Italian translation of Leopold Kampf's *On the Eve*, a play examining the lives of Russian revolutionaries who were radicalized during the years following 1905, and a widely distributed bomb-making manual with the innocent title, *Health is Within You*.

Americans had feared radicals before the war, and distrusted foreigners – people from Southern and Eastern Europe, Russians and Italians, as well as Germans – during it, but the success of the Bolshevik Revolution in Russia in 1917 aggravated existing fears and prejudices. Floods of new immigrants, many from Russia, many with established communist sympathies and inspired by events at home, began to dominate the American communist movement in the late 1910s. Labour unions began to ally themselves with international radical groups; their militancy scared employers. Although the total number of active communists in the United States was probably well under 40,000, they were a vocal minority and the threat of a communist revolution on American shores began to seem a very real one. 'If I had my way, I'd fill the jails so full of them [Bolsheviks] that their feet would stick out of the windows,' declared the evangelist Billy Sunday.

Because radicals, whether they were communists, anarchists, socialists or 'Wobblies' (members of a group called the Industrial Workers of the World), were usually pacifists who had opposed the war, and because so many of them were new to American shores, they were labelled unpatriotic – potential traitors who ought not to be allowed to remain in the United States. Respectable politicians started saying things like, 'My motto for the Reds is S.O.S. – ship or shoot. I believe we should place them all on a ship of stone, with sails of lead, and that their first stopping place should be hell.' (In March 1920 the *New Republic* attributed this quotation to General Leonard Wood who stood against Warren Harding for the Republican presidential nomination that year; Wood publicly denied saying it.)

Intolerance, as the historian Frederick Allen observed ten years later, 'became an American virtue'. Any individual or activity that cast into question 'America' or 'American values' was deemed suspicious. 'In popular parlance a Bolshevik was anybody "from the dynamiter to the man who wears a straw hat in September" while the name "radical" covered all those whose shades of opinion ranged "from a mild wonderment over 'what the world is coming to' to the extremists of the left wing"'.

This anxiety about outsiders, especially non-Northern European foreigners, was given pseudo-scientific credence by a series of books and studies claiming to prove that certain 'races' were physically and mentally inferior to others. Writing in the popular *Saturday Evening Post*, published from Philadelphia, Kenneth Roberts called Polish Jews 'human parasites' and denounced free immigration on the grounds that it would produce 'a hybrid race of people as worthless and futile as the good-for-nothing mongrels of Central America and South-Eastern Europe'.

In the spring of 1919 post-war inflation hit hard. Workers had less to live on; they needed higher wages just to keep up with rising prices. But the companies they worked for were making less and had little inclination to pay them more. A wave of hard-fought strikes, like the one Vanzetti had helped co-ordinate in Plymouth three years earlier, swept the United States. It is estimated that four million people – ship-builders in Seattle, construction workers in New York, policemen in Boston, steel workers and coal miners all over the country – went on strike over the course of 1919. These strikes took place against a background of anarchist violence and rioting which allowed local leaders to crush walk-outs by exaggerating the Red menace and discrediting the striking workers as radicals.

Sixteen bombs were found in a New York post office that April by a worker who had read about a brown-paper package exploding in the hands of Senator Hardwick's maid in Atlanta and remembered that he had set aside identical packages at his sorting office because of insufficient postage. On his information, eighteen more were intercepted at post offices across the country.

On the evening of 2 June bombs were set off in eight cities at carefully planned destinations. The most significant was the one aimed at the front door of the Washington house of the new Attorney-General, Mitchell Palmer. The bomber, who apparently stumbled as he went up the steps to Palmer's house, was killed by his own blast. He was an Italian activist, an adherent of Galleani and an associate of Bartolomeo Vanzetti.

Galleani and eight of his closest followers were deported three weeks later, but although the authorities were desperate to root out more of his associates it was almost impossible to penetrate their tight-knit circles and find evidence that would incriminate them.

After this incident Palmer, known before his appointment to the Attorney-General's office in March 1919 as a Wilsonian progressive who had supported women's suffrage and laws to protect child workers, lost no time in mounting a campaign against 'enemy aliens': the 'blaze of revolution', he said, was sweeping across America 'like a prairie fire'. He requested and received extra funds of $500,000 to set up Edgar Hoover (no relation to Herbert) in an anti-radical division of the Department of Justice. Twenty-four-year-old Hoover, a former librarian, quickly built up a meticulously cross-referenced card catalogue of 250,000 suspects. As a subscriber to Galleani's *Subversive Chronicle*, Bartolomeo Vanzetti's name was on Hoover's list.

Using a Labor Department law set up to allow the Government to deport radicals during wartime, Palmer started rounding up suspected anarchists and revolutionaries in November. Despite the appropriation of the Wartime Sedition Act, his tactics were savage and unlawful. Scant attention was paid to individual warrants. Crowded tenement houses were virtually demolished during the raids, staircases ripped out, men beaten and physically torn away from their wives and children. Even the Assistant Secretary of Labor admitted that the attacks were 'intended to be terrifying' and noted that 'the whole red crusade seems to have been saturated with "labor" spy interests' – that is to say agents hired by big companies to generate and intensify industrial tensions.

In Detroit, where eight hundred men were held for ten days in unheated stone cells, sharing a single toilet and water fountain, the Justice Department's agent gleefully announced to reporters that, 'We didn't leave them a scrap of paper to do their business.' Between November and January over five thousand people were arrested in Palmer's raids, of whom five hundred were deported and another third prosecuted.

The Government and the Establishment were united in their support of Palmer's extreme measures. 'There is no time to waste on hair-splitting over infringements of liberty...' said the *Washington Post*. Warren Harding, at the start of his campaign for the presidency, delivered a tub-thumping speech to the Ohio Society. 'Call it the selfishness of nationality if you will, I think it is an inspiration to patriotic devotion – To safeguard America first. To stabilize America first. To prosper America first. To exalt America first. To live for and revere America first... Let the internationalist dream and Bolshevist destroy... We proclaim Americanism and acclaim America.'

The Palmer raids were conducted particularly vigorously around Boston. A large community of immigrants, especially Italians, lived in the Bay area, their presence greatly resented by longer-established residents. About eight hundred people were arrested on 2 January 1920 and half were taken in chains to the immigrant station on Deer Island in Boston Harbour where they too were held in unsanitary, freezing conditions. Two of the prisoners died of pneumonia; another went mad; a third plunged to his death out of a fifth-storey window. Later it emerged that a group of thirty-nine bakers arrested in Lynn, Massachusetts, had been gathered together not to ferment revolution, but simply to establish a co-operative bakery.

It was at this time, and in this atmosphere of suspicion and fear, that two crimes in particular were committed near Boston. In Bridgewater on Christmas Eve, 1919, four men had unsuccessfully attempted to hold up a payroll truck, and fired at the truck as it fled. Four months later, in April, a gang murdered a paymaster and his guard at a South Braintree shoe factory, escaping the scene with $15,000. Suspicion rested firmly on the immigrant community, and the police were under enormous pressure to find and convict the murderers.

The following month, the body of Andrea Salsedo, an Italian anarchist printer, was found smashed on the ground beneath the windows of the Department of Justice's New York office. He and an associate had been held without warrants and probably tortured since their arrests eight weeks earlier. It was unclear whether Salsedo had jumped or was pushed. During his captivity, Bartolomeo Vanzetti had travelled to New York as a delegate from his local Italian society, hoping to stand bail for Salsedo and his friend.

Back in Boston two days after Salsedo's death, Vanzetti and a fellow anarchist, Nicola Sacco, went to get an associate's car out of the garage so that they could drive to the homes of various anarchists, warn them of Salsedo's fate and tell them to hide away any incriminating political pamphlets – probably including the bomb-making manual, *Health is Within You*. They had heard that the area was going to be raided again. Finding that the car did not have a current licence plate, they left the garage and boarded a trolley-bus heading home. The garage owner, acting on official instructions to inform on any Italians who owned cars, called the police as soon as they had left. The police apprehended Sacco and Vanzetti on the trolley-bus and took them into custody.

Visibly nervous, aware that the authorities probably knew of their anarchist connections, the two men lied about the fact that they were carrying weapons and who their friends were. The officers who arrested them interpreted this as 'consciousness of guilt' – although John Dos Passos, who later wrote an impassioned appeal for their release, suggested that it might have been 'consciousness of the dead body of their comrade Salsedo lying smashed in the spring dawn two days before'.

The Department of Justice quickly realized that by convicting Sacco and Vanzetti for the Bridgewater and South Braintree crimes they would be getting rid of two central members of the Galleanist group they had long hoped to smash. Even before they were arrested, Sacco and Vanzetti had been the focus of Justice Department interest. Once they were in prison awaiting trial the Department stepped up its efforts to incriminate them. As many as a dozen spies were placed near them and their friends and families – in neighbouring cells in prison; boarding with Sacco's wife Rosa; one even sat on the committee formed for their defence (and pocketed funds from it for himself). A letter to one of the spies later showed that he was offered $8 a day for his work – two or three dollars more than Vanzetti had earned per week as a dishwasher when he first arrived in New York. But the agents' efforts went unrewarded. Maybe no one knew anything; certainly they weren't telling.

As Sacco, who worked for a shoe factory, had a stamped time-card for Christmas Eve 1919, Vanzetti alone was tried for being part of the attempted robbery in South Braintree. The court case was staged in Plymouth, where he was a known anarchist. Despite the eighteen mostly Italian witnesses Vanzetti produced to testify to his whereabouts selling fish on 24 December (eels are an Italian Christmas delicacy), nine of whom had actually spoken to him, Vanzetti was convicted on evidence such as that of a fourteen-year-old boy who admitted he had not seen the face of the fleeing man purported to be Vanzetti, but swore he 'could tell he was a foreigner by the way he ran'. One witness was asked whether he had ever heard any of Vanzetti's entirely unrelated political speeches to the striking cordage workers, four years earlier. Judge Webster Thayer – who asked for and received permission to preside over the South Braintree case as well – told the jury in his summing-up that the crime was 'cognate' with Vanzetti's radical ideas.

After Vanzetti was convicted and sentenced to fifteen years for attempted robbery at Bridgewater, he and Sacco were tried for their part in the South Braintree murders in a courtroom heavily and dramatically fortified against a potential bomb-attack. Twenty-two of the thirty-five eyewitnesses to the crime were certain that neither Sacco nor Vanzetti had been there; seven were unable to make any kind of identification; of the four who identified Sacco, two were discredited and the other two changed their first accounts to incriminate him; only one, who had elsewhere contradicted the evidence he gave in court, positively identified Vanzetti. Both men had alibis for that day, but these were disregarded by the jury. Although many of the Justice Department agents apparently thought that the theft and murders had been committed by professional highway robbers, one of the detectives working on the case was later quoted as saying, 'They were bad actors anyway and got what was coming to them.' Off the record, Judge Thayer was said to have said that he wanted to see the bastards hanged.

The two men were convicted and sentenced to death by Thayer in July 1921. 'There was not a vibration of sympathy in his tone when he did so,' said Vanzetti later. 'I wondered as I listened to him, why he hated me so. Is not a Judge supposed to be impartial? But now I think I know – I must have looked like a strange animal to him, being a plain worker, an alien, and a radical to boot. And why was it that all my witnesses, simple people who were anxious to tell the simple truth, were laughed at and disregarded? No credence was given to their words because they, too, were merely aliens.'

*

Over the next few years, while Sacco and Vanzetti waited for a retrial, the Red Scare fuelled by Palmer's brutal raids abated. The threat of a widespread Bolshevik rising seemed less and less likely as stability returned to Europe. Despite Palmer's dire warnings of imminent revolution on American soil, the chaos he had predicted did not come to pass. Americans wanted to forget the recent turmoil and concentrate on the future. When Warren Harding came to office seeking 'a return to normalcy' he declared, 'Too much has been said about Bolshevism in America'.

But immigrants continued to flood into America. Between June 1920 and June 1921, the year of Sacco and Vanzetti's first trial, 800,000 people, 65 per cent of them from South-Eastern Europe, landed in Ellis Island. Incoming ships had to be diverted to Boston because the facilities for dealing with new arrivals were overwhelmed. Almost unanimously, Congress passed an emergency act to stall the incursion. 'America must be kept American,' declared the Vice-President, Calvin Coolidge. Supported by the trade unions, the National Origins Act of 1924 was unabashedly discriminatory, limiting immigrants from South-Eastern Europe to pre-1890 levels and prohibiting Asian immigration. On hearing the news Japan declared a day of mourning.

Prejudice, ignorance and intolerance were gradually being institutionalized. One senator declared that the bill would mean 'that the America of our grandchildren will be a vastly better place to live in. It will mean a more homogeneous nation, more self-reliant, more independent, and more closely knit by common purpose and common ideas.'

Only a few lone voices, like that of the *Baltimore Evening Sun*, dared express disapproval of the bill, pointing out that the United States had finally abandoned 'that old and admirable tradition that this land was to serve as a refuge for the oppressed of all nations. No longer is the foreigner, to American eyes, a welcome fugitive from the political, economic and religious oppression of the Old World.'

From the start, liberal intellectuals and political progressives recognized Sacco and Vanzetti's cause as their own. In late 1921 Anatole France wrote an open letter to the people of the United States, describing Sacco and Vanzetti's crime as one of 'opinion' and their sentence as 'iniquitous'. 'It is horrible to think that human beings should pay with their lives for the exercise of that most sacred right which, no matter what party we belong to, we must all defend,' the French writer wrote, urging Americans to save the two men 'for your honour, for the honour of your children, and for the generations yet unborn'.

The following year, in an article in *Harper's*, the writer Katharine Gerould declared that America was no longer a free country. 'No thinking citizen, I venture to say, can express in freedom more than a part of his honest convictions,' she wrote. 'I do not of course refer to convictions that are frankly criminal. I do mean that everywhere, on every hand, free speech is choked off in one direction or another.' Her piece provoked hundreds of responses, as many denouncing her as a dangerous radical as rejoicing that someone had at last dared tell the truth.

For the six years following their conviction, Bartolomeo Vanzetti and Nicola Sacco were held in different prisons, Vanzetti serving hard labour in Charleston and Sacco in solitary confinement for twenty-three hours out of twenty-four in Dedham, Iowa. Both were affected profoundly by their incarceration. At one point Sacco went on hunger strike, refusing food for thirty days; Vanzetti became so depressed and paranoid that he spent four months in a prison asylum.

When they were well, the two men wrote to each other from their cells with fraternal affection. They had known one another since 1917, when they had spent six months in Mexico avoiding the draft. Neither had supported what they saw as a war to defend capitalist interests. From that point on, bolstered by their shared ideals and commitment to Galleanist principles, their friendship had flourished.

Burly Nicola Sacco, at thirty years old in 1921 three years Vanzetti's junior, had arrived in America in 1908, within months of Vanzetti, but he had gone straight to Boston. His family were prosperous peasant farmers from the foothills of the Apennines in southern Italy. Unlike Vanzetti, Sacco was married with two young children and had a steady and relatively well-paid job; like his friend, though, he had been a socialist and anarchist since 1913. On the day he was said to have committed the South Braintree robbery and murders, Sacco claimed he had been at the Italian consulate in Boston, getting passports for himself and his family to return to Italy for good. He had saved almost $1,500, enough to start a new life at home.

Vanzetti had no plans to return to Italy, although like Sacco he had been frustrated, humiliated and demoralized by the discrimination and hostility he had encountered in the United States. After a seven-day crossing in steerage, he had sighted New York from the ship, looming 'on the horizon in all its grandness and illusion of happiness'. But from his first steps on land he was shocked to find that he and his fellow arrivals were treated like animals. In his characteristically idiosyncratic prose, Vanzetti remembered seeing terrified children weeping as they went through immigration procedures. 'Not a word of kindness, of encouragement, [were given] to lighten the burden of tears that rests heavily upon the newly arrived on American shores. Hope, which lured these immigrants to the new land, wither [sic] under the touch of harsh officials'.

Friendless, empty-handed and unable to speak or understand English, twenty-year-old Vanzetti was typical of many Southern and Eastern European immigrants to the United States. Al Capone's family, which had arrived fourteen years earlier, had at least had each other. 'Where was I to go? What was I to do? Here was the promised land. The elevated [railroad] rattled by and did not answer,' remembered Vanzetti, his words unwittingly echoing Charlie Chaplin's first frightened response to New York. 'The automobiles and the trolleys sped by, heedless of me.'

The single contact Vanzetti had in New York could not find him space to sleep in his crowded, rat-filled tenement, so Vanzetti slept in the park. He did help him get work as a dishwasher, for which Vanzetti was paid $5 or $6 — as much as a worker on Ford's plant would earn in a day, a few years later — for an eighty-eight hour week. Although he hated baking, Vanzetti eventually managed to find work as a pastry-chef (the trade he had been trained in as a boy), but time and again he was sacked for no reason after a few months in the job. It turned out that the head chefs were paid by the employment agencies every time they hired a new worker, so they never kept anyone for long. Over the next few years, as he made his way slowly eastwards towards Boston, Vanzetti preferred to find manual labour under the open sky in furnaces, quarries and railyards.

Vanzetti never married; his life was spent alone. What sustained him through these hard years was his inner life, his almost spiritual understanding of social justice. He read everything he could get his hands on (in Italian), from the *Divine Comedy* to Charles Darwin to Maxim Gorky to the Italian anarchist Errico Malatesta. Vanzetti started to see himself as a champion of 'the weak, the poor, the simple and the persecuted': the character of the man who would inspire the Plymouth cordage workers and then a generation of discontented intellectuals began to take shape.

'I understood that man cannot trample with impunity upon the unwritten laws that govern his life, he cannot violate the ties that bind him to the universe,' he wrote while he was in prison. 'I grasped the concept of fraternity, of universal love. I maintained that whosoever benefits or hurts a man, benefits or hurts the whole species... I wanted a roof for every family, bread for every mouth, education for every heart, light for every intellect... I maintain that liberty of conscience is as inalienable as life... I am and will be until the last instant (unless I should discover that I am in error) an anarchist-communist, because I believe that communism is the most humane form of social contract, because I know that only with liberty can man rise, become noble, and complete.'

Neither Sacco nor Vanzetti had spoken, read or written English with any fluency when they were arrested. Sacco did not read or write much until 1922, but Vanzetti began to study from the moment he was imprisoned. Visitors commented on his 'keen interest in world affairs, and his thirst for knowledge'.

Smiling benevolently beneath his substantial walrus moustache, in prison Vanzetti became an icon of the left. In letters to friends and supporters, he embraced his role as a political symbol, developing and expanding his philosophy and almost mystical sense of mission. 'I cannot share your confidence in "better government", because I do not believe in the government, any of them, since to me they can only differ in names from one another,' he wrote to one new friend in the spring of 1925. 'Mutual aid and co-operation and co-operatives shall be the very base of a completely new social system, or else nothing is accomplished.'

To another, later that year, he made it sound almost as if arrest and imprisonment had allowed him to serve his principles: 'We did not come to [be] vanquished but to win, to destroy a world of crimes and miseries and to re-build with its freed atoms a new world. I am disappointed, but not crushed. I have not become a rat or a renegade. And I can carry my burden to the last, and only that counts.' He refused to recant his beliefs and continued to call for vengeance, which he hoped would be realized as freedom for all. 'But till then, the struggle goes on... till then, to fight is our duty, our right, our necessity.'

The Department of Justice would have seen these words in the context of Vanzetti's links to the violent anarchist movement – and so they were meant; documents signed by Vanzetti and Sacco while they were in prison contain pointed references to *Health is Within You*. But they also inspired their liberal supporters with a vision of Vanzetti, in particular, as a 'philosophical' anarchist, a harmless dreamer, a would-be intellectual. Instead of a ferocious activist, they saw a poet and an idealist behind the large moustache.

Vanzetti contemplated his end with serenity and dignity. 'Were I to recommence the "journey of life," I should tread the same road, seeking, however, to lessen the sum of my sins and errors and to multiply that of my good deeds.' With all the lyricism of the incarcerated, he wrote of his lost hopes of living 'free among the green and in the sunshine under an open sky'.

He thanked well-wishers who had sent him flowers for his cell: 'My window here is peopled of recipients, it is a riot of blissing colors and beauties forms: A giranium plant, a tulip and plant both from Mrs Evans. White flowers, pink carnations, roseate peaches buds and flowers, bush-yellow flowers from Mrs Jack, and a bouquet of May flowers from Mrs Winslow.' How could Mrs Evans or Mrs Winslow see this gentle, nature-loving man as a murderer?

Sacco and Vanzetti's adherents focused on the 'noble' characters of the accused men, swearing that no one who knew them could believe either man capable of committing the crimes with which they were charged. Visitors and correspondents described them as warm, poetic, simple-hearted and sincere; every contact they had with them, they claimed, made the conviction of their innocence stronger. Judge Thayer, however, thought differently.

After six appeals their case was reopened in 1927. One of Sacco's fellow prisoners in Dedham, Celestino Madeiros, had confessed to being part of the South Braintree gang and specified that neither Sacco and Vanzetti had been there. He named his fellow conspirators as the Morelli brothers – one of whom bore a striking similarity to Nicola Sacco. Madeiros was able to demonstrate that he had received a large sum of money, his fifth-part share of the robbery. No money had ever been associated with either Sacco or Vanzetti, the alleged thieves.

Madeiros's evidence corroborated the generally held

opinion of the Boston Department of Justice agents that the South Braintree crimes had been committed by a professional gang of highwaymen, but Judge Thayer (again presiding) dismissed it. The Department of Justice refused to open their files to disprove evidence gathered against them of spying and manipulating evidence and witnesses. A Justice Department agent who had placed a spy in prison with Sacco insisted that his 'only motive in trying to clear up the mystery was to aid justice'.

Sacco and Vanzetti's lawyer protested: 'A government that has come to honour its own secrets more than the lives of its citizens has become a tyranny whether you call it a republic or a monarchy or anything else,' but there was nothing he could do to change Thayer's mind. As the journalist Heyward Broun would later point out, Thayer was acting out of a genuine commitment to what he saw as the public interest. His belief in Sacco and Vanzetti's guilt was that of a 'solid and substantial' citizen, and it chimed 'with all our national ideals and aspirations'. Whether as ungrateful, un-American immigrants, common criminals, dangerous radicals or godless anarchists, Sacco and Vanzetti could not be allowed to triumph. A woman in the courtroom cried out, 'It is death condemning life!'

'There could not have been another Judge on the face of this earth more prejudiced and more cruel than you have been against us,' said Vanzetti later. 'We know, and you know in your heart, that you have been against us from the very beginning, before you see us. Before you see us you already know that we were radicals, that we were underdogs, that we were the enemy...'

Vanzetti spoke proudly in court after Thayer had passed sentence. 'My conviction is that I have suffered for things that I am guilty of. I am suffering because I am a radical, and indeed I am a radical; I have suffered because I am an Italian, and indeed I am an Italian; I have suffered more for my family and for my beloved country than for myself; but I am so convinced to be right that if you could execute me two times, and if I could be reborn two other times, I would live again to do what I have done already.' Sacco echoed him, but with a more overtly political tone. 'I know the sentence will be between two class, the oppressed class and the rich class, and there will always be collision between one and the other... That is why I am here today on this bench, for having been the oppressed class.'

After sentencing, the two men were moved into the same prison for the first time. Between April and July they were held in Dedham, and for the final six weeks before their execution they were moved to Charleston. Still both refused to renounce the political ideals they had held so dear and for which they believed they were being punished. 'Both Nick and I are anarchists – the radical of the radical – the black cats, the terrors of many, of all the bigots, exploiters, charlatans, fakers and oppressors,' said Vanzetti in May. 'Consequently we are also the more slandered, misrepresented, misunderstood and persecuted of all.'

He proudly rejected a suggestion that they recant in order to sue for pardon. 'We cannot make it [a refutation of their ideals], because it is a thing against our understanding and conscience... I cannot explain you why... But we too have a faith, a dignity, a sincerity. Our faith is cursed, as all the old ones were at their beginning. But we stick to it as long as we honestly believe we are right... We have renounced voluntarily to almost all of even the most honest joys of life when we were at our twenties. Lately we have sacrificed all to our faith. And now that we are old, sick, crushed, near death:... should we now quack, recant, renegate, be vile for the love of our pitiable carcasses? Never, never, never... We are ready to suffer as much as we have suffered, to die, but be men to the last.'

Interviewed by the *New York World* at about the same time, Vanzetti expressed the strange sense of vindication that accompanied their final defeat. The newspaper chose to emphasize his foreign accent and imperfect English. 'If it had not been for these thing, I might have live out my life, talking at street corners to scorning men. I might have die, unmarked, unknown, a failure. Now we are not a failure. This is our career and our triumph. Never in our full life can we hope to do such work for tolerance, for joostice, for man's onderstanding of man as now we do by accident.'

Despite the efforts of their Defence Committee and a vocal international group of prominent supporters including Eugene Debs, H. G. Wells, Marie Curie, Albert Einstein and Bertrand Russell, Sacco and Vanzetti's death sentences were confirmed. The journalist William Allen White was among those who wrote to Massachusetts governor Alvan Fuller pleading for clemency, but to no avail. 'I now know why the witches were persecuted and hanged by upright and godless people... This is a tremendously important case for America. It seems to me that our courts would be vastly more discredited before the world if we executed innocent men than they would be if we refrained to execute innocent men when there was even a shadow of doubt as to their guilt.'

On 21 August Sacco and Vanzetti formally thanked the Defence Committee that had supported them since their arrest. 'That we have lost and have to die does not diminish our appreciation and gratitude for your great solidarity with us and our families. Friends and Comrades, now that the tragedy of this trial is at an end, be all as of one heart. Only two of us will die. Our ideal, you our comrades, will live by millions; we have won, but not vanquished. Just treasure our suffering, our sorrow, our mistakes, our defeats, our passion for future battles and for the great emancipation.'

That same day, Vanzetti wrote to Nicola's thirteen-year-old son, Dante, of how his father had 'sacrificed everything dear and sacred to the human heart and soul for his fate'. He hoped, he said, that Dante would understand that they had died for their principles, honour their memories, and perhaps one day take his father's place 'in the struggle between tyranny and liberty'.

Last-minute appeals went unheeded. An editorial in the *New York World* summed up the views of those who still hoped that eleventh-hour pardons might be issued. 'The Sacco–Vanzetti case is clouded and obscure. It is full of doubt. The fairness of the trial raises doubt. The evidence raises doubt. The inadequate review of the evidence raises doubt. The Governor's inquiry has not appeased these doubts. The report of his Advisory Committee has not settled these doubts. Everywhere there is doubt so deep, so pervasive, so unsettling, that it cannot be denied and it cannot be ignored. No man, we submit, should be put to death where so much doubt exists.'

At three minutes after midnight on the morning of Tuesday 23 August, Celestino Madeiros entered the execution room in Charleston prison. Nine minutes later he was dead. Nicola Sacco came in at 12.11, having refused the ministrations of a priest, and was strapped to the electric chair shouting, 'Long Live Anarchy!' in Italian. He was pronounced dead eight minutes later.

Finally Bartolomeo Vanzetti was brought into the room, having also refused the last rites. He declared his innocence one final time, expressed his forgiveness for those who had brought him to this point, and shook his warden, William Hendry, warmly by the hand, thanking him for all his kindness. For most of the past seven years this prison had been his home. Hendry was so overcome that he was barely able to confirm that Vanzetti was dead at twenty-six minutes past twelve. The three executions had taken less than half an hour.

As they had hoped, Sacco and Vanzetti's demise set off a series of retaliatory demonstrations, riots and bombs targeting

United States embassies in Paris, Rome and Lisbon as well as all across America. Five hundred Italian immigrants protested against the executions in Boston's North End. Writers John Dos Passos, Dorothy Parker and Edna St Vincent Millay were among many arrested for picketing the Boston State House the day before Sacco and Vanzetti died.

Millay was not alone in crediting their deaths with awakening her social conscience. 'It is impossible for me to be an Anarchist, for I do not believe in the essential goodness of man,' she wrote afterwards, contrasting her own disillusionment with Sacco and Vanzetti's unflinching idealism. 'The world, the physical world, that was once all in all to me, has at moments such as these no road through a wood, no stretch of shore, that can bring me comfort. The beauty of these things can no longer at such moments make up to me at all for the ugliness of man, his cruelty, his greed, his lying face.'

People involved in their conviction – the brother of the garage owner who had informed on them, Governor Fuller who had refused them clemency, one of their jurors, the executioner, Judge Thayer himself – were the focus of specific violent attacks. Thayer's home was destroyed by a bomb and he spent the rest of his life living under permanent guard at his club in Boston.

It is still unclear whether or not Sacco and Vanzetti did commit the crimes for which they were killed. Upton Sinclair, whose novel *Boston* was an attempt to place the events surrounding their purported crime and trial in a believable fictional context, was convinced that both were innocent – until his interview with their first lawyer, Fred Moore, who told him that although he had never heard them confess to it, he thought they were guilty. Sinclair considered Moore unreliable (he was sacked from the defence team because he was a cocaine addict) but his faith in his heroes was shaken.

It seems unlikely that Vanzetti was involved either with the murders and robbery at South Braintree or with the attempted robbery at Bridgewater. Ballistics experts over the years have linked Sacco's gun to the bullets fired at South Braintree, although others claim that the gun or the bullet-casings found in his pockets were tampered with at the time or afterwards. In the 1980s, the son of an anarchist associate of the two men said everyone in their inner circle knew that Sacco was guilty but Vanzetti was not.

What they were clearly and proudly guilty of was political radicalism, but this was not the offence for which they were tried. Their trial was a shameful attempt by the Government to rid itself by the only means it knew how of two men who symbolized forces that it feared and would not try to understand. But much of America would have agreed with Judge Thayer's unofficial verdict that Nicola Sacco and Bartolomeo Vanzetti were 'bastards' who deserved to die, regardless of the means used to achieve that end. It was these people who rushed in their millions to join the revived Ku Klux Klan.

8

The Ku Klux Klan Redux

THE POST-CIVIL WAR Ku Klux Klan had faded out of public consciousness in the late nineteenth century, but in 1915 the Kentucky-born director D.W. Griffith made a movie adaptation of Tom Dixon's best-selling novel of a decade earlier, *The Clansman*. *The Birth of a Nation*, starring Lillian Gish, showed the revival of the devastated post-war South as in large part due to the patriotism and loyalty of the Klan. Although Griffith claimed that his film merely reflected the period as he had read about it in history books – which it did; the history books of the time were uniformly racist – *The Birth of a Nation* served as inspiration to a new generation of fearful, prejudiced Americans who distrusted blacks as much as they resented immigrants.

One man observing the success of *The Birth of a Nation* with enraptured interest was Colonel 'Doc' Simmons, a lonely 35-year-old alcoholic recuperating in Atlanta after being hit by a car. Tall and impressive-looking, Simmons's inflammatory oratorical skills (and zeal for the sound of his own voice) were reflected by his fiery red hair. One acquaintance described him as being 'as full of sentiment as a plum is full of juice'. He had been a Methodist circuit preacher; he was also an inveterate joiner of churches and societies. In 1915 he wore the lodge pins of thirteen groups including the Masons, the Knights of Pythias and the Woodmen of the World, for which he worked as promoter. Simmons assumed his title, Colonel, from the honorary rank he held in the Woodmen; the 'Doc' came from a medical degree he claimed to have taken at Johns Hopkins University, but of which no evidence has been found.

On Thanksgiving night, 1915, just before the Atlanta première of *The Birth of a Nation*, Simmons took thirty-five men – including two former members of the Reconstruction Klan – up Stone Mountain, sixteen miles outside the city. Declaring that his society had 'the same soul in a new body' as the post-Civil War Klan, Simmons lit a fiery cross, his symbol of the old Klan, and led his followers in an oath of allegiance to his new order. They swore to protect female chastity and uphold and promote morality, 'Americanism', Protestantism and white supremacy.

Nothing in Simmons's original aims would have jarred with a large proportion of 'native-born' Americans at the time. He was simply expressing values that, to many, represented their existing ideas about their place in the world. Nor was he explicitly advocating violence against other races, although the use of the name, Ku Klux Klan, was in itself provocative.

Evidence suggests that instead of using feathers for tarring and feathering miscreants Simmons would have preferred them to adorn a splendid headdress that he could have worn at the head of a procession. What he loved was the Klan's regalia, its secret ceremonies, grandiose titles and arcane rituals, all devised by him, and his own position as leader of the movement. In the Kloran (the Klan book of ritual), Simmons described his role, that of Imperial Wizard, as 'a wise man; a wonder worker, having power to charm and control'.

Although Simmons inducted ninety-two members in the first two weeks and by 1920 had about three thousand followers in the Atlanta area, he was vague and impractical and had little idea of how to mould or expand his 'invisible empire'. Noticing Simmons's administrative difficulties, in June 1920 a young Klansman introduced Simmons to his mother-in-law, Bessie Tyler. The charismatic, determined Tyler had been married at fourteen and left widowed, with a baby, a year later. She and her lover, Edward Clarke, then formed the Southern Publicity Association. Despite the fact that in 1919 Clarke and Tyler had been arrested inebriated and in a state of undress in a house owned by Tyler, they had previously promoted the Anti-Saloon League (the driving force behind the Prohibition movement) as well as the Red Cross and the Salvation Army. Soon their most important client was the Ku Klux Klan.

Clarke and Tyler had no compunction about using the Klan for their own personal financial gain; Tyler later admitted that she was in it for the money. In return for 80 per cent of the fees collected from new Klan members, Clarke invested $7,000 of his own savings into putting the Klan on to the kind of profitable, business footing being used all over America by travelling salesmen. He divided the country into nine regions ruled by Grand Goblins and placed a King Kleagle in each state to oversee a troupe of local Kleagles, or Klan agents.

Each new Klansman who signed up paid $10. The Kleagle who had recruited him kept $4 and sent $6 to his King Kleagle; the King Kleagle kept $1 and sent $5 to his Grand Goblin; the Goblin kept 50 cents and sent the remainder to Klan head-quarters in Atlanta where Clarke and Tyler pocketed $2.50 and put $2 into the Imperial Treasury. The members' requisite white robes and hoods, intended to resemble the ghosts of the Confederate dead, cost an additional $6.50 and were soon being made in factories run by Clarke.

Within less than a year of Tyler and Clarke being hired, over a thousand Kleagles were actively pursuing new members all over the United States. By 1923, when nationwide membership was approaching the million mark, the Klan's annual income was $3 million – comparable to that of the Capone–Torrio organization in Chicago at the same time.

The Klan made a point of presenting itself as a force for social cohesion and improved morality and integrating itself into a community's daily life. An elderly woman from Indiana who was interviewed in the 1980s by the historian Kathleen Blee remembered that 'the good people all belonged to the Klan' in her youth and described it as a positive social force.

Her testimony was, however, somewhat disingenuous (no doubt unwittingly) because in practically the same breath as she denied that the Klan was xenophobic she commended it for getting rid of Catholic influence in her area.

A cross would be burned on a hillside to signal the Klan's arrival to the local population. Then a group of masked, robed men would appear at church services, bearing flowers and singing 'Onward Christian Soldiers', and offering money to church charities. One of the Klansmen might be invited to preach. New members would be initiated in the glow of a ring of car headlights, kissing the American flag and swearing loyalty to the order. Meaningless generalities about 'much needed local reform', 'just laws' and 'pure Americanism' were spouted.

Apparently innocuous Klan-organized barbecues, picnics, spelling-bees, concerts and rallies drew the local population in. Financial contributions would be made to local hospitals and schools. On Klan Day at the Texas State Fair in 1923 rodeo riders competed in full Klan regalia, a Klan-sponsored orphanage was declared open and, later on, fireworks blazed in the night sky above seven thousand masked marchers.

To demonstrate what they liked to think of as their paternalistic benevolence, the Klan even donated money to black causes. In 1921 a chapter in Memphis gave $500 to the black victims of an explosion. 'Be it known and hereby proclaimed,' read a Klan advertisement in a Dallas newspaper in 1921, 'that no innocent person of any color, creed or lienage [sic] has just cause to fear or condemn this body of men. That our creed is opposed to violence, lynchings, etc., but that we are even more strongly opposed to the things that cause lynchings and mob rule... Your sins will find you out. Be not deceived. You cannot deceive us and we will not be mocked. This warning will not be repeated.' The blues singer Bessie Smith was forcibly bundled into a car, driven off and horsewhipped in Dallas. She refused ever to go back to Texas.

Marcus Garvey, leader of the separatist United Negro Improvement Association (UNIA), went to Atlanta in the summer of 1922 to discuss possible Klan support for his 'Back to Africa' movement with Edward Clarke, although nothing came of their meeting. According to his widow, Garvey believed that most white Americans were only prevented from demonstrating the racism that the Klan made explicit by hypo-critical 'culture and refinement'. From his point of view, at least the Klan was honest.

Kleagles haunted showings of *The Birth of a Nation* and deliberately pandered to local fears and prejudices about illegal drinking, immoral behaviour, striking workers or influxes of blacks and immigrants to the area. Advised by the weekly newsletters Bessie Tyler produced, Kleagles scape-goated local 'enemies'. In California they played on hatred of the Japanese; in New York, on anti-Semitism; in Texas, on fear of Mexicans.

Once a local chapter had been established, Klansmen began targeting immigrants, blacks and political radicals. Cowed newspaper editors feared losing advertisers and readers if they spoke out against the Klan. Elections might be monitored and potential voters warned to stay away from the polls if they were not going to vote for a candidate sympathetic to the Klan; local businesses were bribed to boycott Jews, blacks and Catholics; non-Klan homes and shops were burned; bootleggers, immigrants, blacks, or even people sympathetic to them were flogged, acid-burned or occasionally killed. The Klan's victims were just as often whites who had transgressed as blacks or immigrants, like the two young men who had criticized the Klan in Louisiana and were kidnapped and murdered by being run over again and again by a large road-grading tractor before being dumped in a lake, or the white divorcee beaten to unconsciousness in her own home.

The revived Klan was by definition racist and anti-black but its activities were far from limited to the persecution of blacks. As the black-owned *Savannah Tribune* commented in July 1922, no lyncher felt he needed to put on a hood to kill a black man: 'They do not think it necessary to join a secret society, pay initiation fees and buy regalia when Negroes are the quarry.' Southern chapters of the Klan did take part in vigilante violence because lynching was an established part of their culture, but nationwide the Klan did not promote it per se. Although Bessie Tyler recommended that blacks be sterilized, in many areas fears about Southern and Eastern European immigrants were stronger and more potent than fears about blacks. Tyler best summed up the Klan's philosophy when she said that to be *for* the white race meant to be *against* all others – and that meant against anyone who was not Protestant and of Northern European descent.

Catholics were a particular focus of Klan mistrust. According to one mid-1920s newspaper article, devotion to the Pope was evidence of Mediterranean people's 'servility', while 'the spiritually-minded, chivalrous, and freedom-loving Nordic peoples have always been hostile to Rome'.

Ironically, given this pervasive antipathy to Catholicism, the Klan's secret rituals were strangely reminiscent of the Catholic Church (and of the Masons, with whom their membership often overlapped). Klansmen were baptized and anointed, made to swear oaths of fealty and introduced to a world of mysterious and complex symbolism. The mask, rendering members anonymous, represented altruism and the denial of the self; the fiery cross denoted members' noble self-sacrifice to a higher cause.

Lurid conspiracist tales of female enslavement and exploitation by gangs of perverted priests and Jews fed into the fears and prejudices of potential Klan members. In Muncie, Indiana, a woman claimed that Catholics had developed a powder that would bleach the skins of black men – so that they could trick unsuspecting white girls into marrying them.

Fundamentalist Protestants were seen as particularly sympathetic to the Klan cause. Kleagles were ordered to approach fundamentalist ministers when they arrived in new towns and Klan preachers promoted fundamentalism in their sermons.

These men were deliberately non-intellectual inheritors of the 'Know-Nothing' tradition of the Southwest. In the words of the evangelist Billy Sunday, 'I don't know any more about theology than a jack-rabbit knows about ping-pong, but I'm on my way to glory!'

Just as Bruce Barton's best-selling book *The Man Nobody Knows* reinvented Jesus not as the mild lamb of God but as a manly, driven leader, so too did the Klan deliberately project to its members a virile Christian militancy very attractive to men who found themselves emasculated and excluded by the onward march of modern society. Parading around town in a sheet was seen as empowering. Klan discipline and its code of loyalty – and the severe punishments meted out to those who betrayed it – reinforced this sense of brotherhood and masculinity.

The Klan used its connections with the Church as a way of sanctifying and justifying its actions. Klansmen were constantly reminded that the movement was 'not a lodge' but 'an army of Protestant Americans' fighting to protect their birthright. 'The Klan is engaged in a Holy Crusade against that which is corrupting and destroying the best in American life,' declared its newspaper, the *Searchlight*.

While the Church was passive, the Klan saw itself as an active force for moral reform: the defender of America's trad-itional values against modernity, urbanization, secularization, divorce, immigration and the sinful influence of the movies and jazz. 'The Klan stood for the same things as the Church, but we did things the Church wouldn't do,' said one Pennsylvania Klan's Exalted Cyclops (local leader). 'They talked about morals in the churches, but if some young fellow got into trouble or some couple was about to get a divorce, the churches wouldn't mess in it. We acted.'

Local chapters of the Klan posted signs reading, 'Fooling around the other fellow's home is not wise' and 'Wife-beaters, family deserters, home-wreckers, we have no room for you'. The Denver Grand Goblin placed his Klan recruits at the disposal of the Chief of Police to aid the local fight against crime. Klansmen conducted 'Clean Up Your Town' campaigns and worked closely with the Anti-Saloon League. Enforcing Prohibition (despite its leaders' private fondness for the bottle) became one of the Klan's most important functions.

Although people recognized that the Klan was 'commercializing' prejudice, in general its appeal to 'their patriotism and their moral idealism' was more potent than its appeal to 'their hates'. Membership promised not just mystery and excitement, but valuable opportunities for networking and a sense of community. For many, joining the Klan was a positive decision, not a negative one.

Promoting this Babbittish idea of Americanism – small town, Protestant, white, clean, sober, hard-working, family-minded – meant promoting cultural conformity, a humourless cult of 'oneness'. In Middletown, observed Robert and Helen Lynd, 'being "different" is rare, even among the young'. Middletown high-school students overwhelmingly agreed with statements such as 'The white race is the best race on earth' and 'The United States is unquestionably the best country in the world'.

The Lynds described the Klan coming 'upon Middletown like a tornado', spreading tales of Catholic, Jewish and black plots to take over the world, and recruiting 3,500 (or one in ten) locals by 1923. Most Middletown Klansmen were more anti-Catholic than anti-black, probably because only about 6 per cent of Middletown's population was black. They blamed immigrants for violating Prohibition, sexual licence, for introducing worrying new political trends and challenging their own prosperity and control of their area, and saw the Klan as a way of eradicating these evils from their society.

'The true story of the 1920s Klan', writes Kathleen Blee, 'is the ease with which racism and intolerance appealed to ordinary people in ordinary places... These citizens, comfortable in daily lives in which racial, ethnic and religious privilege were so omnipresent as to be invisible to their possessors, found in the Klan a collective means to perpetuate their advantages.' It might be argued that they also found there other forces than themselves to blame for the changes that were transforming American society.

Not every American was seduced by the Ku Klux Klan. The journalist William Allen White described the Klan to a colleague as 'a self-constituted body of moral idiots'. The trouble with the Klan, he said, 'is that it is based upon such deep foolishness that it is bound to be a menace to good government in any community'. In a similar vein, a professor of sociology asserted that 'the most dangerous weakness in a democracy is the uninformed and unthinking average man'. Even Thomas Dixon, author of the novel that had inspired D.W. Griffith's *The Birth of a Nation*, spoke out against the revived Klan (albeit from the perspective of a paternalistic racist): 'If the white race is superior − as I believe it is − it is our duty as citizens of a democracy to lift up and help the weaker race.'

Steps were taken in some places to combat the Klan's rising popularity, often using vigilante techniques that reflected those of the Klan. Klan meeting houses were torched and Klan parades met with mobs wielding rocks and bottles. Catholics organized themselves into groups like the Red Knights or the Knights of the Flaming Circle, intending to defend themselves and their homes from Klan aggression. A bomb destroyed the offices of *Dawn*, the Chicago Klan's newspaper. Spies infiltrated Klan meetings and exposed Klan members' identities to the press.

Local politicians might also resist the Klan's appropriation of their area, for example by banning the wearing of hoods or masks in public, but in many cases resistance was futile. When the governor of Oklahoma instituted martial law to remove the Klan from his state, the Klan-dominated state legislature impeached him and removed him from office. In Dallas the Citizens' League, while in agreement with the Klan about white supremacy, questioned its religious intolerance and restrictions on freedom of conscience. Seeking to restore peace to the community, the mayor asked the Klan to disband. This it refused to do. In 1922 Klan membership in Dallas was nudging 10,000.

On tour in North Carolina, the singer Bessie Smith formed her own anti-Klan league. One of her performers went outside during a show and found six Klansmen trying to collapse the tent – in the South, black artists travelled on their own trains and performed in their own tents, rather than in public halls, from which they were banned. Hearing what had happened, Bessie came out and confronted the men, one hand on her hip and shaking the other at them. 'What the fuck you think *you're* doin'? I'll get the whole damn tent out here if I have to. You just pick up them sheets and run!' The Klansmen would not move at first, but as Smith continued to scream obscenities at them they faded into the night. She turned back to the watching prop boys: 'I ain't never *heard* of such shit. And as for you, you ain't nothing but a bunch of sissies.'

In October 1921 one former Klansman from east Tennessee, Henry Fry, revealed his experiences as a member of the Ku Klux Klan to the *New York World*. Over the past twenty years, Fry said, he had joined the Masons, the Knights of Pythias, the Odd Fellows, the Red Men, the United American Mechanics, the Royal Arcanum, the Woodmen, the Elks, the Eagles, the Owls, and the Theatrical Mechanics' Association. In January 1921 he had added one more society to his list: the Knights of the Ku Klux Klan.

At first Fry found his fellow Klansmen normal, church-going, prosperous family men, but he quickly noticed that the Klan gave them a licence to lawless behaviour which he could not condone. 'The mere fact of being a member of an organization that can go abroad in the land white-robed and masked is a suggestive force that encourages men to take the law into their own hands.' As time went by, he began to realize that the organization was less fraternal than political, masking its profit-making objectives with badly written, pseudo-religious ritual and seeking to achieve its aims locally by stirring up prejudice and hatred.

After watching a local Klan leader, a doctor, make a speech attacking blacks, Jews and Catholics, and urging the Klan to 'organize and arm itself for the purpose of protecting the city' from the 'murderous' designs of the Catholics, Fry resigned his membership. He found the rhetoric overblown and deluded. Not only were there very few Jews or Catholics in his area, but the black population was hard-working and well-respected. Klan assertions that white supremacy was a 'sacred constitutional right' sat uneasily with him.

Fry listed a series of Klan crimes to the *New York World*. These included, at random: 'April 1, 1921 – Alexander Johnson, a Negro bell boy, of Dallas, Texas, was taken out by masked men, whipped, and the letters "K. K. K." burned on his forehead with acid. He was said to have associated with white women... April 26, 1921 – At Houston, Texas, J. W. McGee, an automobile salesman, was whipped by masked men for annoying high school girls... July 12, 1921 – At Enid, Okla., Walter Billings, a motion-picture operator, was given a coating of cotton and crude oil, after being whipped by masked men.'

In all, the *World* reported that 'four killings, one mutilation, one branding with acid, forty-one floggings, twenty-seven tar and feather parties, five kidnappings, forty-three individuals warned to leave town or otherwise threatened, fourteen communities threatened by posters, sixteen parades of masked men with warning placards' had taken place during the period from October 1920 to October 1921.

The *World* also exposed the corruption at the head of the Klan, revealing very un-Klan-like behaviour on the parts of Edward Clarke and Bessie Tyler. Clarke's previous investigation for embezzlement was revealed, as was his having abandoned his wife for Tyler and their having been arrested together by the police for disorderly conduct. Loyal Klansmen in Atlanta bought all 3,000 copies of the *World* in an effort to prevent the story spreading. The Klan's own weekly newsletter declared that the attacks upon Tyler showed that America's pure womanhood was 'unsafe from the millionaire newspaper owners'.

Tyler showed her true mettle in response to the *World* articles. Clarke, frightened, tried to resign his Klan post but his furious mistress denounced him as 'weak-kneed' and persuaded him to brazen it out at her side. She argued that any publicity was good publicity – and she was right. Although the *World* had belittled the Klan as 'nightie Knights' and described them as a cancer destroying American society from the inside out, its articles intrigued as many readers as they horrified. A rash of fresh membership enquiries across the country followed the two-week long exposé.

Even satire bounced off the Klan. The *American Journal of Sociology* published the following parody of Klan beliefs in 1925 but, commented a French professor, it still seemed 'to express to the letter the attitude of the mass of Americans in the middle West': 'We are the greatest people on earth. Our government is the best. In religious belief and practise we (the Protestants) are exactly right, and we are also the best fighters in the world. As a people we are the wisest, politically the most free, and socially the most developed. Other nations may fail and fall; we are safe. Our history is a narrative of the triumph of righteousness among the people. We see these forces working through every generation of our glorious past. Our future growth and success are as certain as the rules of mathematics. Providence is always on our side. The only war we Americans ever lost was when one-third of us was defeated by the other two-thirds. We have been divinely selected in order to save and purify the world through our example. If other nations will only accept our religious and political principles, and our general attitude toward life, they soon will be, no doubt, as happy and prosperous as we are.'

Alerted by the *World* articles to the Klan's mushrooming popularity, Congress opened an investigation into their activities. It found that Bessie Tyler had 'a positive genius for executive direction' combined with courage and determination. 'In this woman beats the real heart of the Ku Klux Klan today,' it admitted with grudging respect.

Doc Simmons was called to the stand. Although he did not wear his favourite spangled purple silk robe, the Imperial Wizard milked every ounce of drama from his moment in the spotlight. Appearing polite and sincere, he denied the *World*'s accusations and compared himself to Julius Caesar, George Washington and Jesus Christ. The Klan, he insisted, was a 'purely fraternal and patriotic organization', motivated not by racial hatred but by racial pride. He said that the mask and robe his members wore were mere fancy-dress and 'as innocent as the breath of an angel'.

Towards the end of his three-day session he was asked, 'Has it occurred to you that this idealistic organization that you have given birth to and have fostered so long is now being used for mercenary purposes by very clever people or propagandists who know how to appeal to people in this community or that for membership?' 'Nothing has come to my view that would prompt me to have such an opinion,' Simmons replied.

He concluded with a rhetorical crescendo. 'I cannot better express myself than by saying to you who are persecutors of the Klan and myself, "Father, forgive you, for you know not what you do," and "Father, forgive them, for they know not what they do." Mr Chairman, I am done.' Then, rendered unconscious by his own eloquence, Simmons collapsed on to the table in front of him.

Afterwards he declared that 'Congress gave us the best

advertising we ever got'. Apparently even Warren Harding, like Simmons an inveterate joiner of fraternal societies, was impressed. Former Imperial Klokard Alton Young boasted on his deathbed of being one of the Klan's five-member 'Imperial Induction Team' led by Simmons who had initiated Harding into the Klan in a secret meeting at the White House, after which the President gave each of them a special War Department tag for his driving licence, allowing them to violate traffic regulations. If this is true, Harding, who responded to allegations that he had black blood with a casual, 'one of my ancestors may have jumped the fence' and was the first president to call for an end to lynching, seems, like many other Americans, to have seen in the Klan only what he wanted to see: a patriotic Christian fellowship. The next few years would demonstrate how naïve that view of the Klan was.

One misapprehension about Klan membership in the 1920s is that it attracted principally poor, downtrodden Americans who felt marginalized by the forces of modernity and urbanization sweeping through the country and eradicating the steady, modest rural lives they valued. These people, it is argued, joined the Klan because it offered them a sense of belonging. As the saying went, 'a nobody in the world became somebody in the Klan'. 'You think the influential men belong [to the Klan] here?' asked a non-Klan member in Indiana. 'Then look at their shoes when they march in parade.'

However, new studies have shown that although these men

did join the Klan, just as often Klansmen were middle-class middle Americans, members (like Simmons) of other respectable clubs like the Kiwanis. The typical Klan member in Athens, Georgia (where, unusually, membership records survive), was married and probably a father, and lived in his own home. There were a few local grandees – men who sat on committees or participated in local government – and a few more unskilled labourers, but most were owner-managers of small businesses.

That the Klan was an exclusively rural, Southern organization was another popular misconception. In fact, during the early 1920s when recruitment was at its peak, Southern and Southwestern membership levelled off while membership in the North Central states (Indiana, Ohio and Illinois) went up by five times. Kleagles even had real success in pockets of the traditionally tolerant, progressive North Atlantic states, for example around Portland, Maine, and in Worcester, Massachusetts, and on the West Coast.

In the spring of 1921 Doc Simmons paid a private visit to Denver, Colorado, where he initiated the area's first few Klansmen. A few months later, the Klan officially announced its arrival there. Denver was a city of just over 250,000 people, predominantly white and Protestant, with few blacks and hardly any immigrants. The one worrying section of the population – or encouraging, from the Klan's point of view – was the rising proportion of Catholics who by the mid-1920s constituted nearly 15 per cent of Denver's population.

Initially, against the national background of the *New York World* exposé and the Congressional investigation into Klan activities, local opposition to the Klan was strong. The regional tax office began looking into the Klan's failure to pay taxes on its initiation fees; Denver's liberal newspaper published revelations of Klan secrets. The Klan seemed to fade away.

But in January 1922 it resurfaced, this time using more aggressive tactics. It donated to the Young Men's Christian Association; it gave an impoverished widow $200; it made visits and contributed to Denver's churches. At the same time a warning was sent to the president of the local branch of the National Association for the Advancement of Colored People and a black janitor was accused of having had 'intimate relations with white women' and told to leave town (which he did, before the charges against him were proved).

The unwillingness of the local government to condemn these acts, and the passivity of the majority of the population, meant that almost by default the Klan survived and began to regain strength. Denver was a prosperous city, but it had a high crime rate. Violent crime, trafficking in illegal drugs and alcohol, and prostitution were relatively commonplace. The Klan seized on this as a way to appeal to Denver's citizenry, promising that it would succeed in cleaning up Denver where its own leaders had failed.

Chicago was another major city where the Klan made surprising inroads. Unlike Denver, Chicago's population was richly diverse, made up of immigrants, Catholics, Jews and blacks as well as 'Nordic' Protestants. Despite this multiplicity of races — or perhaps because of it — in August 1921 4,650 people were initiated into the Klan in a single day and by the end of the year Chicago had the largest Klan membership of any American city.

As in Denver, at first the Klan had to combat local resistance. The City Council officially condemned its activities; the American Unity League was formed as an opposition group and published the names, addresses and jobs of Klan members in its magazine. But the Klan still thrived, fuelled by the deep-seated insecurity and nostalgia of its members who felt, as blacks and immigrants encroached on their jobs and neighbourhoods, that only the Klan could restore their dignity and place in society. For these northern, urban Klansmen, the Klan was a 'salve for [their] wounded pride'.

By contrast, the Klan never managed to gain a foothold in New York City, perhaps because the black and immigrant communities were too well-established there. In 1922 the Catholic Irish-dominated police were ordered to deal with Klan gatherings as they would with 'Reds and bomb-throwers'. In the suburbs, though, where concerns about bootleggers and immorality ran higher, the Klan made better progress. The *New York Times* estimated that there were 200,000 New York State Klan members, mostly in provincial centres like Rochester, Syracuse and Albany.

In Pennsylvania, the Klan exploited the traditional friction between Catholics and the descendants of the original Dutch settlers, whose militant Protestantism merged easily with the Klan's philosophy. Here, as elsewhere, Klan preachers presented the 'true' American as a victim, robbed of his birthright by interlopers and liberals. Official records don't survive but based on documents concerning an accusation of embezzling Klan membership funds it seems that over 250,000 men may have joined the Pennsylvania Klan by 1923.

The population of Carnegie, Pennsylvania, was almost evenly divided between Catholics and Protestants. Its mayor forbade the Klan from marching through the city, but this was exactly the kind of opposition that spurred the Klan into defiant action. Robed Klansmen went ahead with their procession, and in the riots that ensued a young Klansman was shot. This tragedy was a public relations triumph for the Klan; its leaders rubbed their hands together with glee and speculated that the young marcher's death would mean 25,000 new members. It published an incendiary pamphlet entitled *The Martyred Klansman*, beginning, 'This is the story of the murder of a native-born American in his native land, at the hands of a ruthless mob...'

Just as the Klan's tentacles stretched widely out across the country in the early 1920s, so too did it deepen its hold on American society by extending its reach beyond its existing members to their wives and children. Entire families were invited to Klan picnics and days out; members were encouraged to have Klan weddings, funerals, and baptisms. Boys and girls joined the Junior Klan and the Tri-K Klub, respectively.

Before the Women of the Ku Klux Klan (WKKK) was formed in 1923, informal auxiliary groups sprang up to cater for women interested in supporting Klan activities. Bessie Tyler was a member of the Ladies of the Invisible Eye (LOTIE), which inducted over a thousand members in a single month in 1922. Members proclaimed their racial, religious and political allegiances, and swore fealty to 'pure Americanism'.

When the Klan was reaching its peak in terms of member-ship and profitability Simmons's leadership was challenged. In 1922 Hiram Evans, a dentist from Dallas, was made Kligrapp (secretary of the order). In a dramatic coup at the Thanksgiv-ing Klonvocation (nationwide gathering) later that year, Evans replaced Simmons as Imperial Wizard. He sacked Clarke and Tyler (who had apparently been keeping Simmons drunk in order to maintain control over the organization; Clarke had been arrested for possession of alcohol two months earlier) and scrapped the recruitment incentives from which they had made their fortunes.

A vicious struggle for leadership of the Klan continued well into 1923, played out perhaps most clearly over the issue of the WKKK. Fighting for support, both Simmons and Evans attempted to bolster their positions within the Klan by appeal-ing to women. In March 1923, Simmons appointed Bessie Tyler head of a short-lived women's Klan group, the Kamelia; Evans retaliated by founding the Women of the Ku Klux Klan which numbered perhaps half a million members by 1925.

Eventually, in February 1924, Doc Simmons was bought off,

agreeing to cede all his rights over the Klan to Evans for $145,000. Edward Clarke, facing charges of mishandling church funds, transporting liquor and white slavery, briefly fled the country; Bessie Tyler, already suffering from ill-health, died later that year.

Evans saw the Klan not as a money-making venture, but as a political party with five million potential voters. He encouraged Klansmen to elect local officials, congressmen, governors and senators and led a procession of 40,000 hooded Klansmen down Washington's Pennsylvania Avenue in August 1925.

The man who had engineered Evans's takeover was the energetic and unscrupulous Grand Dragon of Indiana, David Stephenson, known as Steve. After helping oust Simmons, Stephenson claimed as his reward the lucrative position of head of promotion in twenty-three Northern states. Under his regime, from 1923 recruitment standards fell and meetings were held monthly, not weekly, eroding the cohesive spirit Tyler and Clarke had worked so hard to instil. Membership continued to grow, complained a Pennsylvania Klan leader to Evans, 'but the old spirit wasn't there'.

Stephenson's main area of influence was Indiana, where perhaps a third of the male population were Klansmen who proudly walked the streets in their robes with their hoods thrown back to show their faces. Klansmen had elected Indiana's governor and both its senators as well as most of its local officials; there was no county that did not have its own

Klavern (local branch). On parade nights policemen directed traffic in their robes.

Steve had grown rich and powerful since his appointment as Indiana's King Kleagle in 1921, travelling everywhere in an aeroplane and wearing a purple robe like the one favoured by Simmons. He established a band of vigilante policemen called the Horsethief Detectives who broke up 'petting parties' and raided bootleggers', all the while acting as his own private police force; he created an elaborate network of spies who kept him informed of everything that went on in Indiana.

Concerned, like Simmons and Evans, with the role women might play in tightening Klan control, Steve formed a society called the Queens of the Golden Mask made up of Klan wives and daughters. These women planned Klan functions like fundraisers and picnics, lobbied schools to get rid of non-Klan-sympathizing teachers and organized consumer boycotts; they also acted as informal 'poison squads', spreading rumours about people who opposed the Klan and gathering information that the power-hungry Stephenson might find useful.

During the 1924 elections Stephenson distributed cards to voters reading 'Every criminal, every gambler, every thug, every libertine, every girl ruiner, every home wrecker, every wife beater, every dope peddler, every moonshiner, every crooked politician, every pagan papist priest, every shyster lawyer, every K. of C., every white slaver, every brothel madam, every Rome-controlled newspaper, every black spider is fighting the Klan. Think it over. Which side are you on?'

But despite his professions of morality Stephenson was everything he pretended to abhore, except Catholic: crooked to the core, a violent, hard-drinking abuser of women. He held wild, drunken orgies in the mansion and on the yacht he had bought with Klan money. In 1924 a secret Klan trial found him guilty of attempted rape and banished him from the organization, but he refused to accept the ban.

In early 1925, Stephenson turned his attentions to Madge Oberholtzer, the wholesome 28-year-old Superintendent of Public Instruction in Indianapolis. Steve had saved her job from being abolished and expected some thanks. He invited Madge to his house but when she found him there drinking with his henchmen, she tried to leave; he had her bundled into a car and on to an overnight train heading for Chicago. That night he raped her violently and repeatedly, biting her all over her body. A witness said it looked as though she had been 'chewed by a cannibal'.

The next morning they disembarked at Hammond, Indiana, and Oberholtzer, pretending she needed medicine for her visible injuries, bought and took an overdose of mercury tablets. It took Stephenson two days to return her, suffering terribly, to Indianapolis and her parents. By that time it was too late for doctors to help her although she was able to give a full statement to the police before she died.

In the sensational trial that followed, Stephenson was convicted and sentenced to life. People were horrified by the savagery of his crime, his contempt for the judicial system 'and his smug belief that he would escape punishment' because he was so close to the centre of Indiana's government. The governor he had brought to power, Ed Jackson, refused to pardon him and in revenge Stephenson blew the whistle on Klan activity in Indiana. His evidence brought the mayor of Indianapolis, a Congressman, a county sheriff, several other local officials and very nearly Jackson himself to jail.

After this public outrage, the Klan could no longer claim to be the guardian of America's morals and its decline was dramatic. Other scandals erupted, including the imprisonment of Colorado's Grand Dragon for tax evasion, although he was also tried for threatening to castrate a high-school student if he didn't marry his pregnant girlfriend. In Buffalo, New York, where a local policeman and a Klan member had been shot during a gun battle in 1924, a local Klan leader was arrested for illegally selling contraceptives.

It was clear that once in power, the Klan had licensed the very evils it had promised to eradicate. Its leaders had shown themselves weak and corrupt. More importantly, as America grew more prosperous, immigration was restricted and relations between the races improved in the mid-1920s, and the social and political fears the Klan had played on to achieve power seemed less urgent. Klan membership in Pennsylvania, which had peaked at about 300,000 in early 1925, was down to 5,000 five years later. Indiana had less than 7,000 Klansmen in 1928. In Middletown, according to the Lynds, the Klan had all but disappeared by 1925, 'leaving in its wake wide areas of local bitterness'.

Hollywood royalty: Mary Pickford and her second husband, Douglas Fairbanks, boating in the lake at their Beverley Hills Mansion, Pickfair

Charlie Chaplin as the Tramp in his masterpiece, *The Gold Rush* (1925). Along with director D.W. Griffith, Chaplin, Pickford and Fairbanks co-founded United Artists in 1919

Comedian Fatty Arbuckle, in bow-tie on the right, at his trial for rape and murder, September 1921

The plutocrat setting off on vacation:
automobile magnate Walter Chrysler
in the late 1920s

Henry Ford and his replacement for the horse-drawn cart, the Model T,
available in any colour 'so long as it's black'

President Warren Harding, looking as if he is already part of Mount Rushmore, and his wife Florence, wearing the black velvet ribbon around her neck that became known as a 'Florrie', in 1921

Anarchists Bartolomeo Vanzetti and Nicola Sacco, shackled together, on their way to their retrial for robbery and murder in 1927

The Ku Klux Klan marches openly down Pennsylvania Avenue, 1926. Note the US Capitol in the background

Glamorous exiles Caresse and Harry Crosby and Harry's sister Kitsa on the beach at
Deauville, September 1929. Narcisse Noir reclines at their feet

Caresse at a typically bohemian picnic at the Moulin de Soleil, 1928;
the donkeys were used for games of donkey-polo

9

In Exile

THE PETTY XENOPHOBIA THAT fed the revived Ku Klux Klan was anathema to one small but vocal section of American society: its writers and artists. Feeling themselves and their values stifled by what they saw as the jingoism, philistinism and repression of their parents' generation, these self-conscious rebels turned their backs on what the poet Harry Crosby called 'all this smug self-satisfaction'.

'Red drug-stores, filling stations, comfort stations, go-to-the-right signs, lurid billboards and automobiles swarming everywhere like vermin... How I hate this community spirit with its civic federations and its boyscout clubs and its educational toys and its Y.M.C.A. and its congregational Baptist churches,' wrote Crosby during a visit home to the US from Paris in 1926, inadvertently describing the Klan's heartlands. 'Horribly bleak, horribly depressing.'

Harry Crosby had left America four years earlier, running from his respectable banking job and the expectations of

his fond parents – all the pressures of what one of his contemporaries called 'the American high bourgeoisie'. The family
into which Crosby had been born in 1898 was American
aristocracy. His uncle and godfather, J. P. Morgan Jr (the
financier John Pierpont's son, known as Jack), epitomized
the values of the American Establishment in all its 'worldly
Puritanism, class-consciousness [and] self-righteousness'.
Jack Morgan was scrupulously Protestant, Republican,
Anglophile, loyal to company and government and morally
conservative. His staff at the Morgan bank were not permitted
to divorce; money (despite his profession) he looked upon
with a certain lofty disdain; brilliance and individualism he
distrusted – even in his nephew, of whom he was very fond.
But Harry wanted nothing in life but brilliance.

Like so many young men of his generation, he had spent the
last year of the war driving ambulances in northern France. It
was a bloody initiation into adulthood for a protected boy. By
the time he arrived back in Boston in the spring of 1919 Harry
had watched two of his closest friends die in action, as well as
numerous others. Narrowly evading death himself had left him
convinced that he had been saved by his already idiosyncratic
faith in God.

Returning home, Harry reluctantly got back on to the time-
honoured treadmill where he had left off. Harvard was the
accepted next step after prep school, and to please his parents
Harry took a two-year wartime degree, *honoris causa* – the
kind of diploma Jay Gatsby claimed to have received from

'Oggsford'. In 1921 he moved to New York to start work at the Morgan bank, but the seeds of his flight had already been sown.

Two years earlier, soon after his return to Boston, Harry had fallen in love with Polly Peabody, a married woman seven years his senior. For both it was love at first sight, the kind of passion that sweeps away every consideration before it. Polly was struck at their first meeting by the vividness of Harry's personality and his combination of wisdom and naïveté: 'He seemed to be more expression and mood than man... he was taut as a tangent, his eyes blazed like mica, his mouth was large and it quivered ever so slightly when he was nervous, and his hands were like a musician's hands, sensitive, compelling.'

Separated from Polly while she tried to repair her marriage – the scandal of a divorce was something neither the Crosbys nor Polly's family relished – Harry barely made the effort to turn up to the office each morning. He drank so much that his mother offered him $100 to give up for the month of January 1922; the terse entry in his diary on 7 February reads, 'Wasn't worth it.' Finally he handed in his notice. Still hoping to save Harry from a rash match, his mother arranged a job for him in Paris. Harry, delighted to be set free, celebrated by drinking 'to excess' and crashing a friend's new car 'slap-bang into an iron fence'. This was the life he chose: intensity, exile, intemperance, destruction. As Polly said, 'any "middle" whatsoever was anathema to Harry'.

Polly – to whom Harry soon gave the invented name,

Caresse – came to Paris to marry him later that year. She had found it impossible to return to her old life without him. 'Once one has known rapture,' she wrote, 'security is not enough.'

Their adopted city, devastated by the war, was battered but still beautiful. With almost an entire generation dead, arriving Americans remarked on how few young people they saw on the streets. But the Parisians, who had survived more than a century of revolutions and two German invasions, still knew how to live. Other refugees gathered in Paris – émigré Russians, rich and debauched Indian princes, discontented, pleasure-seeking English aristocrats, all belonging to crumbling orders of one type or another – and it was into this world of 'sparkling cynicism' that Harry and Caresse flung themselves.

By contrast to Europe, America represented everything that was sordid and ugly: industrialized and 'pustulant', stinking of 'bananas and cocacola and ice cream'. Harry was, he wrote elsewhere after lunch with two small-minded Americans, 'Glad I am *déraciné*.' As Caresse put it, they were 'escapists': 'I became a rebel the moment I married Harry.'

Caresse had two small children by her first marriage, six-year-old Billy and five-year-old Polleen, or Polly. Harry, who hated reality imposing on his life of fantasy and self-indulgence, bitterly resented their calls on his adored wife's time and attention. The children were soon sent off to boarding school in Versailles and the Crosbys moved into a tiny apartment on the Île Saint-Louis.

At first Harry went through the motions with his job at

Morgan, Harjes et Cie. Every morning, dressed in her bathing costume, Caresse paddled her husband up the Seine in a red canoe, dropping him off near the Tuileries gardens so that he could walk to the office in the Place Vendôme. He quit after eighteen months. Banal office work he neither enjoyed nor did well. Besides, it wasn't worth it for $75 a month – less than the salary he paid his driver, and peanuts compared to his unearned annual income of about $12,000. He had decided to become a poet.

Their various relations brought them into contact with grand literary Americans-in-Paris like Edith Wharton and aristocratic French families in Saint-Germain who frowned on their eccentric evening clothes – a Vionnet man's jacket and short skirt in cloth-of-gold for Caresse and a black silk gardenia in Harry's buttonhole. The company they preferred was that of exiles, of artists and writers, émigrés from convention like themselves: the sculptor Alberto Giacometti, the poet Archibald MacLeish and his wife Ada, Frieda and D. H. Lawrence, a sprinkling of rich divorcees and bohemian wanderers.

Each year the Crosbys attended the art students' riotous Bal des Quatz'Arts. After one ball, Harry wrote: 'The room was hot and reeked with cigarette and cigar smoke, with fard [an archaic French word for cosmetics] and sweat and smell of underarms... there were shrieks and catcalls and there was a riot. I remember two strong young men stark naked wrestling on the floor for the honour of dancing with a young girl (silver paint conquered purple paint) ... and in a corner I watched two savages making love.'

One year Harry recorded arriving home in a taxi completely naked, his toga 'and even my drawers to which I had pinned a hundred francs' lost in the frenzy. Another year Caresse rode to the party on a hired baby elephant dressed as an Inca princess, stripped to the waist and wearing a long blue wig. She got home to find Harry in their huge bath with three girls, washing off each other's body paint – and hated pink bubble bath from that moment on. There were seven sleepers in their bed that night.

Harry's devotion to Caresse and the intensity of their relationship – 'Your body is the golden spoon by means of which I eat your soul,' he wrote to her in one poem – did not curb his appetite for other women. He believed that 'one should follow every instinct no matter where' it led. To save Caresse's feelings he tried to be discreet but he could not accept restraints on his behaviour or desires. Some of the relationships with his many mistresses were short-lived, women he met on the street or at the races and seduced over an afternoon or a few weeks; others were friends as well as lovers, and long-lasting. On these women Harry bestowed extravagant titles that fitted into his personal mythology: the Lady of the Golden Horse, the Sorceress, the Tigress, the Youngest Princess.

Soon after they were married Caresse tried to revolt 'against sharing with anyone the queenship of my heart', but Harry's refusal to change forced her to accept his other women as long as she was pre-eminent among them, a queen (in his private lexicon) above the princesses. The fact that she too had other demands on her love was held against her. 'He made me believe that my children balanced our account.' Ultimately she claimed to recognize only one real rival: Jacqueline, the Grey Princess, an imaginary woman Harry believed was his soul-mate, whose name he had tattooed across his chest. 'She was the dream – the girl of infinite mystery,' wrote Caresse. 'No other loves were quite as true'.

Caresse consoled herself with her own cadre of admirers. Over the years her lovers included the Chilean painter Manolo or Manuel Ortiz; a glamorous war pilot, Cord Meier, whom Harry called 'the Aviator'; an English lord, Gerard Lymington; and the duc de Doudeauville, Armand de Rochefoucauld, later their landlord, whom she described as 'short, sandy-haired, full of love and the devil'.

Harry also insisted that Caresse occasionally join him in bouts of mutual promiscuity about which, according to a friend in whom she confided, she was loyally uncomplaining but less than enthusiastic. They and two other couples would drive to the Bois de Boulogne at night, draw their cars up in a circle with the headlights on (bizarrely recalling the Ku Klux Klan's head-lit initiation ceremonies) and swap partners. On hashish-fuelled trips to North Africa and the Middle East they paid young girls to dance for them, and sometimes took them to bed. 'O God when shall we ever cast off the chains of New England,' Harry wrote after one such episode.

Drugs were another important part of Harry's rejection of convention. Their circle in Paris was well acquainted with cocaine. Harry's diary entries record days at Longchamp races accompanied by 'much sniffing [cocaine] and taking of aspirin tablets' and Montmartre nights of 'oysters and caviare, champagne and whiskey, cocaine and dancing'.

Opium, with its elaborate rituals, its literary heritage and its dreamily hallucinogenic qualities, was Harry's favourite drug. He first tried it in 1924 and quickly became a regular user. In Morocco he and Caresse bought 'four jars of the best brand of opium' and when they got back to Paris stored them in little Polly's toy chest. 'And the bubbling sound of another pipe and another and another and the round contour of a breast and the touch of delicate fingers delicately gently snow upon snow and the metamorphose into oblivion beyond the beyond,' Harry wrote. 'And all day across my soul red icebergs have been drifting like tombs across the sun.'

But for much of the 1920s the most important thing in either Harry or Caresse's lives, more than the fleeting attractions of narcotics or lovers, was each other and their shared relish for the immoderate, unorthodox life they had chosen. Their black whippet, Narcisse Noir, had gold-painted claws and a gold collar; they named his pearl-pink mate Clytoris. They went on holiday stopping only in places with names of one syllable. To Harry, one friend said, getting lost was 'the best hors d'oeuvre for the belated dinner, still far away, the spice of adventure. Any fool can find his way, a poet alone knows how to lose it.'

One spring they walked and hitch-hiked across Europe to Florence. Harry, lithe and elegant as a faun, carried a pack of books and wore his usual dark blue suit, patent pumps and soft shirt, always bareheaded at a time when no gentleman went hatless; Caresse travelled in a tweed suit and lisle stockings. They arrived dusty and ragged at the Grand Hotel on a straw-covered cart carrying Chianti. Thankfully the hotel was expecting them. Their Hermès luggage and a telegram from the Morgan bank with their reservation had arrived just before they did. Within minutes they were being served martinis in an immense marble bathtub.

Harry sought meaning in literary as well as in sensual debauchery, in the writers and works which helped form his own decadent, mystical views: Baudelaire, *The Picture of Dorian Grey*, Proust and especially Rimbaud. He loved books, words, certain colours, names, list-making. From 1922 he kept a diary, a mesmerizing portrait of his life but at the same time strangely detached and self-absorbed. It was dedicated to his obsessions – ritual, hedonism, gambling for high stakes, the sun and sunbathing, extravagance – and framed an increasingly complex personal philosophy that revolved around sun-worship and an impulsion towards the final, longed-for obliteration into the sun – death, the ultimate escape from reality.

'Life is pathetic, futile save for the development of the soul; memories, passionate memories are the utmost gold; poetry is religion (for me),' Harry wrote in an effort to define his own

'Castle of Beauty'. Except for those closest to him, people were almost irrelevant beside his intense interior life. He was utterly elitist and misanthropic generally (*'Je suis royaliste,'* he wrote. 'I hate the multitude') but tenderly generous to individuals, bringing coffee daily to the old woman who sold him violets in the street and buying her a special folding stool with a seat-back.

Harry's friend Stuart Gilbert never heard him speak harshly or ill of anyone and never saw him refuse a service to anyone. 'His only enemies were Mrs Grundy and Mr Bowdler.' He was less arrogant than curiously remote, distracted by his unflinching gaze towards the sun. As Gilbert said, Harry 'feared the *terre à terre*, the normal, as most of us fear celestial heights'.

In 1927 Harry and Caresse, who avoided politics and current events and had long since banished all newspapers and magazines except the *Nouvelle Revue Française* and *transition*, started their own tiny publishing house, the Black Sun Press. Over the next two years they brought out editions of their own poetry as well as works by friends including Lawrence, James Joyce and Hart Crane.

Harry's own poems were mildly surrealist, richly decadent and heavily indebted to Rimbaud and e.e. cummings, a fellow rebel against the Bostonian Establishment two years Harry's senior. The short prose poem 'White Slipper' makes reference to several of Harry's fixations: aeroplanes; symbolic colours; the sun; Harry's favourite word, 'Yes': 'A white aeroplane whiter than the word Yes falls like a slipper from the sky. You come dancing over the silver thorns of the lawn and by holding up the corners of your rose-and-white skirt you catch the white slipper which I kick down to you from the sun.'

Aware of how privileged he was to be able to afford to pursue his passions, Harry enjoyed supporting struggling writers and artists. The entirely undomesticated Hart Crane wrote much of his epic poem 'The Bridge' at the Crosbys' house just outside Paris, on a typewriter Harry had bought him, in between manic episodes of drinking, making aggressive sexual overtures towards male house-guests and destroying furniture. Later, Crane was arrested for brawling in Paris. Fuming at the fact that the police hadn't allowed the poet pen and paper in his cell, Harry rushed to pay his fine and vouch for Crane's good character. What he was most impressed by was the fact that it had taken ten gendarmes to bring the raging Crane in.

Friends unlucky enough not to have modern plumbing were invited over to sink into steaming Floris's Rose Geranium-scented baths followed by feasts of caviar, alligator pears and champagne. When their friend Kay Boyle, another impover-ished and as yet undiscovered writer, found herself unhappily pregnant Caresse hunted down a doctor and Harry paid for the abortion. They left her their grass-green Voisin motor-car, complete with monkey-fur throw for her knees and their notoriously inebriated driver Gus, 'an incurable collector of contraventions', when they went on holiday.

In the spring of 1928 Eugene Jolas, editor of *transition*,

received the following letter from Harry: 'I have inherited a little money, and if you approve, I would like to send you $100 (strictly anonymous) for you to send to the poet who in your judgement has written the best poem in the first twelve numbers of *transition*. But for God's sake, don't make a prize out of it. Instead of going to some fathead organization, I should like this small amount to go to someone who will spend it on cocktails and books rather than on church sociables and lemonade. If you accept this, please forget it as quick as possible.'

Tiring of city life in 1928, Harry and Caresse rented from Armand de la Rochefoucauld a mill-house outside Paris where Jean-Jacques Rousseau had once lived. They called it Le Moulin de Soleil. A caravan of glamorous friends arrived and left to a background of repeating jazz records imported from Harlem – 'orchestras hot and sweet' – and signed their names on the staircase wall: 'poets and painters and pederasts and lesbians and divorcees and Christ knows who', as Harry gleefully described them. They included Douglas Fairbanks, the exquisite Maharani of Cooch Behar, another girlfriend of Arnaud's who played baccarat for stakes as high as Harry did, Brancusi, the surrealist artist Max Ernst, Nathalie Barney, Picasso, the Mountbattens. At the Moulin they swam and played ping-pong and donkey-polo, or they drove, invariably drunk and far too fast, to the casinos at Deauville or to the Bois de Boulogne for the races. Exile had come to feel like home.

*

The Moulin was a fantasy world, as full of shadows as it was of the sun, and it did not enchant every visitor. The American writer Robert McAlmon spent the last night of 1928 there with the Crosbys and various other revellers and found it 'too damned depressing... so depressing I can't even get drunk. They're wraiths, all of them. They aren't people. God knows what they've done with their realities.' He should have known that reality was not something in which Harry dealt.

Even Caresse had moments of misgiving although she recognized the impossibility of questioning any aspect of her life with Harry. As he desired, she had moulded herself to him and there could be no separation save a violent one. More and more they argued, about his lovers and hers, always making up but with the arguments increasingly bitter. 'I knew it would be treason ever to wish for a simpler love,' she admitted.

Harry himself was living at an unsustainable peak of rapt intensity. As Kay Boyle said, when Harry was happy 'every atom of him [was] radiant – for I've never known anyone who could shine with it as he does so absolutely'. In July 1929 he cabled his father: 'PLEASE SELL TEN THOUSAND DOLLARS WORTH OF STOCK. WE HAVE DECIDED TO LEAD A MAD AND EXTRAVAGANT LIFE' – as if his life up until that point had been staid and dull. He was pursuing oblivion as ardently as he could: soaking up the sun as if it would absorb him, learning to fly stunts in an aeroplane, drinking and taking opium and making love with even more than his usual feverishness. 'How fast the year has gone the fastest I can remember like a flash of lightning not one vibration of a clock since a year ago and perhaps now I can destroy time,' he wrote.

He was hurtling towards his longed-for destiny. 'For the Seekers after Fire and the Seers and the Prophets and the Worshippers of the Sun, life ends not with a whimper [as T. S. Eliot suggested in 'The Hollow Men'], but with a Bang – a violent explosion mechanically perfect,' he wrote. 'While we, having set fire to the powderhouse of our souls, explode (suns within suns and cataracts of gold) into the frenzied fury of the Sun, into the madness of the Sun into the hot gold arms and hot gold eyes of the Goddess of the Sun!'

Harry's friends indulged his manic eccentricities with varying degrees of tolerance and amusement. Ernest Hemingway sent him a clipping from the *New York Times* describing a new fad: sun-worship. 'The sun is definitely de rigueur... The smartest girls come into town looking like figures moulded in old Cordovan leather... This new version of an old cult has its fanatics, its would-be martyrs, its meta-physicians who would make philosophic systems out of personal desires.' Others took Harry's plans for death more seriously. One said that by 1929 he could no longer bear to shake Harry's hand – his friend had already become a corpse.

Harry had long been fascinated by suicides, drawing up a list of those he admired, including Sappho, Seneca, Jesus (Harry thought him self-martyred) and Modigliani, in a prose poem from 1929 entitled 'Sun Death'. For him, choosing the moment one died was a privilege reserved for the strongest, the bravest, those who recognized 'the point of finality, irrevocable as the sun', when the spirit and the body were united in their desire 'to be reborn, in order to become what you wish to become, tree or flower or star or sun, or even dust and nothingness'. He was not afraid to die because he believed so strongly in a world to come.

In his earliest letters to Caresse, Harry had spoken of the joy of lovers dying together. Three years after they married he persuaded her to set a date for their joint deaths, writing out a contract which they both signed and which he carried around with him for the rest of his life. On 31 October 1942, the day on which the earth would be in perihelion, closest to the sun, they were to fly over a forest and jump from the plane. Their bodies would be cremated – 'purify me with fire,' Harry wrote – but there would be no funeral. 'I want my ashes to be taken up in an aeroplane at sunrise and scattered to the four winds... Let there be no mourning or lamentation (what have I ever had to do with lamentation)'.

He had even had their gravestone made, a plain slab carved with their interlocking names:

C
A
H A R R Y
E
S
S
E

But for Harry, the obsession with choosing the moment of his own death and the way in which that death would inextricably join him to the person with whom he did it – for he had no intention of dying alone – was becoming more important than waiting for his Cramoisy Queen to say yes.

In November 1929 Caresse and Harry made one of their regular trips back to America. For Harry it was an opportunity to see the woman he called the Youngest Princess or the Fire Princess, Josephine Bigelow, a 22-year-old girl, newly married, whom he had met while sunbathing on the Lido at Venice the summer before. Their transatlantic affair had been as violent and ecstatic as Harry could have wished. She was waiting impatiently for him in Boston when they docked.

In early December Harry and Josephine went to Detroit for a few days away from everyone they knew in Boston or New York. They gorged themselves on opium and caviar and spent their time fighting and making love, or both at the same time. 'All night we catapult through space, J and I in each other's arms visions security happiness' reads Harry's notebook. 'Little Harlot... Little Animal... Little Yes.'

Glittering with mania, Harry returned to New York and Caresse. Twice over the next few days he invited her to jump with him from their window on the twenty-seventh floor of the Savoy Hotel. She refused. 'I did not guess,' wrote Caresse later,

> I did not guess
> That madder beauty waited unawares
> To take your hand upon the evening stairs.

Four days afterwards, Harry didn't turn up for tea with Caresse, his mother and his uncle Jack Morgan. By dinnertime Caresse was frantic. One of their few articles of faith was never to miss appointments with each other. She rang Stanley Mortimer, whom she knew Harry had seen earlier that day. Harry had arranged to meet Josephine at Mortimer's studio after lunch.

Mortimer went to the studio soon after 9.30 p.m. but the door was bolted on the inside. He and the caretaker broke down the door. Harry and Josephine were lying on the bed, dressed, facing each other, their left hands entwined and Harry's right arm around Josephine's neck. Harry was thirty-one, Josephine ten years younger. Neat bullet-holes adorned their temples. e. e. cummings wrote,

> 2 boston
> Dolls; found
> with
> Holes in each other
>
> 's lullaby.

Harry's feet were bare, showing his red-painted toenails and the tattoos on their soles, a cross on one and a symbol of the sun on the other. In his pockets were the tickets he had bought that morning for himself and Caresse to return to Paris several days later; over $500 in cash; a telegram from Josephine that he had received on the *Mauretania* three weeks earlier; and a telegram from another mistress reading simply, 'Yes'. According to the medical examiner Harry had waited two hours after shooting Josephine before shooting himself. The gun he had used was one he had been carrying for the past year, a little Belgian automatic that he had had engraved with the sun.

There was no note, but Harry's diary was record enough of his inexorable ascent towards the sun. The last entry reads, 'One is not in love unless one desires to die with one's beloved' and, beneath that, 'There is only one happiness it is to love and to be loved'. Neither Caresse nor Harry's other great love, Constance Crowninshield (the Lady of the Golden Horse), had been willing to make the final sacrifice for him and trust in his belief that if they died together they would be together through all eternity, although he had asked them both. Josephine was bold and crazy and desperate enough to possess him that she said the 'yes' he had been waiting to hear. As she wrote to him the day before they died, death would be their marriage – and Harry's ultimate flight from reality.

D. H. Lawrence, depressed by the news of Harry's death, wrote to his friend and publisher, Dino Oriolo, that Harry 'had always been too rich and spoilt: nothing to do but commit suicide'. This was only partly fair. Harry Crosby's ability to insulate himself from the real world may have been exceptional, but in life the things he was running from were far from unique and a fascination with death was common among his contemporaries.

Born around the turn of the century, the young men who would become the voices of their generation came to maturity during the First World War, when many of them served as soldiers or ambulance drivers. Not just Harry but friends and acquaintances including Ernest Hemingway, e. e. cummings, Malcolm Cowley, Louis Bromfield and John Dos Passos had watched their companions die in the bloody mud of northern Europe and glimpsed adulthood and freedom in the bars and brothels of Paris.

Stimulated by a rich new culture but disillusioned by the carnage and senselessness of war, in France these men felt the first stirrings of their distinctive identity: a 'spectatorial attitude' to life, a sense of emptiness and detachment from reality; a feeling, because ultimately they survived the war, of being both chosen and undeserving; finally, a restless rootlessness that would colour much of their subsequent work with a faint but unmistakable wash of nostalgia. 'What shall we do tomorrow?' asked T. S. Eliot in *The Waste Land*. 'What shall we ever do?'

Writers of the period didn't want, as Malcolm Cowley put it, to 'write stories in which salesmen were the romantic heroes'. They had to fight to find their own material. Even the one novel that did achieve Cowley's improbable transformation, Sinclair Lewis's *Babbitt*, expressed the same unformed yearnings, the unfocused nostalgia, that characterized their generation and sent so many into exile.

One way of turning their backs on the past was to celebrate

modernity and the future. Hart Crane's poetry, like Langston Hughes's and Carl Sandberg's, used experimental language to convey with a new immediacy the effect produced upon him by jazz, machinery, laughter, debauchery, alcohol, sex, slang. His most famous work – the one written at the Moulin de Soleil – was an ode to the Brooklyn Bridge. Crosby was fascinated by cars, aeroplanes and speed; Gerald Murphy's paintings presented machines and engineering as works of art.

Believing their world had been wrecked by the generation that had preceded them these writers set about wholeheartedly rejecting their parents' values. 'They give us this thing, knocked to pieces, leaky, red-hot, threatening to blow up; and then they are surprised that we don't accept it with the same attitude of pretty, decorous enthusiasm with which they received it, way back in the '80s,' wrote John Carter furiously in *Atlantic Monthly* in 1920, expressing the views of so many of his contemporaries. 'We have been forced to live in an atmosphere of "tomorrow we die," and so, naturally, we drank and were merry.'

'They're all desperadoes, these kids, all of them with any life in their veins,' said one of the maturer characters in Warner Fabian's best-selling novel, *Flaming Youth*. The disenchanted younger generation strove to maintain their inner purity while living as dissolutely as they could, turning their backs on the complacency and conformity that sucked the vitality from life. 'Depravity was their prayer, their ritual, their rhythmic exercises: they denied sin by making it hackneyed in their own bodies, shucking it away to come out not dirtied but pure,' wrote the poet William Carlos Williams of the English debauchees Iris Tree and Nancy Cunard, whom he met in Paris at this time. Scott and Zelda Fitzgerald also saw their fast living almost as a dare, as if they were challenging something inside them to be tainted by their excesses.

Harry, too, was obsessed with purity. For all his womanizing, he was never attracted to the tawdry or the easily available. At Harvard he had declared that 'he'd rather kiss a nice girl than screw a chippie' and his amours were defined by his being able to find something to venerate about the women with whom he became involved. On his thirtieth birthday he pledged (among other things) 'to continue rites but to abolish superstitions ... to be ascetic not hedonistic ... to be bright and delicate and gentle and chaste to worship the Sun with a chaste heart and a chaste soul and a chaste body'.

And yet hedonism was what Harry's generation would be remembered for. Fearlessly they embraced the sins Middle America blamed on immigrants and hoped the Ku Klux Klan would eradicate: adultery, profanity, homosexuality, divorce, alcohol, extravagance, perversity, drugs, individuality, liberty and libertinism. For to them there were worse sins, outlined by the critic Edmund Wilson in an essay on *The Waste Land*: 'people grinding at barren office routine in the cells of giant cities, drying up their souls in eternal toil whose products never bring them profit, where their pleasures are so vulgar and feeble that they are almost sadder than their pains.'

Any catastrophe was preferable to living incarceration in a town like Sinclair Lewis's fictional Zenith or the Lynds' very real Middletown. Richmond Barrett wrote an essay in 1928, 'Babes in the Bois', satirizing a group of pretentious young lotus-eaters he met sailing from New York to Paris. '"I may make a mess of my life," said one. It was obvious that he rather hoped he would – a glorious, passionate kind of mess. "But at least I won't be a ready-made, the sort that's turned out by hundreds."'

Security was stultifying. Only by challenging himself with danger and movement could the thrusting young intellectual of the 1920s find inspiration. The cost mattered naught; in fact the cost was part of the prize. As Harry wrote of two of his literary heroes, Byron and Edgar Allan Poe, 'in these semi-madmen, these geniuses, lies the true aristocracy of mankind'. Talent was hardly talent if it didn't burn you up entirely.

Youth, too, was exalted. Like moderation, experience and wisdom were apologies for those who could not keep up. Scott Fitzgerald saw youth as its own justification – the only one. He longed for life but hated the marks it left on him. Above all he feared losing the idealistic sheen that youth had bestowed upon him. 'You remember I used to say I wanted to die at thirty,' he wrote to his editor as he was finishing *The Great Gatsby*. 'Well I'm twenty-nine and the prospect is still welcome.' Part of this was bravado; part of it was what he thought an artist should feel; but part of it was genuine. 'Youth is the only thing worth having,' said Oscar Wilde's Dorian

Gray, poster-boy for the 'Lost Generation'. 'When I find that I am growing old, I shall kill myself.'

'They long to be doomed,' wrote Richmond Barrett of his immature shipmates. 'If destruction threatens to be tardy, they'll rush to meet it half-way by committing suicide.' Suicide was popularly thought to be a twenties malaise. Barrett referred to the 'dozens of sensational scare-heads on the subject of suicide among American students' and admitted that the fact that people were brooding on self-destruction was a worrying social development.

Harry Crosby was not the only one. Hart Crane threw himself off a ship in the Gulf of Mexico in 1932. Harry had recognized their kinship: 'He is of the Sea as I am of the Sun.' Members of a suicide club in Paris drew lots once a year to see which of their number was to take his life; for them, committing suicide was the purest, bravest expression of contempt for life and its futility. The heroine of Carl Van Vechten's *The Tattooed Countess* travelled with a loaded gold-and-black Toledo-work revolver and a vial of bichloride of mercury tablets, just in case her acute sensitivity to life (and her desire for death) overcame her. Suicide had become a cipher for a kind of glamorous vulnerability, for clear-eyed courage, aestheticism and decadence.

Self-imposed exile of some other kind was an easier route for most. Rather than risk conforming to society or being rejected by it, intellectuals had no choice but to become, as the writer Glenway Westcott put it, 'spiritual expatriates... a band of revolutionaries or a cult of immoralists'. Feeling like strangers at home, attached to the United States but in an obscure way rejected by it, they sought escape and refuge. Millions of Americans pursued the exotic in films like *The Sheik* or in mah-jong tiles; the heiress and art collector Mabel Dodge Luhan fled to Mexico and the Southwest; Carl Van Vechten hailed a taxi to take him to Harlem.

Civilization in the United States came out in the same year that Harry and Caresse emigrated to France. The thirty contributors collected together by its editor Harold Stearns were unanimous in their view 'that American civilization itself is responsible for the tragedy of American talent'. In a later article, Stearns asked himself, 'What should a young man do?' and replied, 'A young man had no future in this country of hypocrisy and repression. He should take ship for Europe, where people know how to live.' Stearns, who had left New York in 1921, had already followed his own advice – although with little success. Six years later Hemingway immortalized him in *The Sun Also Rises* as the failure, Harvey Stone, counting his pennies in a Montparnasse café.

At first, being in Paris made it easier to believe in 'a *patrie* of the imagination'. It was, wrote Malcolm Cowley, another voluntary exile, 'a great machine for stimulating the nerves and sharpening the senses. Paintings and music, street noises, shops, flower markets, modes, fabrics, poems, ideas, everything seemed to lead toward a half-sensual, half-intellectual swoon'. e. e. cummings said Paris continually expressed the

'humanness of humanity', as opposed to American cities pros-
trate before the machine. It was also wonderfully cheap: a
dollar bought eight francs in 1919 and twenty-five in 1926.

'They were not in Paris because they were Americans,'
wrote Archibald MacLeish of Gerald and Sara Murphy, another
expatriate couple in the Crosbys' circle. 'They were in Paris
because it was Paris. And not only the Paris of the damp,
sweet-smelling mornings with their flooded gutters and their
high-wheeled carts but the Paris of the difficult work – the
work of art.' No one in America ever did things with the 'vast,
magnificent, cynical disillusion with which Gerald and Sara
make things like their parties,' wrote Fitzgerald.

Harry Crosby was by no means the most talented writer of
his generation, nor the most representative, but he encapsu-
lates so many of the things that inspired his peers: the feeling
of alienation, the desire for self-expression and freedom, the
conflation of pleasure and happiness, the philosophy of living
for the moment, the pagan worship of the body, the belief that
by continuing to move one would find meaning. Even his
suicide was part of a broader pattern. In a strange sort of way
he achieved the 'grace under pressure' that Hemingway said
was all a man could hope for from himself. Harry found
meaning in death; others would find it by returning home.

By late 1929, when Harry and the Fire Princess died, most
Americans-in-Paris were already making their way back. The
French had complained for years that they only heard
American-accented English spoken in the boulevard Saint-

Germain and that high prices were driving them out of their favourite restaurants, but for the first time Europe-based Americans were beginning to get a sense that they were transplanting their own materialistic, progress-obsessed culture to Europe as much as absorbing that of Europe themselves. Writing in *Harper's* magazine in March 1929, the historian Charles Beard spoke out against the Americanization of Europe: 'prose against poetry; dollars against sacrifice; calculation against artistic abandon'. What was the point of having a *patrie* of the imagination if you turned it into a mirror image of the sordid reality from which you were trying to escape?

Bored, discontented exiles, running from themselves, had even managed to make Paris dreary. 'From the Dome to the Rotonde, thence to the Select they march,' wrote Richmond Barrett of his weary 'trail-blazers' doing the rounds of literary Montparnasse nightspots. 'The next move is around the corner to the Parnasse; across the street someone beckons from the window of the Dingo. The dogged band leaves the Dingo at last for a round of Russian cocktails at the Viking. So the time passes – day after day, week after week, and still they congratulate themselves upon having escaped the rut!'

The more insightful among them recognized that, paradoxically, living abroad made it possible to look more clearly at the United States, to better judge and comment on what they had left behind. Their time away actually intensified their Americanness, rather than diluting it, and this became a powerful inspiration for many. Then, too, returning Americans found that they liked being back home – that the familiar had charms more potent than they remembered. Harold Stearns, finally back in New York after a decade away, rediscovered his homeland with a sense of wonder: 'after all, there is a real world here'.

10

The New Yorker

THE IRONY ABOUT THE literary world of the 1920s was that although it bemoaned the dearth of culture and inspiration in America, it was in fact experiencing a period of vibrant growth. The generation that delighted in the title 'lost' – Hemingway's epigram to *The Sun Also Rises* was a quote from Gertrude Stein describing him and his friends as a 'Lost Generation' – found itself through creative endeavour.

As Archibald MacLeish later wrote, it was 'precisely because the bottom had fallen out of the historical tradition' that his contemporaries wrote so bravely, so innovatively, so freely and tragically. 'It was not the Lost Generation which was lost: it was the world out of which that generation came.' This idea of what Edmund Wilson called 'the starvation of a whole civilization' allowed MacLeish, Hemingway and their friends – even Harry Crosby – to produce from the rubble something entirely, compellingly new.

From the First World War onwards, artists followed Ford

Madox Ford's maxim: 'the business of art is not to elevate but to render'. The very fact that Crosby, whom friends described as an Elizabethan adventurer in spirit, should have desired to be a poet above all other things shows how crucial the role of literature was to 1920s America, as criticism, conscience, mirror and diviner. Ezra Pound, who was commissioned by Caresse to write a posthumous appreciation of Harry's work, described the role of the 1920s artist:

> Ruffle the skirts of prudes
>   speak of their knees and ankles.
> But, above all, go to practical people –
>   go! Jangle their door-bells!
> Say that you do no work
>   and that you will live forever.

While some Americans with literary or artistic aspirations spent long periods of time away from the United States, many more gravitated to New York. The leafy, brownstone-lined streets of Greenwich Village had for decades been the province of the bohemian, women with short hair and men with long, both sexes in flowing, brightly coloured clothes. Their ideals of personal liberty and self-expression were quickly adopted by the post-war generation who added to them their own sense of affected disillusionment and an emancipating dose of Freud.

Some of the more adventurous ventured up to Harlem in

search of exotic drum-beats. Hoping to break free from the repressive shackles of society and civilization, they believed they would find in 'primitive' black culture a freer, more spontaneous, less inhibited life. Despite these avowedly high ideals, the practice was invariably low-life. Harlem may have been a place of inspiration for its own artists and writers but it did little more than service the darker needs of its white visitors.

For 1920s intellectuals, though, the earnest idealism of the Village and the fleshpots of Harlem could not compete with the allure of a smoky table in a back dining-room at the Algonquin Hotel. Here, writers and critics 'whose IQ was as high as their talk was rowdy' (in the words of the scriptwriter Anita Loos, an occasional guest) gathered informally but regularly to discuss work and love affairs, to drink and gamble, and to tease each other mercilessly about their shortcomings.

The Round Table was more a lunchtime meeting of friends, 'wits, poker and cribbage players, critics and writers', than a networking opportunity. None of them, in the early years, were especially successful but all were ambitious. In 1920 Franklin Pierce Adams, known as FPA, was at thirty-nine the oldest member of the group. He chronicled this insular little coterie in his Saturday column in the *New York Tribune* (up to 1922) and then in the *World*, the 'Diary of our own Samuel Pepys'. His chief pleasure was promoting the work of up-and-coming writers – many of whom, like Dorothy Parker who quipped that he 'raised her from a couplet', were Round Table regulars.

Several were drama critics, like the morose ladies' man

George Kaufman (also a director and playwright) and the effeminate Alec Woollcott, nicknamed Louisa May Woollcott. They invited their theatrical friends, including Noël Coward, who had arrived in New York with £17 in his pocket in 1921 on the first of several visits, the as-yet-unknown Harpo Marx and his brothers, the hard-drinking but charming womanizer John Barrymore and a dazzling teenager, Tallulah Bankhead, whose chief desire in life at that time was to seem more experienced than she really was. The drama critic and editor George Jean Nathan occasionally brought along the movie star Lillian Gish, with whom he had an enduring affair. She said that when she lunched with Nathan and Henry Mencken both talked 'at once, neither listening to the other, each keeping up a barrage of observations and witticisms... Scott and Zelda Fitzgerald often joined us, drinking their whiskey as if it were water and with seemingly no effect'.

Journalist-editors like Mencken – 'the personification of shrewd good nature' and the voice of his generation – joined columnists like Heywood Broun and fiction writers like Ring Lardner, venerated by his contemporaries, who occasionally abandoned his splendid isolation in Great Neck, Long Island, to grace the Algonquin and flirt with Dorothy Parker. Bob Benchley was a noted humorist; lanky Bob Sherwood, with his Chaplinesque moustache, was an editor and, later, playwright and screenwriter. He was so shy that he dictated his copy sitting on the floor with his back to the stenographer, but at the Algonquin he blossomed.

Although female Round Tablers were outnumbered by their male counterparts they held their own. Jane Grant was the first female writer placed on general assignment by the *New York Times*. Along with her friend Ruth Hale, a Broadway press agent, she founded the Lucy Stone League, a feminist advocacy association named for a nineteenth-century activist; both women fought to retain their maiden names after they married. Anita Loos, whose husband lived off her earnings, was an early member of the League.

Dorothy Parker, the only female drama critic in New York, had started her career writing captions for the fashion pages at *Vogue*. One of her first assignments was to write the copy for an underwear spread: 'Brevity is the soul of lingerie.' She had been sacked as a staff writer at *Vanity Fair* in 1920 for observing in print that the powerful impresario Florenz Ziegfeld's actress wife was too old for ingénue roles. Supported by friends and colleagues Bobs Benchley and Sherwood, Parker was the best-known woman at the Round Table – or the Vicious Circle, as it was known.

Vicious maybe; merciless assuredly. Even Parker's own wit could not always defend her from that of her friends. Unhappily married to an alcoholic and morphine addict and herself prone to severe depression, she returned to the Algonquin after one suicide attempt with enormous bows tied around her gauzed wrists, complaining, 'Eddie [Parker, her husband] doesn't even have a sharp razor.' On another occasion, after she took an overdose of the sleeping powder

Veronal, Bob Benchley drawled: 'Dorothy, if you don't stop this sort of thing you'll ruin your health.'

The Round Table's brittle charms did not have universal appeal. The aristocratic intellectual Edmund Wilson, a class-mate of Scott Fitzgerald's at Princeton and, as literary editor of *Vanity Fair*, a sometime stable-mate of Parker, Benchley, Sherwood, Broun and Woollcott, found them at bottom provincials masquerading as urban sophisticates. Only people from the same small-town, middle-class backgrounds could despise and mock their roots with such malice and yet be unable to escape them. Dorothy Parker was the one who stood out for Wilson: she alone, he thought, was genuinely witty as well as being able to move in circles other than her own.

Wilson's circle was higher-brow than the wise-cracking, small-town mob at the Algonquin – a group of aspiring poets rather than hack journalists. He and his friend John Peale Bishop competed for the affections of the untamed Edna St Vincent Millay. Their literary tastes, shaped by their years at ivy-covered colleges, were self-consciously aesthetic and deca-dent; their heroes were James Joyce, T. S. Eliot and Ezra Pound.

When Henry Mencken and George Nathan founded the *American Mercury* magazine in 1924, the first issue carried a parody of the 'Aesthete: Model 1924', a composite portrait of the literary intellectual of the period by Ernest Boyd, drawing on Wilson, Gilbert Seldes, John Dos Passos, e. e. cummings and others. Born with the century, wrote Boyd, the Aesthete had a proprietary attitude towards his times. He had been moulded by evening parties at Harvard and Princeton against a background of 'red plush curtains and chairs but recently robbed of their prudish antimacassars'. A spell in France during the war had given him a veneration for Proust and Cézanne, a florid rhetorical style and a taste for inaccurate and spurious French phrases. 'The Aesthete holds that a cliché, in French for preference, will dispose of any genius.'

Accessibility was not the Aesthete's aim. Although he adored French literature its allure would have been tarnished if it had been widely popular. 'What he wants to do is lead a cult, to communicate a mystic faith in his idols, rather than to make them available for general appreciation.' But the appeal of 'the esoteric editorial chair where experiments are made with stories which "discard the old binding of plot and narrative"' had to compete with 'the sales manager's desk, where, it appears, the Renaissance artist of today is to be found'. Like the habitués of the Round Table, even the Aesthete was learning to be commercial.

Dorothy Parker and her friends at the Algonquin were riding the tide of a revolution in the writing business. Although they would have hated the comparison, the literary industry, as Malcolm Cowley put it, 'was becoming like General Motors… The book trade was prospering, new publishers were competing for new authors, and suddenly it seemed that everybody you knew was living on publishers' advances.' Authors' advances, which made it possible to live while writing a book rather than just being paid from royalties after it came out, were a new development, pioneered during the 1920s by firms like Knopf, Viking and Random House. The number of new books published doubled between 1919 and 1929. An eager, if credulous, audience awaited: it almost seemed as if anyone who felt the urge could call themselves a writer and make a living from their pen.

The young editor Max Perkins transformed old-fashioned Charles Scribner's Sons by pursuing (and in large part creating) the stars of the new generation: Scott Fitzgerald, Ring Lardner, Ernest Hemingway and Tom Wolfe. Sixty-six-year-old Charles Scribner II, known at the firm as 'old CS', had headed Scribner's Sons since 1889 with his brother, Arthur. They were cigar-smoking, handsomely moustached, cautious with their money and suspicious of new writers, preferring to rely on established authors who needed very little editing like John Galsworthy, Edith Wharton and Henry James.

Against their better judgement, Perkins persuaded the Scribner brothers to publish Fitzgerald's first novel, overseeing three rewrites over a period of two years before his elders agreed to take the manuscript. His faith was amply rewarded. Encapsulating the dreams of the generation that grew up in the wake of the Great War, *This Side of Paradise* was the seminal novel of the early 1920s and a runaway bestseller. 'I am the man, as they say in the ads, who made America Younger-Generation conscious,' Edmund Wilson imagined his friend Fitzgerald boasting after its publication.

Fitzgerald respected Perkins enormously and liked being able to bring him into contact with friends whose work he thought Perkins might want to publish. He introduced Perkins to Ring Lardner, his neighbour on Long Island in 1923, and Perkins helped Lardner make the transition from sports-writer to one of the most celebrated short-story writers of the era.

When Fitzgerald moved to Paris in 1924 and met Ernest Hemingway he lost no time in letting Perkins know about his discovery. 'This is to tell you about a young man named Ernest Hemmingway [Fitzgerald never learned to spell Hemingway's name], who lives in Paris, (an American) writes for the transatlantic Review + has a brilliant future... I'd look him up right away. He's the real thing.'

Through this introduction Perkins went on to publish the second seminal novel of the 1920s, *The Sun Also Rises*, which inspired a generation of imitators. It was Perkins who per-suaded Hemingway to call his novel by this title rather than *Fiesta*, and both Perkins and Fitzgerald edited Hemingway's 'careless' and 'unpublishable' manuscript heavily to produce the pared-down power of the final version. 'Nowadays when almost everyone is a genius, at least for a while, the temptation for the bogus to profit is no greater than the temptation for the good man to relax,' Fitzgerald wrote in his ten-page critique. 'This should frighten all of us into a lust for anything honest that people have to say about our work.'

Hemingway's story of a group of expatriates drifting around

Europe drinking, arguing and making love encapsulated the glamorous disaffectedness that characterized the Lost Generation. Malcolm Cowley described people fresh from visits to Paris swapping stories about their hero and talking in what Cowley called the 'Hemingway dialect – tough, matter-of-fact and confidential'. Smith College girls in New York were wearing leather commissars' jackets and modelling themselves on Brett Ashley, although their cheeks were too healthily pink for authenticity.

The one future bestseller Perkins failed to persuade Charles and Arthur Scribner to publish was the advertising executive Bruce Barton's spiritual self-help book, *The Man Nobody Knows*. Sex and profanity they could learn to live with; making Jesus into a business adviser was a step too far.

Scholarships and fellowships like the Guggenheim Foundation, set up in 1925, supported male writers (as well as scientists and composers) including Wilson, Hart Crane, e.e. Cummings, W. H. Auden, Conrad Aiken and Langston Hughes. Its declared aim was to seek out 'men who were wilful, uncompromising, quarrelsome, arrogant and creative' – qualities not previously valued by American society.

Readers as well as writers felt part of a vibrant new literary movement characterized by the proliferation of experimental journals like the *Transatlantic Review*, *Broom* and *transition* and by mass-market magazines like the *Saturday Evening Post* which paid so much for witty, contemporary short stories that Fitzgerald could keep Zelda in diamonds and furs almost throughout the decade. In 1890 the Middletown public library had offered its readers nineteen periodicals; by 1925 its shelves groaned with 225.

Condé Nast's glittering *Vanity Fair* was edited by Frank Crowninshield, uncle of Harry Crosby's mistress Constance Crowninshield, his Lady of the Golden Horse. Founded in 1913, it had quickly become America's most successful chronicle of the international world of arts and letters. The writings of T. S. Eliot, Gertrude Stein, Aldous Huxley and P. G. Wodehouse were featured alongside the photographs of Albert Steichen and the drawings of Pablo Picasso and Henri Matisse. Its office's location near the Algonquin Hotel on West 44th Street was one reason the Algonquin had become Parker, Benchley and Sherwood's regular meeting place.

An insatiable national appetite for current events meant that daily papers proliferated as well. Fifty-five publishing chains controlled 230 daily newspapers with a combined circulation of over thirteen million. Although many of these papers were 'sex and sensation' tabloids like W. R. Hearst's *Daily Mirror*, and most placed as much importance on the twenties obsessions of sport and entertainment as on politics or international affairs, this was a publishing revolution. Increasingly Americans observed events through the media, rather than participating directly in them.

The *American Mercury*'s ambitious Aesthete was at the heart of this publishing boom. Although not yet thirty, as 'Editor-in-Chief, Editor, Managing Editor, Contributing Editor,

Bibliographical Editor, or Source Material Editor' of a newspaper or magazine he had 'an accredited mouthpiece, a
letterhead conferring authority, a secure place from which to
bestride the narrow world in which he is already a colossus'
and he revelled in his influence and fame.

Mencken himself, the editor who had commissioned
Ernest Boyd's parody of the Aesthete, could not have been
further from Boyd's precious creation. Grinning good-
humouredly, Mencken revelled in sending up the pretentious
and the sententious – anyone who took themselves too seriously. His *Smart Set* and, later, *American Mercury*, attacked what
he called 'boobus Americanus' and catered for a 'civilized
minority': 'men and women', as he jokingly put it, 'who had
heard of James Joyce, Proust, Cézanne, Jung, Bertrand Russell,
John Dewey, Petronius, Eugene O'Neill, and Eddington; who
looked down on the movies but revered Charlie Chaplin as a
great artist, could talk about relativity even if they could not
understand it, knew a few of the leading complexes by name,
collected Early American furniture, had ideas about progressive education, and doubted the divinity of Henry Ford and
Calvin Coolidge'. More than any other writer of the day,
Mencken swept provincialism and pettiness from America's
literary culture.

Like the poet Langston Hughes, who found inspiration in
Harlem street slang and the strains of popular music, Mencken
celebrated the vitality of modern American culture. 'Nothing
could exceed the brilliancy of such inventions as joy-ride,

high-brow, road-louse, sob-sister, frame-up, loan-shark, nature-faker, stand-patter, lounge-lizard, has-foundry, buzz-wagon, has-been, end-seat-hog, shoot-the-chutes, and grape-juice diplomacy,' he wrote admiringly of his countrymen's newly invented words in *The American Language* in 1919. 'They are bold; they are vivid; they have humor; they meet genuine needs.'

Despite this embarrassment of literary riches, there was still room, according to Howard Ross, a straight-talking young editor and regular at the Round Table, for one more publication. Ross had been dreaming of editing his own magazine since returning from military service in Europe where he had run the US army's newspaper, *Stars and Stripes*.

Born in Aspen, Colorado, in 1892, Harold Ross had started his first job on a newspaper at fourteen years old as a stringer for the *Salt Lake City Tribune*. Over the next nine years he wrote and edited for seven different papers before leaving for France in 1917.

Ross met his future wife, the journalist Jane Grant, in Paris during the winter of 1918–19. Grant took one look at him and 'decided he was really the homeliest man I'd ever met – he'd *have* to be good with that face and figure'. Ross's fidgety ungainliness did nothing to soften the impression of his huge hands and feet, widely spaced teeth, big mouth and thick butternut-coloured hair in a 'high, stiff pompadour, like some wild gamecock's crest' but he was engaging and modest and there was immense charm in his awkwardness. 'He was always in mid-flight, or on the edge of his chair, alighting or about to take off.'

Years later James Thurber described Ross fuming over news that Thurber had been imitating him, to the delight of their friends. '"I don't know what the hell there is to imitate – go ahead and show me,"' Ross snarled at Thurber. 'All the time his face was undergoing its familiar changes of expression and his fingers were flying. His flexible voice ran from a low register of growl to an upper register of what I can only call Western quacking. It was an instrument that could give special quality to such Rossisms as "Done and Done!" and "You have me there!" and "Get it on paper!"'

Janet Flanner, a friend of Grant who worked for Ross for over a decade, found him 'a strange, fascinating character, sympathetic, lovable, often explosively funny, and a good talker who was the most blasphemous good talker on record'. His swearing was constant, unconscious and entirely chaste. Ross's 'goddam' and 'Geezus' were simply interjections – they had nothing to do with any deity. Thurber said Ross was virtually unable 'to talk without a continuous flow of profanity... it formed the skeleton of his speech, the very foundation of his manner and matter, and to cut it out would leave him unrecognizable to his intimates, or even to those who knew him casually'.

Ross's sense of morality was as innocent as his swearing. Flanner remembered him discussing a couple having an affair:

'I'm sure he's s-l-e-e-p-i-n-g with her.' He was, she said, 'the only man I've ever known who spelt out euphemisms in front of adults'.

Their post-war gang in Paris included Alec Woollcott, Heywood Broun, Ring Lardner and Franklin Pierce Adams. When they returned to New York the collective friendship flourished against a new backdrop – the smoky back room of the Algonquin Hotel.

Ross and Grant married in 1920 and three years later moved into two large converted tenements on West 47th Street in the virtual slum of Hell's Kitchen. Their huge, elegant house, run by Chinese houseboys, was always open for an after-hours drink or a game of poker – complete with the added thrill of the possibility of being robbed while arriving or leaving. Guests included everyone from the outspoken nightclub hostess Tex Guinan to the boxer (and wannabe intellectual) Gene Tunney. They had two tenants, also Round Tablers, Hawley Truax and the temperamental Alec Woollcott whom Ross described receiving visitors 'like a fat duchess holding out her dirty rings to be kissed'.

Woollcott was the frequent victim of his friends' mockery. 'He was not so much a mere participant in his own daily life as he was the Grand Marshal of a perpetual pageant, pompous in demeanour, riding a high horse, wearing the medals of his own peculiar punctilio and perfectionism,' wrote James Thurber. 'His men friends loved to put banana peels in his portentous path to bring him down, high horse and all, while his women friends, whom he could slay in the subject of a sentence and eulogize in the predicate, loved to catch him before he could fall, or to pick up his outraged bulk.' Wolcott Gibbs, later writer and copy editor at the *New Yorker*, thought his friends tolerated Woollcott's 'insults because he also called them, or most of them, geniuses'.

In the early 1920s Ross edited *The Home Sector*, a magazine devoted to veterans' issues, and, for a miserable few months in 1924, he worked at the humorous magazine *Judge*. From the time he had arrived back from France he had dreamt of creating and editing his own magazine, and he and Grant had been saving money to fund it since their marriage. 'He carried a dummy of the magazine for two years, everywhere,' said his friend George Kaufman, 'and I'm afraid he was rather a bore with it.'

Ross's vision, as laid out in the mission statement he produced in the autumn of 1924, was a reflection of the considerations which governed his own and his friends' and associates' attitudes to life and work. The tone of his magazine, he said, would be marked by 'gaiety, wit and satire' and though it would not be highbrow it would be sophisticated. 'It would hate bunk.' It would be *au fait* with current events but 'interpretative rather than stenographic' in its attitude to them, and would deal neither in 'scandal nor sensation'. 'It hopes to be so entertaining and informative as to be a necessity for the person who knows his way about or wants to.' Illustrations would be a distinguishing characteristic and it would carry 'prose and verse, short and long, humorous, satirical and miscellaneous'.

Ross intended his magazine's selling point to be avowedly directed at 'a metropolitan audience'. With no disrespect intended, he said, he was not concerned with the tastes of the 'old lady in Dubuque' whom editors of national magazines had to consider. New York residents hoping to decide what to do in the evening would find news of the latest supper clubs and cabarets; local incidents and personalities would be reported upon in a pastiche of 'the small-town newspaper style' with which Ross had grown up.

The prospectus was compelling, but in person Ross was less prepossessing. At the Round Table he was a listener rather than a performer, better at parry than thrust in repartee. His wit never sparkled like Dorothy Parker's or Alec Woollcott's. Although several of his friends agreed to allow Ross to use their names on his editorial board, they thought his ambitions ridiculous. As George Kaufman observed, Ross was 'completely miscast as an editor' and none of their friends thought he had a chance of getting his magazine into print. 'How the hell could a man who looked like a resident of the Ozarks and talked like a saloon brawler set himself up as pilot of a sophisticated, elegant periodical?' asked the playwright Ben Hecht.

Ross's first stroke of luck came in the person of Raoul Fleishmann. Fleishmann, who preferred the Round Table (and its regular poker game) to the bakeries in which his family had made their millions, agreed in 1924 to invest

$25,000 in Ross's idea, more than matching Ross and Grant's own savings of $20,000. Another Round Table habitué, a Broadway press agent called John Toohey, provided Ross's idea with a name — the *New Yorker* — and was amused to be given shares in the magazine as thanks. He did not anticipate that they would ever translate into anything tangible.

The first issue of the *New Yorker* came out on 17 February 1925. Despite art director Rea Irvin's characteristic typesetting (still used today) and his cover illustration of a dandy examining a butterfly through a monocle, which straight away conveyed the sophisticated, self-reflective feel for which Ross was striving, the articles were laboured and the editing jumbled. The wit was immature; jokes were printed with the punch-lines first; pieces were featured in more than one issue; typos abounded. 'So I went to Florida for a rest,' read one supposedly humorous comment on the Florida housing boom in April 1925. 'Of course I left all my money there in real estate, and had to return by boat.'

Frank Crowninshield, editor of *Vanity Fair*, went through the first edition in his office with one of his writers. He was all too aware that as several of his contributors were friends of Ross's the *New Yorker* might become a rival. 'Well, Margaret,' he said to his colleague as they finished, 'I think we have nothing to fear.' Ross needed to learn, commented Niven Busch (who later became a *New Yorker* writer), 'that there is no provincialism so blatant as that of the metropolitan who lacks urbanity'.

The *New Yorker* was 'the outstanding flop of 1925'. Advertisers failed to materialize. Circulation dipped below 3,000. In early May, Ross, Fleishmann, Hawley Truax (Ross's tenant and a director of the magazine) and the professional publisher John Hanrahan met at the Princeton Club and decided to cut their losses. The initial investment of $45,000 had gone and Fleishmann was owed another $65,000. It was costing between $5,000 and $8,000 a week to keep the magazine afloat. As they walked away from the meeting, Fleishmann overheard Hanrahan say, 'I can't blame Ross for calling it off, but it surely is like killing something that's alive.' Hanrahan's words struck Fleishmann deeply, and when he saw Ross later that afternoon he told him that he was willing to try and raise outside capital to help the *New Yorker* survive.

Success was slow in coming and for a while the *New Yorker* was a standing joke even among its contributors. When Ross asked Dorothy Parker why she hadn't come into the office to write a piece for him, she replied tartly, 'Somebody was using the pencil.' Although magazine word rates were high during this period, Ross could afford to pay his writers very little. In the magazine's first ten months he used 282 different contributors.

The editorial board Ross had assembled from among his Round Table friends often found it difficult to contribute, either because they were too busy or because contractual obligations to other publications (most often *Vanity Fair*) forbade it. To hide their identities they sometimes wrote under pseudonyms. Parker, who would become literary editor in 1927, turned in only one article and two poems in 1925. Bob Benchley, from 1929 the *New Yorker*'s drama critic, didn't write anything for the magazine until it had been running nearly a year. Alec Woollcott's column 'Shouts and Murmurs' was not introduced until 1929. Henry Mencken only started contributing in the 1930s.

Ross's friends' early reticence was actually a blessing in disguise, because it forced him to seek out new talent, like E. B. White, James Thurber and the first 'Talk of the Town' writer, Ralph Ingersoll, who perfectly captured the mood of 'dinner-table conversation' that Ross hoped for. Gradually Ross and his team of writers and editors found their voice: informed but offhand, detached and amusing, always slightly tongue-in-cheek. By the end of their first year Scott Fitzgerald was writing to Maxwell Perkins from Paris asking for 'all the gossip that isn't in *The New Yorker* or the *World*'.

In the summer of 1925 Jane Grant wrote to her friend Janet Flanner, an aspiring writer who had just moved to Paris and was living on her 'hopes and good bistro food on the Left Bank'. Grant told Flanner about Ross's new magazine, and asked her if she would like to write for it. What was it called, Flanner asked – and was it any good? It was called the *New Yorker*, wrote Grant, and though it was not yet any good, it was going to be. Flanner was the *New Yorker*'s Paris correspondent for the next fourteen years.

Ross's leadership was idiosyncratic. He was conscientious,

enquiring, demanding and critical. James Thurber saw him as a mass of contradictions: 'a visionary and a practicalist, imperfect at both, a dreamer and a hard worker, a genius and a plodder, obstinate and reasonable, cosmopolitan and provincial, wide-eyed and world-weary'. One day Ross called Thurber into his office. 'Now in this casual way of yours here, you use a colon where anybody else would use a dash,' he said. 'I'm not saying you can't do it. I'm just bringing it up.' Thurber argued his point and Ross 'agreed to let the colon stand, for he was, as I have said and now say again, at once the most obdurate and reasonable of editors'.

Ross's own areas of knowledge were patchy in the extreme and he was profoundly suspicious of 'anything smacking of scholarship'. Literature, music and art were virtually unknown to him. In 1931 the English painter Paul Nash came into the *New Yorker* offices to meet Ross, who greeted him with the words, 'There are only two phoney arts, painting and music.' Nash was a little surprised. 'He is like your skyscrapers. They are unbelievable, but there they are.'

Dorothy Parker thought Ross 'almost illiterate'. The only novels he had read were *When Knighthood Was in Flower* and *Riders of the Purple Sage*. He stuck his head around the corner of the subs' office one day to ask, 'Is Moby Dick the whale or the man?'

From the start the *New Yorker*, under Wolcott Gibbs's careful gaze, prided itself on its scrupulous copy-editing. When Henry Mencken referred to a European restaurant in which he said

Wits of the Round Table: writer Dorothy Parker (left) and Harold Ross (right), editor of the *New Yorker* until his death in 1951

Celebrated lawyer Clarence Darrow, in braces, leaning on the desk in front of his defence team in Dayton, Tennessee, July 1925. The defendant, science teacher John Scopes, is in a white shirt with his elbows on the desk behind Darrow

The Spirit of St Louis before Lindbergh's record-breaking flight,
May 1927

Evangeline Lindbergh bidding her son Charles
goodbye before his solo flight from New York
to Paris; note their reserved expressions and
body language. She wrote to him, 'For the first
time in my life I realise that Columbus also
had a mother'

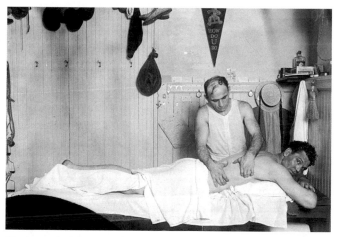

The boxer Jack Dempsey being given a massage by his trainer in 1925.
Although he had been World Heavyweight Champion for six years, at this point
Dempsey was more focused on his Hollywood career than on defending his title

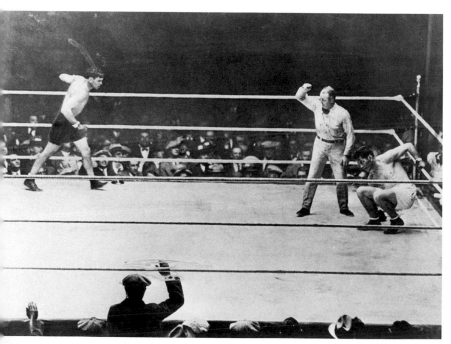

Dempsey coming towards the fallen Gene Tunney during the Long Count in Chicago, 1927.
The box-office take for the fight was $2.5 million

The nearly-finished Chrysler Building,
autumn 1929, when it was on track to overtake
the Eiffel Tower as the tallest building in the world.
It held that title for less than a year before the
Empire State Building overtook it in 1931

The Chrysler Building's architect,
William Van Alen, dressed as his
creation, with his wife at the Society of
Beaux Arts Architects ball, 1931

he had eaten but of which the subs could find no record, they refused to include it. Not until Ross brought the restaurant's menu into the office would they accept that it existed. 'Ross has the most astute goons of any editor in the country,' said Mencken.

By 1927 the *New Yorker* was beginning to flourish. *Vanity Fair* featured Ross in its Hall of Fame for the year: 'and finally because he is now editor-in-chief of *The New Yorker*'. The British journalist Beverley Nichols, sent to New York in 1928 to model the *American Sketch* in the *New Yorker*'s image, said Ross was producing a 'high-powered, streamlined little magazine' that impressed its rivals – namely Nichols's publisher, George Doran. That year, for the first time, the *New Yorker* turned a profit. Not only had it survived but it had thrived, and would continue to do so. Today, in much the same form as Ross first imagined it, his creation continues to disregard the old lady of Dubuque. Somebody once asked James Thurber whether he thought the *New Yorker* had succeeded 'because, or in spite of, Harold Ross?' His answer was that the magazine had been 'created out of the friction between Ross Positive and Ross Negative'.

By the time the *New Yorker* had rounded the corner, the heyday of the Round Table was over. Most of the regulars had moved on, going to Hollywood to write for the movies or producing their own plays on Broadway rather than merely reviewing them. Ross and Jane Grant's marriage broke up and they sold the house in Hell's Kitchen.

Harold Ross, who would marry twice more, never found a greater passion than the *New Yorker*. Every apartment he lived in became an extension of his office until, appropriately, he moved into the Algonquin just before he died in 1951 – having edited every single edition of the *New Yorker* up until that point. Incurably restless to the end, it was said that after he died a fat envelope marked 'Getaway Money' was found in his safety deposit box.

11

'Yes, We Have No Bananas Today'

It is possible that the place in America least prepared to welcome journalists of the stamp of Harold Ross and his wearily sophisticated writers was the small mountain town of Dayton, Tennessee, population 1,800. But in the summer of 1925, according to the journalist Joseph Wood Krutch, Dayton was 'selected as the site of an Armageddon'. Over two hundred eager reporters, one from as far away as London, moved into this pious, provincial town to chronicle a great clash between the forces of progress and the forces of conservatism.

In the 1920s the Deep South was dominated by evangelical Protestant fundamentalism which taught a literal acceptance of the Scriptures. If one could not believe that Christ actually rose from the dead, ministers argued, then one could not believe a word of what He said. Fundamentalists celebrated ignorance, preaching that simple faith was more important than all the learning in the world. Books, apart from the Bible, were violently mistrusted. If their contents were true, then they should already be in the Bible; if false, then reading them would imperil the soul. One Georgia assemblyman said that a man needed only three books: the Bible, as a guide to behaviour; the hymn book, for poetry; and the almanac, to predict the weather.

This return to the source was, like the revival of the Ku Klux Klan (which exploited fundamentalists in its recruiting process), a howl of protest against the forces of modernity sweeping the United States – urbanization, industry, immigration, technology, immorality. Anyone who dissented from their view of the universe was by definition a sinner, a heretic and an enemy. 'The modernist juggles the Scripture statements of His deity and denies His virgin birth,' raged one fundamentalist minister, 'making Him a Jewish bastard, born out of wedlock, and stained forever with the shame of His Mother's immorality.' Hearing this at the Algonquin, Dorothy Parker and her friends would have screamed with laughter and called for another cocktail. The chasm between the two groups was unbridgeable.

Perhaps the bloodiest battleground between fundamentalists and modernists was the relatively new science of evolution. Darwin's *On the Origin of Species* had been published in 1859. Just over twenty years later, when Darwin was still alive, the presidents of nine leading Eastern colleges were asked by the New York *Observer* whether their faculties taught evolution; the response was a shocked and unanimous no. Even though the theory of survival of the fittest would be used to promote racism and eugenics during the early twentieth century, at this stage the mere idea that man was descended from apes was unthinkable.

By the 1920s, though, progressive intellectuals had accepted Darwinism (and the concept that science would one day explain everything) so entirely that it had become an article of modernist faith. When a bill prohibiting the teaching of man's evolution from animals was brought before the Delaware legislature, it was facetiously referred to the Committee on Fish, Game and Oysters.

But pious Southerners still believed that the entire truth about the creation of the universe was contained in Genesis: 'In the beginning God created the heaven and the earth. And the earth was without form, and void; and darkness was upon the face of the deep. And the Spirit of God moved upon the face of the waters. And God said, Let there be light: and there was light.'

The notion that man was descended from apes was seen as blasphemy. As a French visitor to the United States in the mid-twenties observed, one of the frightening implications of Darwinism, for Southerners who believed implicitly in white supremacy, was its message to black people. 'If the monkey can become a man, may the Negro not hope to become white?' The Ku Klux Klan added Darwinists to their list of anti-American conspiracists which included Catholics, blacks, Jews and Bolsheviks. After being ousted from the Klan's high command in 1924, Edward Clarke became an anti-evolution campaigner.

Throughout the early 1920s the fundamentalist crusade to ban the teaching of evolution in schools gained pace. When the Texas legislature rejected a bill permitting censorship of school books, the state governor, 'Ma' Ferguson, declared, 'I am a Christian mother, and I am not going to let that kind of rot go into Texas textbooks.' She blacklisted or bowdlerized the offending books to remove any mention of Darwinism.

In early 1925 the state of Tennessee became a particular focus for the anti-evolutionists, headed by William Jennings Bryan. Known as the 'Great Commoner', the charismatic Bryan was a Southern folk hero, a sincere, energetic Jacksonian democrat with an abiding mistrust of education. 'The only morality comes from the Bible, all our institutions and our social life are founded on an implicit belief in it, and without that belief there is no ground on which moral teaching may be founded.'

Bryan had three times run as Democratic candidate for president (and twice more as an independent) and served in President Wilson's Cabinet before resigning when Wilson led the United States into the First World War. Having moved to Florida hoping to improve his wife's health, Bryan was also a major beneficiary of the Florida property boom, receiving handsome payment for promoting the 'Coral Gables Land Association'. His political causes – pacifism, Prohibition and female suffrage, as well as anti-evolutionism – sprang out of his twin convictions: a deep religious faith and a passionate commitment to populism and social justice. He blamed Darwinism for the Great War and the decline of faith in 1920s

America, and hoped to prevent schools and 'infidel universities' from teaching scientific theories of evolution. 'What shall it profit a man if he shall gain all the learning of the schools and lose his faith in God?' Bryan thundered. His audiences cheered as he reached his oratorical crescendo: 'You can't make a monkey of me!' he would cry.

At the start of 1925 Bryan and the evangelist preacher Billy Sunday arrived in Tennessee's capital, Memphis, to put pressure on the state legislature to pass a bill proposed by John Washington Butler, a local farmer and Primitive Baptist lay leader. Butler had been worried by news 'that boys and girls were coming home from school and telling their fathers and mothers that the Bible was all nonsense', and proposed to make it illegal 'to teach any theory that denies the story of the divine creation of man as taught in the Bible and to teach instead that man has descended from a lower order of animals'. Masked Klansmen marched in support of the bill, despite Bryan's private disapproval of their order. The Butler Act was passed that March. In New York, the American Civil Liberties Union (ACLU) pledged to support anyone who dared defy this ban on the grounds that it was unconstitutional.

It was the manager of Dayton's coal and iron mine, George Rappleyea, who first had the idea of using Dayton as a test case for the Butler Act. Rappleyea came from New York. He accepted the principles of evolution and, as a member of a modernist Methodist church, did not see it as incompatible with Christianity. Having read about the ACLU's declaration, he suggested to a group of local men gathered in Frank Robinson's drugstore and soda fountain (the hub of Dayton life) that they stage a test case of the Butler Act there. Robinson, who was also chairman of the Rhea County school board, liked the idea of generating some publicity for his sleepy town, as did the School Superintendent, Walter White.

Rappleyea persuaded his friend John Scopes, Rhea county's amiable young maths and science teacher and part-time football coach, to continue teaching biology classes from the state-approved textbook, Hunter's *Civic Biology*, which contravened the Butler Act. Having secured the ACLU's support, Rappleyea prosecuted Scopes for violating the law and Robinson notified the *Chattanooga Times* and the *Nashville Banner* of his action. Associated Press picked up the story and the next day it was carried by every major newspaper in the country.

The ACLU, which would eventually raise a fund of $11 million for Scopes's defence appeal, engaged Clarence Darrow to act as his head lawyer. Darrow had spent his long and distinguished career fighting for the rights of the individual, for freedom of speech and the privilege of dissent. Initial fears that he was too radical, and would allow the opposition to present the case as a clash between religion and godlessness, were finally discounted in view of Scopes's expressed preference for the experienced criminal lawyer.

Darrow himself had hesitated before committing himself to the case until he heard that his adversary would be William

Jennings Bryan. Both men were Democrats, old allies in some causes and old sparring partners in others; in the past Darrow had even supported Bryan's presidential ambitions. Their relationship was cordial but plain-spoken. As an evangelizing agnostic and an impassioned advocate for scientific knowledge in general and evolution in particular, Darrow was the perfect focus for the prejudices and fears of the team prosecuting John Scopes. Secular and anticlerical to the core, he denied the primacy that biblical fundamentalists assigned to man above all other creatures and believed that the Christian doctrine of original sin was 'silly, impossible and wicked'. He said afterwards that he took up Scopes's cause because 'there was no limit to the mischief that might be accomplished unless the country was roused to the evil at hand'.

William Jennings Bryan arrived in Dayton three days before Scopes's trial began, declaring that it would be a 'duel to the death'. Welcomed as the popular hero he was, Bryan spent his time giving lectures to the school board about teaching evolution, preaching, posing for pictures at Robinson's drugstore and attending a banquet in his honour at the Progressive Dayton Club. Two ACLU lawyers from New York, Darrow's associates, arrived two days later, having seen the extensive news coverage of Bryan's pre-campaigning. 'Am I too late for the trial?' asked Dudley Malone, declaring, 'The issue is not between science and religion, as some would have us believe. The real issue is between science and Bryanism.'

In the days before the trial began, hot-dog, sandwich and

ice-cream sellers catering to the unusual crowds mingled with trained chimps and revivalists, evangelists and holy rollers in Dayton's town square. Signs everywhere exhorted the faithful to read their Bibles daily and have faith that Jesus is their saviour. 'The Sweetheart Love of Jesus Christ and Paradise Street is at Hand,' read one. 'Be Sure Your Sins Will Find You Out,' warned another. A few bold booksellers hawked biology texts. Badges reading 'Your Old Man's a Monkey' were sold. A string quartet of black musicians played.

Journalists absorbing the scene reported back to their editors via twenty-two newly installed Western Union telegraph operators. A movie camera platform had been placed in the courtroom and Rhea County's first airstrip was marked off in a field so that film coverage of the trial could be flown out to be shown on national newsreels. Equipment was installed to transmit proceedings to the nation by live radio; it was the first trial to be broadcast nationally.

Reporters flooded into Dayton, filling the town's one hotel and several boarding houses and crowding into Robinson's soda fountain. Inhabitants revelled in the national attention and the chance to boost their home town. The local policeman's van bore a sign reading 'Monkeyville Police'; a delivery man called himself the 'Monkeyville Express'; the regional press declared its delight that the world was 'taking note of the South'. As Clarence Darrow said, 'Most of the newspapers treated the whole case as a farce instead of a tragedy, but they did give it no end of publicity.'

Perhaps the man most enjoying Dayton was Henry Mencken, covering the trial for the *Baltimore Evening Sun*, which had stood for John Scopes to the tune of $500. Mencken could be seen everywhere, his relish for the unfolding events apparent on his broadly smiling face. As Scopes put it, his trial was really 'Mencken's show'. Joseph Krutch, a Tennessean journalist working in the North, was in Dayton reporting for *The Nation*. He said the scene 'seemed arranged for [Mencken's] delight... Had he invented the Monkey Trial no one would have believed in it, but he had been spared the necessity of invention.' Krutch admired Mencken, but, sensitive to his scorn for small-town Southern life, disliked how he charmed everyone on both sides and then wrote 'brutally contemptuous' accounts of them.

'There was a friar wearing a sandwich sign announcing that he was the Bible champion of the world. There was a Seventh Day Adventist arguing that Clarence Darrow was the beast with seven heads and ten horns described in Revelation XIII, and that the end of the world was at hand,' Mencken recounted. 'There was an ancient who maintained that no Catholic could be a Christian. There was the eloquent Dr. T. T. Martin, of Blue Mountain, Miss., come to town with a truck-load of torches and hymn-books to put Darwin in his place. There was a singing brother bellowing apocalyptic hymns. There was William Jennings Bryan, followed everywhere by a gaping crowd. Dayton was having a roaring time. It was better than the circus.'

But Mencken, nostrils twitching for any whiff of hypocrisy,

found that even in Dayton 'there was a strong smell of antino-mianism'. The sweating evangelists preaching Armageddon outside the courthouse were mostly itinerant, hoping to take advantage of the crowds gathered to see evolution dispatched by Bryan once and for all; the townspeople, according to Mencken, did not permit their faith to impede their debaucheries. As a friendly female journalist explained to him, Dayton was, after all, the capital of Rhea County. 'That is to say, it was predominantly epicurean and sinful. A country girl from some remote valley of the county, coming into town for her semi-annual bottle of Lydia Pinkham's Vegetable Compound, shivered on approaching Robinson's drug-store quite as a country girl from up-State New York might shiver on app-roaching the Metropolitan Opera House.'

To Clarence Darrow's surprise, the trial opened on the sweltering morning of Friday 10 July with a long prayer entreating the jury, the accused and the attorneys to be 'loyal to God'. Dayton's courtroom had been freshly painted yellow. It was packed solid by a mixture of journalists and fascinated locals, and loudspeakers conveyed the proceedings to the crowds that had overflowed on to the lawn.

As a concession to the unusual heat, Judge Raulston announced that the trial's participants would be permitted to remove their coats and ties. Only the defence's Dudley Malone managed to keep his jacket on for the entire two weeks, admitting the temperature just so far as to dab his damp forehead with a linen handkerchief and earning Dayton's grudging respect for his stamina. Unusually, smoking was banned from the courtroom, but nicotine addicts (everyone but Bryan) were placated with well-placed spittoons and chewed their tobacco instead of smoking it.

While his defence team were relaxed and eagerly anticipating the upcoming debate, John Scopes, looking like a college student in his slacks and open-necked shirt, was nervous. He had been happy enough to allow Rappleyea to bring him to court – he did not come from Dayton, and had no intention of remaining there; he was unattached and easy-going, with liberal views but no very strong opinions – but once there he found that all the hullabaloo made him uncomfortable. He spent as much of the next two weeks as he could hiding out down at the local swimming hole, escaping public attention. His presence wasn't really necessary, anyway: on leaving for Dayton, Clarence Darrow had declared, 'Scopes is not on trial. Civilization is on trial.' The defence had decided that their client need not testify. As Scopes put it later, he was nothing more than a 'ringside observer at my own trial'.

Bryan sat confidently in court with his stiff collar removed and his sleeves rolled up, fanning himself against the heat and flies with a huge palm leaf. He hadn't prosecuted a case for nearly forty years, but, as the mouthpiece of God, he was unintimidated. Bryan knew 'he represented religion', said Darrow, adding in a damning phrase worthy of Mencken, 'and in this he was the idol of all Morondom'. Behind him, in a wheelchair, sat his invalid wife Mary, who suffered from severe arthritis with quiet dignity.

The judge, John Raulston, an acknowledged supporter of the law Scopes had violated, gave off an air that said, 'Rest assured, we shall assassinate you gently.' For, as Joseph Krutch observed, Raulston 'had probably never in his life heard anyone question in other than timidly apologetic terms the combination of ignorance, superstition, and (sometimes) hypocrisy for which he stood; and he was confident that, so far at least as *his* world was concerned, the debate as well as the legal verdict would be in his and his community's favour'.

That afternoon twelve jurors were selected. They were representative of Dayton's population – mostly regular church-goers, simple, middle-aged farmers with little formal education. According to custom, no women were included among their number. An informal poll conducted during the trial showed that 85 per cent of churchgoing Daytonians professed to believe the Bible literally, though they were more usually moderate Methodists than fervently fundamentalist Baptists.

Clarence Darrow's two-hour opening speech the following Monday was one of the most electrifying of his career, an impassioned defence of tolerance and secularism against fundamentalism. 'Coatless and conspicuously suspendered as if to assure Dayton that he was as plain a man as any of its own citizens', according to Krutch, Darrow burst into a fierce attack on 'what he called the ignorance, intolerance, arrogance and bigotry' of Dayton.

Having decided that there was no point saving his punches until his closing speech, on the basis that Bryan would be the final speaker, Darrow rebutted the prosecution's populist opening argument that the people paying teachers' salaries should be allowed to dictate their curriculum. For years this had been Byran's argument against the teaching of evolution in public schools: a simple defence of majority rule. 'The *right* of the *people* speaking through the legislature, to control the schools which they *create* and *support*, is the real issue,' Bryan had written before the case opened.

Darrow countered that the people of Tennessee had adopted a constitution which granted every single one of them 'religious freedom in its broadest terms'. Violating that freedom by limiting what people were able to teach or learn was thus a breach of their individual liberty. The state of Tennessee, Darrow argued, had no more right to insist in schools that the Bible is a holy book than it had to present as sacred the Koran, the Book of Confucius, or the essays of Emerson. In this way Darrow hoped to show that Bryan was not a defender of democracy but a threat to it. He concluded with a solemn warning: 'We are marching backwards to the glorious age of the sixteenth century when bigots lighted fagots to burn men who dared bring any intelligence and enlightenment and culture to the human mind.'

As Joseph Krutch reported, Darrow's eloquence and passion made even Dayton stop to think. Riveted, the town's inhabitants forgot which side they were on, even bursting into applause for a particularly good strike by either side – but still placed their faith in Bryan as their champion to prove that, as Joseph Wood Krutch put it, 'Learning is useless... Faith alone counts.'

The next day, while electrical storms thundered outside the courthouse, Darrow formally objected to the prayers that initiated each day's proceedings. A supreme court decision permitted prayer in courtrooms, but it was not mandatory. 'When it is claimed by the state that there is a conflict between science and religion there should be no... attempt by means of prayer... to influence the deliberations,' he argued. Prayer, he said, was a personal matter, to be conducted in private. The prosecution team protested but later a compromise was reached allowing modernist ministers to alternate with fundamentalists so that a broader spectrum of faith was represented.

Darrow had not expected Raulston to agree with his opening argument that Scopes's constitutional rights had been violated by the Butler Act, and on Wednesday the judge confirmed this opinion. Furthermore he would not permit the defence's scientific experts to take the stand and try to prove the facts of evolution. Once the parameters of the trial had been set, the proceedings could begin in earnest.

The prosecution called as witnesses some of Scopes's students, hoping their testimony would demonstrate how Scopes's use of the theory of evolution had undermined their faith in God. In response to Darrow's cross-examination, they said that they did not think science had done them any harm.

After the trial, Darrow was delighted to overhear one saying to another, 'Don't you think Mr Bryan is a little narrow-minded?' He did not, perhaps, hear another Dayton teenager, also after the trial, comment, 'I like him [Scopes], but I don't believe I came from a monkey.'

When drugstore owner Frank Robinson took the stand he testified that Scopes had said to him that any teacher using Hunter's *Biology* was violating the Butler Act. Darrow, cross-examining, asked first if Robinson sold Hunter's *Biology* in his shop – he did – and then, as the audience began to laugh, asked him if it were true that he was a member of the school board.

Dudley Malone rose for the defence after Bryan spoke. He questioned Bryan's right to speak for all Christians and stated the defence's conviction that no conflict existed between Christianity and evolution. The newspaper headlines summarized their arguments. Bryan raged, 'They call us bigots when we refuse to throw away our Bibles.' Malone responded, 'We say "Keep your Bible," but keep it where it belongs, in the world of your conscience... and do not try to tell an intelligent world and the intelligence of this country that these books written by men who knew none of the accepted facts of science can be put into a course of science.'

Most journalists, including Henry Mencken and Joseph Krutch, went home during the first week. They had seen enough. After hearing that no scientific evidence was to be admitted, Mencken gave victory to the prosecution: 'The main battle is over, with Genesis completely triumphant.'

Krutch, however, thought that Bryan had failed his devo-
tees. 'Any passionate revivalist from the hills could have been
more effective. He would have believed. Bryan merely refused
to doubt... [retreating] further and further into boastful ignorance.' On one occasion, when asked if he denied that man was
a mammal, Bryan had answered, 'I do' – because he was unsure
of its meaning, Krutch thought – and an incredulous Mencken
fell with a loud crash from the table on to which he had climbed
to get a better view.

None of them had predicted Darrow's masterstroke. At the
beginning of the second week Bryan agreed to stand as witness
in the role of biblical expert, facing Darrow's questioning; it
was understood that Darrow would in turn submit to Bryan's
examination. By this time the heat was so unrelenting and the
crowds so immense that court proceedings had been moved
out on to the lawn in front of the courthouse amid rumours that
the floor was about to collapse.

Darrow, thumbs in his lavender braces, coolly declared that
his intention in questioning Bryan was, 'to show up fundamentalism... to prevent bigots and ignoramuses from
controlling the education system of the United States'. Bryan
leapt from his seat, purple with rage. Pounding his fist on the
table in front of him, he shouted, 'I am simply trying to protect
the word of God against the greatest atheist or agnostic in the
United States. I want the papers to know I am not afraid to get
on the stand in front of him and let him do his worst!'
Although he remained defiant in the face of Darrow's attack,

Bryan's wilful ignorance made him seem a fool; he simply lacked the wit that would have helped him counter Darrow's arguments. As Darrow said, 'He did not think. He knew.'

When Darrow asked Bryan what he thought about biblical miracles like Adam's rib, the Flood and Jonah and the whale, he replied, 'One miracle is just as easy to believe as another.' Pressed further about how he could believe in such improbabilities, he responded, 'I do not think about things I don't think about.' 'Do you think about things you do think about?' queried Darrow. 'Well, sometimes.'

Darrow asked him how old he thought the universe might be – when God had made it and how long the seven days had lasted – and Bryan thundered, 'I am more interested in the Rock of Ages than in the age of rocks.' The triumphant Darrow looked on his opponent with pity: he had 'made himself ridiculous' and still worse, 'contradicted his own faith'. For his part Bryan accused Darrow of insulting the people Bryan called 'yokels' by trying to weaken their faith by making them admit that it was necessary to interpret the Bible. Darrow replied, 'You insult every man of science and learning in the world because he does not believe in your fool religion.' Eventually Raulston adjourned court for the day.

The next day Raulston ruled that Bryan's testimony was irrelevant and struck it from the record, forbidding any cross-examination of Darrow. 'Mr Bryan and his associates forgot to look surprised,' commented Darrow, evidently suspecting collaboration. The two teams were invited to make their closing remarks. Since Scopes had clearly broken the law, Darrow urged the jury to find Scopes guilty so that the case could be appealed to the Tennessee Supreme Court where the constitutionality of the law itself could be assessed.

Many of the jurors were keen for the trial to end so they could start harvesting their peach crop; it took them nine minutes to reach a guilty verdict. The trial had lasted two weeks. John Scopes, who had not once taken the stand, was fined $100. Although Bryan offered to pay his fine in the spirit of goodwill, Mencken's *Baltimore Evening Sun* took care of it.

Both sides claimed victory, although in fact they were both diminished by the trial and the hard glare of national attention that they had endured. Moderate onlookers resented the stark choice they had been offered between atheism and fundamentalism. Most people thought the case had exposed Bryan as a fool and Darrow as a know-it-all, without resolving the issue it had sought to address. And as Joseph Krutch observed, future generations who saw the Scopes case as a witch hunt and compared it to post-war McCarthyism missed 'the fact that it was also a circus' — 'a jape elaborately staged for their own amusement by typical intellectual playboys of the exuberant Twenties, and the real villains were … the responsible citizens and officials of Tennessee who should never have allowed it to happen'.

Immediately after the trial ended, a still defiant William Jennings Bryan began making plans for a national anti-evolution lecture tour to capitalize on the publicity the Scopes case had created for his cause. Undeterred by Darrow's devastating examination, he planned to argue four points: that the theory of evolution contradicted the biblical account of creation; that the theory of survival of the fittest destroyed man's faith in God and love for one another; that studying evolution was spiritually and socially useless; and that a deterministic view of life as propounded by evolutionists undermined efforts to reform and improve society.

Bryan may have been undaunted by Darrow's arguments, but others saw him as a spent force. Krutch felt almost sorry for him. 'Driven from politics and journalism because of obvious intellectual incompetence, become ballyhoo for boom-town real estate in his search for lucrative employment, and forced into religion as the only quasi-intellectual field in which mental backwardness and complete insensibility to ideas could be used as an advantage, he already knew that he was compelled to seek in the most remote rural regions for the applause so necessary for his contentment,' he wrote. 'Yet even in Dayton, as choice a stronghold of ignorance and bigotry as one could hope to find, he went down in defeat in the only contest where he had met his antagonists face to face. Dayton itself was ashamed for him.'

But Bryan would never get the chance to resurrect his reputation by touring the nation. After a few days spent lecturing locally he returned to Dayton where he died in his sleep during an afternoon nap, five days after the end of the trial. A reporter told Darrow, holidaying in the Smoky Mountains, that people were saying Bryan had died of a broken heart because of his cross-examination. 'Broken heart nothing,' said Darrow. 'He died of a busted belly.' In Baltimore, Henry Mencken hooted, 'God aimed at Darrow, missed, and hit Bryan instead.' In private he said to a friend, 'We killed the son-of-a-bitch!'

Gloating such as Mencken's helped turn Bryan into a martyr and Darrow into a villain. As the tributes to him after his death showed, Bryan was still a hugely popular national figure despite his limitations. Even the *New York Herald Tribune* congratulated him for trying 'to do the right thing as he saw it'.

Although modernists claimed their nominal defeat as a triumph, calling the trial 'the last significant attempt to discredit Darwin's theory' as if no further attempts to challenge it would ever be made, two years later thirteen states, both Northern and Southern, were still considering instituting anti-evolution laws. In Mississippi and Arkansas they passed into statute. Even where no changes to the law were made, local school boards increasingly presented science as theory rather than dogma, restricting the teaching of evolution and biology throughout the 1930s. In 1927 when the appeal on the Scopes case reached the Tennessee Supreme Court, it upheld the Butler Act but reversed the original and uncontested judgement of a fine on technical grounds, preventing the case being appealed to the federal courts. The Butler Act was not repealed until 1967, when a teacher successfully claimed that it violated his right to free speech.

Scopes's trial, and the predominantly Northern, urban coverage of it, exemplified the rift in society between the 'old' and 'new' Americas — one traditional, rural, pious, slow-moving, the other fast-paced, industrial, go-getting, high-living. Throughout the 1920s America's population was shifting from predominantly rural to predominantly urban — but defenders of the threatened 'old' values were not prepared to lie down and accept defeat.

12

The Spirit of St Louis

RELIGION MAY HAVE VANQUISHED science (at least according to
the law) in the Scopes case but modernity was a juggernaut that
could not easily be turned back. In the 1920s numerous new
technologies transformed the way people lived and worked,
but the development of flight was perhaps the fastest-paced
and the most revolutionary of the changes taking place. Man
was a terrestrial creature and to imagine him moving through
the air like a bird required a leap of faith and imagination as
well as of machinery. Orville and Wilbur Wright had achieved
lift-off for the first time at Kitty Hawk in North Carolina in
1903. The Frenchman Louis Blériot successfully crossed the
English Channel six years later. The Great War stimulated a
new interest in aviation and by its end in 1918 planes were
being used for fighting as well as reconnaissance. Over 50,000
aircraft were built in Britain alone during the war years.

The French, whose flying aces (aviators who had downed
five enemy aircraft) had found international fame as gladiators

of the air during the war, were as interested in the possibilities of peacetime flight as the Americans. The International Air Traffic Association (IATA) was founded in Paris in 1919. Ten years later it had twenty-three members and its headquarters in The Hague attempted to standardize timetables and safety systems. Established in 1923, Air Union ferried passengers – 75 per cent of whom were Americans in these early years – across the English Channel. It merged with Air Orient in 1933 to form Air France. Early flight conditions were an unsettling combination of discomfort and luxury: passengers were expected to be up at dawn to catch their planes and even the shortest flights might make numerous emergency landings en route, but they were lavished with caviar while on board.

America's first air-mail service began in 1918, shuttling daily between New York and Washington. From 1923 the Post Office started contracting air-mail deliveries to private companies, and the following year letters could be sent across the continent by air mail from New York to San Francisco via Chicago and Cheyenne. In 1926 the Air Commerce Act was passed, giving the US Government power to regulate and encourage commercial aviation by building a national network of post routes, airports, beacons, floodlights, boundary markers and weather stations. The service was almost prohibitively expensive, though: until 1928, when it was reduced to a flat rate of five cents a letter, air-mail postage might cost twenty-five cents at a time when a land-mail postcard stamp cost only one cent.

From the start air mail was closely linked to passenger air travel. Because flying was so expensive, pilots flying the first air-mail routes were encouraged to carry paying passengers. But mail planes could only accommodate one or two passengers alongside the pilot, so transporting people rather than mailbags wasn't initially seen as a viable commercial enterprise. All that would change in 1927.

In the spring of 1922, a shy college drop-out from Minnesota enrolled as the only student at the Nebraska Aircraft Corporation's flying school in the provincial city of Lincoln. At the end of the first week, during which he had begun his practical training as an aviation mechanic, twenty-year-old Charles Lindbergh was taken up for his inaugural flight. He was as captivated as he had known he would be. As a child, Lindbergh had spent long afternoons lying on his back in a field near his house, screened by long grass, dreaming of swooping and floating among the clouds above him.

He used to imagine himself with wings, 'soaring through the air from one river bank to the other, over the stones of the rapids, above log jams, above the tops of trees and fences'. But the reality of flight was even more thrilling than he had hoped. In the air, he wrote later, 'I live only in the moment in this strange, unmortal space, crowded with beauty, pierced with danger.' From the first second of that lift-off he knew that he had found his path in life. Just ten years of flying, he believed, 'would be a worthwhile trade for an ordinary lifetime'.

Flying became for him an almost mystical experience. Lindbergh described flying by moonlight as times of transcendence. 'Its light floods through woods and fields; reflects up from bends of rivers; shines on the silver wings of my biplane, turning them a greenish hue. It makes the earth seem more of a planet; and me a part of the heavens above it, as though I too had the right to an orbit in the sky.'

In 1924 Lindbergh enrolled in the army's new Air Service from which, two years later, he graduated first in his class. An army doctor who examined him during this period noted his perfect hearing and sight, describing him as an 'optimum type – slow and purposeful, yet quick of reaction, alert, congenial, [and] intelligent'. Lindbergh set himself the highest of standards for his conduct as well as his physical achievements, listing fifty-nine qualities towards which he strove including Diligence, Manliness, Zeal, Reserve, Concentration and Balance.

As he perfected his craft during the early 1920s Lindbergh notched up his hours working as a stunt pilot, barnstorming through the country offering rides to anyone with $5 or performing tricks under the name 'Daredevil Lindbergh'. Parachute-jumping and wing-walking were both regarded as suicidal – especially when the plane was looping the loop – but the fearless Lindbergh insisted that with careful preparation and precautions the risks were minimal. At college, he and a friend had amused themselves by shooting coins out of each other's fingers at fifty feet; being wired up to a wing at a hundred miles an hour, even if it was upside down, was hardly a frightening prospect by comparison.

When the St Louis air-mail service opened in April 1926 Lindbergh was chosen as the route's chief pilot. He and two other aviators flew five round trips a week between Chicago and St Louis for the handsome salary of $400 a month. Their planes were army-salvage de Havilland observation bi-planes with single engines, fondly known as Flaming Coffins because so few pilots survived crashing them.

Two hundred people came to St Louis's Lambert airfield to watch the dedication ceremony before Lindbergh took off on the city's first official mail flight. He and his fellow pilots, postal clerks and executives 'felt we were taking part in an event which pointed the way toward a new and marvellous era'. But to Lindbergh's disappointment, popular interest declined after that first burst of enthusiasm. For him, flight combined 'science, freedom, beauty [and] adventure' and he was evangelical about the future of aviation, taking immense pride in being part of 'man's conquest of the air'. To ordinary people, though, an air-mail letter or even a flight in an aeroplane at a county fair were diverting gimmicks rather than heralds of a dazzling new future.

Lindbergh and his team were the explorers of the age, flying long distances in uncertain conditions in insecure planes. To begin with, they flew without night-flying equipment, carrying only a pocket torch ('pilot furnished', Lindbergh wryly noted) and an emergency flare, although eventually they were given red and green navigation lights. Despite these conditions Lindbergh's St Louis–Chicago run had the best record among the routes converging on Chicago, successfully completing 99 per cent of their scheduled flights.

Several times, in poor weather, Lindbergh was forced to make crash landings on to Midwestern cornfields and cow pastures. He became known as the only pilot to have successfully saved his own life four times by parachuting out of his failing plane. His former Staff Sergeant wrote to congratulate him on his escapes: 'It appears to me as though you are favoured by the angels'.

Although Lindbergh loved the camaraderie and pioneering spirit of mail-route life, he was soon made restless by its monotony. As he flew along the same route day after day he dreamed up new challenges for himself, the most persistent of which was the idea of flying the Atlantic. In 1919 two English pilots, John Alcock and Arthur Brown, had flown the 2,000 miles from Newfoundland to Ireland. In the same year Raymond Orteig, a French-born hotelier living in New York, had focused pilots' attention on the 3,600-mile New York–Paris route by offering a prize of $25,000 for the first non-stop flight in either direction.

By 1926 several failed attempts at the Orteig prize had been made. Lindbergh thought he knew why: the planes were too heavy, carrying too many engines and too many pilots and crew members. One French team of four had set off in a magnificent triple-engine bi-plane upholstered with red leather and equipped with a bed and a batch of croissants; only the two pilots had survived the crash at take-off. Lindbergh reckoned that the more weight and engines a plane had, the greater the possibility of failure. What he wanted was simple: 'one set of wings, one engine, one pilot'.

Money was his first objective. His own savings of $2,000 wouldn't cover an aircraft engine, let alone an entire plane. Emphasizing the as-yet-untapped commercial possibilities of air travel and its benefits to St Louis in particular if it were to become an 'aviation city', Lindbergh persuaded a consortium headed by two businessmen he had taught to fly and his former commanding officer, and supported by the St Louis Chamber of Commerce and the *St Louis Globe-Democrat*, to guarantee him the $15,000 he estimated he would need. His successful crossing would, he promised, 'promote nationwide interest in aeronautics, demonstrate [the] perfection of modern equipment' and help make America 'first in the air'.

Finding a plane was more difficult. Lindbergh was well-known in Midwestern and military flying circles, but on the East Coast, where the major aeronautical companies were based, he was a nobody. Fokker turned his request down flat. They told him he would need at least $90,000 to buy and outfit one of their specially made planes, but even if he could afford their fee they would reserve the right to veto any pilot attempting an Atlantic flight. And only a fool, they implied, would attempt the flight with fewer than three engines.

Lindbergh deliberately set up his appointment with the

Wright Aeronautical Corporation using a five-dollar long-distance telephone call from St Louis to ensure that he would 'get past the girl at the desk'. He invested in a tailor-made suit and a new blue overcoat and suitcase for his trip to New Jersey where the company was based. But his efforts to impress came to nothing. The Wright executive was friendly but told him that the plane in which he was interested, the Wright-Bellanca, was only a prototype. He suggested Lindbergh speak to its designer, Guiseppe Bellanca, and arranged a meeting between them for the following evening. Bellanca was encouraging but, lacking his own production facilities, could only offer Lindbergh the chance to buy a plane in an existing three-motored design for $29,000, double Lindbergh's entire budget.

Several months later Bellanca got in touch with Lindbergh again. The aggressive young owner of the prototype in which Lindbergh had been interested was willing to sell it for $15,000. Although Lindbergh hesitated over the price, his backers agreed to cover the cost. But as he held out the cheque, Charles Levine, the plane's owner, added a caveat: he, too, reserved the right to choose the plane's crew. 'You understand we cannot let just anybody pilot our airplane across the ocean.'

Furious, Lindbergh had just one option left: the tiny Ryan Aeronautical Company in San Diego, which had started out building planes from war-surplus aircraft parts. He went to California to discuss the plane he hoped they could build him. Ryan was based in the port area of San Diego and comprised one dilapidated building with 'no flying field, no hangar, no sound of engines warming up; and the unmistakable smell of dead fish from a near-by cannery [mixed] with the banana odour of dope from drying wings', but Lindbergh was immediately impressed by its workmanlike approach. With a Wright-Whirlwind engine and any extras included at cost-price, Ryan would charge Lindbergh and his sponsors $10,580 to build the *Spirit of St Louis*.

While his plane was being built Lindbergh spent his days meticulously studying nautical charts, planning his route (using fifty-cent drugstore maps for his journey over American land) and writing endless 'To do' lists. He worked closely with Ryan's chief engineer, Donald Hall, to mould the plane around his needs, adapting everything to his long-distance flight plans and his own experience.

Flight efficiency was to be the primary consideration, then safety in case of a crash, and finally Lindbergh's own comfort. Everything unnecessary – even night-flying equipment, a radio, a sextant and gauges on the gasoline tanks – was jettisoned for the sake of weight. Every pound saved meant the plane could travel further without refuelling. Lindbergh turned down the idea of an additional cockpit because the space could be used to store more gasoline. 'I'd rather have extra gasoline than an extra man.'

The empty plane, made of spruce and piano wire and covered in cotton finished with cellulose acetate dope in silver-grey, weighed 2150 lb, of which five hundred pounds was the air-cooled, 223-hp radial Wright-Whirlwind propeller engine stored in the nose of the fuselage. 'Nine delicate, fin-covered cylinders of aluminium and steel,' mused Lindbergh. 'On this intricate perfection I'm to trust my life across the Atlantic Ocean.'

The *Spirit of St Louis* stood just under ten feet tall. She was nearly twenty-eight feet long, with a wingspan of forty-six feet, and carried 450 gallons of gasoline and forty spare pounds of oil. She was a monoplane, because single wings could cope better with ice in the freezing night-time conditions high above the North Atlantic. Lindbergh's seat in the cockpit was made of lightweight wicker.

Her accident equipment was minimal: a small black rubber raft weighing ten pounds; a knife; some flares and matches stored in bicycle inner-tubes; basic fishing equipment; a hacksaw; some 'awful' crumbly army-ration chocolate-like stuff. A parachute, weighing twenty pounds, was rejected – it meant losing twenty minutes' worth of fuel. Even drinking water Lindbergh thought would weigh too much; he ordered the prototype of a newly invented cup that would convert moisture from his breath into water.

Lindbergh himself was the last item, six foot two tall and (clothed) weighing a slim 170 pounds. He planned to wear a zippered flying suit made of wool-lined waterproof cloth weighing nine pounds, specially chosen because it would keep him warm if he crashed, even when wet. Underneath the flying suit he would wear army breeches and boots, a shirt and light jacket and a red-and-blue-striped tie. His vulnerability on the flight, alone and out of all contact, would be intense. 'For the first time in my life,' his mother Evangeline wrote to him, 'I realize that Columbus also had a mother.'

Spirit was ready towards the end of April 1927. Inspired by Lindbergh's quiet determination, knowing that other teams were preparing to make their own attempts at the flight, Ryan's thirty-five men had worked for long hours, often without pay, to finish her as quickly as possible. Lindbergh spent ten days performing twenty-three test flights. *Spirit*'s top speed was 128 mph and he tested her take-off carrying 350 gallons of fuel. He was delighted to find that her performance was far beyond what he had hoped for.

Further encouragement had come that March with news of the arrival in Paris of a French team from Tehran, a non-stop journey of 3,200 miles, admittedly overland. In April information arrived about some of the other teams attempting the New York–Paris flight. Two of the US teams, a $100,000 Fokker and the Bellanca owned by Charles Levine (who had decided to use his own pilots to make his own bid for the prize), had encountered problems and were waiting for repairs to be completed; a pair of French former flying aces had crashed during their final test flight and been killed; a two-man team sponsored by the American Legion had also crashed, killing both pilots. Lindbergh was shaken by his fellow pilots' bad luck, but the fact that his rivals' planes were large, multi-engine craft confirmed his conviction that the *Spirit of St Louis* was the aeroplane best fitted to successfully fly the Atlantic.

On 10 May Lindbergh took off from San Diego headed for New York, stopping for a night in St Louis to consult with his backers about the competition – and casually breaking the records for the fastest times from the Pacific coast to St Louis, and from the Pacific to the Atlantic coasts. Two days earlier two French flying aces had taken off for New York from Le Bourget airfield outside Paris in their single-engine bi-plane, *L'oiseau blanc*. By the time Lindbergh landed at Curtiss Field in Long Island on the afternoon of 12 May, hopes of the French team arriving in New York were fading.

The two American planes waiting to make their Atlantic attempts were in nearby hangars, and Lindbergh was surprised to find a spirit of co-operation and shared endeavour among the engineers and aviation companies there. People who had been unwilling to help him when he wanted to find a plane to fly across the Atlantic, or who were attached to one of the other teams waiting to make their attempt, were happily making repairs to Lindbergh's instruments, checking over his engines, sharing weather information or offering him free use of their runways. Men who had been far-off heroes to Lindbergh – one of those who had developed the Whirlwind engine in his plane, the French flying ace René Fonck, and aircraft manufacturer Anthony Fokker – stopped by his hangar to wish him luck.

Lindbergh's youth, his good looks and the courage of his decision to fly solo all combined to make him the focus of unrelenting journalistic attention for the first time since he had declared his intention of competing for the Orteig prize. At press conferences he was asked questions like, 'Have you got a sweetheart?' and 'How do you feel about girls?' Reporters called him the Flyin' Fool and pushed their way into his bedroom hoping to steal a picture of him shaving in his pyjamas; from then on, Lindbergh locked his door. So many journalists crowded the airfield when he landed after one test flight that he broke his tail skid trying to avoid them.

Thirty thousand enthusiasts came out to Curtiss Field on the Sunday before Lindbergh's flight. He received hundreds of good-luck letters and telegrams from fans, many offering advice or hoping to interest him in business propositions, many more hoping he would post their letters in Paris. Interested grandees like Theodore Roosevelt Jr and Harry Guggenheim wished him well. Lindbergh fended off requests from theatrical agents and Hollywood producers promising to make him a star.

When his mother arrived from Detroit to say goodbye she refused to kiss him for the photographers, protesting that they came 'of an undemonstrative Nordic race' (the Lindberghs' independent, non-conformist Swedish– Scottish bloodlines made them the anti-immigration lobby's idea of ideal Americans) but a tabloid faked one of them kissing anyway. The usually unperturbed Lindbergh was angry. 'They didn't care how much they hurt her feelings or frightened her about my flight, as long as they got their pictures and their stories.'

After ten days, Lindbergh heard that the overcast weather

was forecast to break the next day and he decided to leave the following morning – before his rivals, who he guessed would wait until they knew for sure that the cloud cover was clearing. Only a mail pilot, with flying experience in all weathers, would have dared start his journey in such uncertain conditions.

After a sleepless night, Lindbergh took off from Roosevelt Field at 7.51 on the windless, rain-sodden morning of 20 May in front of a crowd of several hundred. *Spirit*, fully laden with 451 gallons of gasoline, bounced along the runway and cleared the telegraph wires at the end of the field by just twenty feet. A newspaper plane flew alongside him as far as Long Island Sound. News came over the wire that Lloyd's of London were not taking bets on Lindbergh's arrival in Paris because they considered he had too slim a chance of making it. Fortunately, without a radio he would not have heard it.

The thirty-five-mile stretch of ocean between Long Island and Connecticut was the longest expanse of water Lindbergh had yet flown over. When he reached the Atlantic coast, 'looking ahead at the unbroken horizon and limitless expanse of water', he was 'struck by my arrogance in attempting such a flight'. His little *Spirit* resembled nothing more than 'a butterfly blown out to sea' but to him she felt more like 'a living partner in adventure than a machine of cloth and steel'.

America held its breath. 'Alone?' demanded Harold Anderson in the *New York Sun*. 'Is he alone at whose right side rides Courage, with Skill within the cockpit and Faith upon the left? Does solitude surround the brave when Adventure leads the way and Ambition reads the dials? Is there no company with him for whom the air is cleft by Daring and the darkness is made light by Enterprise?... Alone? With what other companions would that man fly to whom the choice were given?'

For the next twenty-eight hours Lindbergh fought off sleep, kept awake by the instability of his plane – 'this little box with fabric walls' – an unexpected blessing because it meant he could not switch off for a second. He preferred not to eat, knowing that his empty stomach would also keep him alert, and kept the plastic windows out of their frames, fearing the barrier they would create between him and the outside elements, the crystal 'communion of water, land and sky'.

He was acutely conscious of his vulnerability as he flew over Newfoundland. 'Nine barrels of gasoline and oil, wrapped up in fabric; two hundred and twenty horsepower, harnessed by a layer of cloth – vulnerable to a pin prick, yet protecting an airplane and its pilot on a flight across an ocean, between the continents – suspended at this moment five hundred feet above a frigid, northern land.'

And yet there was also a strange sense of security and peace. Life had suddenly become wholly simple. His cockpit was tailored to him 'like a suit of clothes': 'Each dial and lever is in the proper place for glance or touch; and the slightest pressure on the controls brings response.' The only thing he had to do was fly, and that felt 'like living in a hermit's mountain cabin after being surrounded by the luxury and countless responsibilities of a city residence'. He became minutely conscious of every detail of his surroundings – the weld marks on the tubing, a dot of paint on the altimeter's face – and 'the grandeur of the world outside. The nearness of death. The longness of life.' He was utterly alone.

The urge to sleep was strongest in the dark, when he was over open water. It felt like a leaden coat pressing down upon his shoulders. He forced himself to squeeze his dry eyes open and shut, to stamp on the floor of the cockpit, shaking the tiny plane, to flex his cramped muscles as he sat. Concentration was his only weapon against sleep – the power of his mind over his body. Relentlessly he made himself think of possible problems and how he would deal with them, created imaginary emergencies, checked and rechecked his route, envisaged how he would cope if he crashed.

Throughout the freezing, misty, moonless night, ghostly spirits crowded around him in the tiny cockpit, 'neither intruders nor strangers', speaking intangible messages of great importance, discussing the flight, offering advice, reassuring him. Dazed with exhaustion, Lindbergh accepted them as normal because he was so far removed from everyday life, existing only in 'this strange, living dream'. The next day he could not remember a word the spirits had said to him.

Mirages of land appeared on the horizon in front of him alongside shimmering ice cakes and vast icebergs. For a time he flew with his head thrown back, looking up through the skylight at the stars just visible in the thickening night fog and the mountainous clouds, racing perilous ice-storms. He was entirely 'conscious of the minuteness of my plane and of the magnitude of the world'.

'Aren't my silver wings fully as remarkable as those Daedalus made of wax and feathers?' Lindbergh wondered. 'Sometimes, flying feels too god-like to be attained by man.' The implications of his record-breaking solo flight, should he survive it, pressed upon him. 'Will men fly through the air in the future without seeing what I have seen, without feeling what I have felt? Is that true of all things we call human progress – do the gods retire as commerce and science advance?'

Waiting for dawn in the unmarked night over cold unfriendly seas, on the second morning of his journey (and the third without sleep), he felt senseless, accomplishing only what he needed to do to survive in a state of semiconsciousness. After more than twenty hours of flight, Lindbergh remembered that he had smelling salts in his medical kit. He broke open one of the capsules but was so out of touch with reality that he could not smell it and his eyes did not water. He felt as though he was hanging in space, divorced from his body. Finally he saw beneath him harbingers of land: a porpoise leaping through the water, then a gull, then the black specks of fishing boats – and at last the emerald-green fields of the west coast of Ireland.

When he reached the mouth of the Seine nearly five hours later he remembered that he had neither eaten nor drunk anything since leaving New York. Someone had handed him five drugstore sandwiches as he left and he attempted a few mouthfuls before packing them carefully away. His mouth was too dry to swallow and he didn't want to taint his landing with discarded sandwich wrappings. He flew over Paris, which looked like a 'lake of stars', and circled the Eiffel Tower (then the tallest man-made structure in the world) at 4,000 feet, waggling his wings.

Lindbergh's moment of greatest confusion came when he arrived at Le Bourget airfield on the outskirts of Paris, just over thirty-three hours after he had lifted off. Where the empty field should have been was an erratic pattern of lights, dimming the beacons he was expecting to see, and a long string of pairs of lights reaching off into the distance. Flying past a second time, he realized that these were the headlights of thousands of Parisians coming out to greet him.

In the crowds beneath him were Harry and Caresse Crosby, marvelling at the crowds, the coloured flares and the great floodlights sweeping the sky. Lindbergh's engine whirred like a toy as he circled the field in preparation for landing. Lost and then captured in the moving lights, the *Spirit* gleamed and flashed in the night sky like a shark darting through water. A mood of suspense built as they waited for his approach. 'Then sharp swift in the gold glare of the searchlights a small white hawk of a plane swoops hawk-like down and across the field – C'est lui Lindberg [sic], LINDBERG! And there is a pandemonium, wild animals let loose and a stampede towards the plane... thousands of hands weaving like maggots over the silver wings of the Spirit of Saint-Louis... scratching and tearing'.

The 150,000-strong crowd surged on to the runway as *Spirit* landed and the mob lifted Lindbergh out of the plane. He said later that 'it was like drowning in a human sea'. A couple of French pilots, realizing how disorientated Lindbergh must be, quickly threw a coat over his shoulders, took off his helmet and placed it on the head of a nearby American reporter, and spirited him into the airfield's office, leaving his substitute to the crowds, who carried the wrong man triumphantly towards the official reception committee. His hosts laughed off Lindbergh's worries about not having a French visa; France was his, they said. After meeting the American ambassador, at whose house he was to stay, his new friends bundled him into a car bound for Paris by back roads. *Spirit* was left under armed guard to protect her from souvenir hunters.

News of the hero's safe arrival was wired to New York and bells rang out across the country. That night, at the Savoy Ballroom in Harlem, a new version of the charleston, the Lindy Hop, was danced in Lindbergh's honour to accompanying screams of 'Lindy's done it, Lindy's done it!'

Ambassador Herrick's motorcade took so long to get back to Paris through the celebrating throngs that Lindbergh had eaten his first meal in two days (light soup and an egg) and had a bath by the time his host arrived home at 3 a.m. After a short press briefing Lindbergh got into bed, sixty-three hours after he had last slept.

Herrick cabled Evangeline Lindbergh in Detroit: 'Warmest congratulations Stop Your incomparable son has honored me by being my guest Stop He is in fine condition and sleeping sweetly under Uncle Sams roof.' When she went out to meet the press, Evangeline's usual restraint failed her. With tears in her eyes, she said that although she had never doubted that her son would complete his journey, 'I am so happy that it is over, more happy than I can ever tell... He has accomplished the greatest undertaking of his life, and I am proud to be the mother of such a boy.'

The next few days – and weeks, and months – passed in a whirl. When, next afternoon, Herrick led Lindbergh on to a balcony to wave to the cheering crowds below, he realized that his flight had transformed his life for ever. Aged twenty-five, he had become public property. Everywhere he went people pressed forward to shake his hand, to touch his clothes, to congratulate and applaud him. From then on, he reflected years later, life 'could hardly have been more amazing if I had landed on another planet instead of at Paris'.

Harry Crosby and his father were among hundreds who called on Herrick to meet Lindbergh the day after his landing. Thousands more lined the streets every time he ventured out in public. Lindbergh insisted on calling on the parents of the French airmen who had disappeared while making their Atlantic attempt two weeks earlier. He paid his respects to Louis Blériot, who told him that he was his heir 'and the prophet of a new era'. Most of his time was spent at receptions and meeting the press. He was presented with the Legion of Honour. Everywhere his behaviour was marked by patience, good-humour, courtesy and humility – an achievement, as one historian observes, even more impressive than his flight.

After a week of official engagements and adulation, Lindbergh left Paris for England, spending a night in Belgium en route. In London he met the Prime Minister, Stanley Baldwin, and was personally congratulated by the King and Queen at Buckingham Palace. George V presented him with Britain's highest peacetime honour, the Air Force Cross, but a more private matter was of greater interest to him: 'Now tell me, Captain Lindbergh. There is one thing I long to know. How did you pee?'

At the beginning of June, Lindbergh returned to the United States aboard the USS Memphis. As the gunship cruised up the Potomac towards Washington, Lindbergh was given a twenty-one-gun salute – a tribute previously reserved for heads of state. Over the next three months Lindbergh toured the country attending parades, receptions and benefits in his honour, promoting and 'stimulating popular interest in the use of air transport'. Countless reams of ticker tape filled the air as an estimated thirty million people turned out to see him in eighty-two cities. During his tour he was only late for one appointment.

Hoping to tempt Lindbergh into starring in a biopic opposite Marion Davies, W. R. Hearst hosted a dinner for him in New York at which the bashful young aviator sat between

Davies and Mary Pickford. Halfway through, Pickford slipped Davies a note: 'He won't talk.' Davies wrote back, 'Talk about airplanes.' In Detroit, Lindbergh took Henry Ford up for his first flight. Al Capone was on Chicago's official welcoming committee when Lindbergh landed on Lake Michigan in a seaplane.

Lindbergh's solo flight created an extraordinary level of interest in aviation. Harry Crosby was not the only man in spired by Lindbergh to take to the skies ('I *do* know how to fly in the *final* and *real* sense of the word that is in the soul Flights to the Sun but now I want to learn also in the Lindbergian sense of the word,' he wrote). As Gloria Swanson put it, after Lindbergh's flight, 'everybody wanted wings'.

Applications for pilots' licences went up by 300 per cent in 1927. New airfields were laid; the manufacture of aircraft soared. Ryan Aircraft, who had made the *Spirit*, received twenty-nine orders for new aircraft within weeks of Lindbergh's flight and were soon manufacturing three planes a week. In 1928 Wright Aeronautical stock soared from 69 points to 289.

The companies that would become United Airlines, American Airlines, Eastern Airlines and Trans-World Airlines were founded, carrying twelve or fifteen passengers rather than the one or two whom mail pilots had occasionally transported. In 1928, the same year that the Havana Air Convention established the first rules for air traffic in the Americas, Pan American Airways used Lindbergh to publicize their international mail routes between the US, the Caribbean and South and Central America. By the spring of 1929 there were sixty-one US passenger airlines and forty-seven air-mail companies.

The popularity of flying mirrored the advent of the motor-car at the start of the century, which had brought with it a host of new industries and infrastructures, from a network of roads to soaring steel, rubber and petroleum production. People began speaking of transatlantic passenger and mail routes as certainties, rather than as science-fiction. In an era transformed by technological developments from the telephone to nylon to typewriters to electricity, a new airborne world had arrived. Lindbergh, who had loved 'the sky's unbroken solitude', feared what the spread of aviation might lead to. 'I feel like the western pioneer when he saw barbed-wire fences encroaching on his open plains. The success of his venture brought the end of the life he loved.'

In the rush towards the future, the negative aspects of progress and technological advancement were ignored. Nature was seen not as a treasure to be conserved and husbanded, but as a resource to be used up. In Middletown even before Lindbergh's flight, people no longer walked or rode their bicycles, they scorned home-grown and home-made food in favour of shop-bought and were unable to fish the town's polluted river, stinking with industrial run-off. But as the Lynds observed, people themselves had changed far less than the objects they dealt with every day: 'Bathrooms and electricity have pervaded the homes of the city more rapidly than innovations in the personal adjustments between husbands and wives or between parents and children.' Those would come later.

Another fundamental social change revealed by Lindbergh's flight and his extraordinary personal popularity was the introduction of the idea of modern celebrity. Americans made Lindbergh into a symbol of all that was best and purest about their country. He was modest, idealistic, a prophet of the future and yet untainted by modernity, radiantly handsome, virtuous, disciplined, self-reliant — in short everything that Americans aspired to be, as well as a blank canvas on to which people could project their dreams and fantasies. Former Secretary of State Charles Evans Hughes declared that Lindbergh had 'displaced everything that is petty, that is sordid, that is vulgar'; a journalist said that Lindbergh had 'shown us that we are not rotten at the core but morally sound and sweet and good'. He was, wrote Frederick Allen, a 'Galahad for a generation which had forsworn Galahads'.

Lindbergh's achievement brought him fame, riches and a wife (Anne, the daughter of Dwight Morrow, a J. P. Morgan banker and the US ambassador to Mexico; as a modern 1920s woman, she learned to navigate so that she could work alongside her husband), but it also brought him tragedy. On 1 March 1932, Charles and Anne's baby son was kidnapped. After ten agonizing weeks his corpse was found nearby. The publicity surrounding the disappearance of the 'Lindbergh baby' and the trial of his abductor was too much to bear. In 1935 the Lindberghs left the United States and spent the next few years in Europe. They returned home in 1939 when war broke out, but Lindbergh's association with the Third Reich (he received the same award as Henry Ford, the Grand Cross of the German Eagle, in 1938) and his arguments for non-intervention in the Second World War tarnished his public image. In the years before his death in 1974 he was an ardent conservationist, seeking the balance between nature and technology he had meditated upon during his epic transatlantic flight.

In 1927, only the worldly-wise writers at the *New Yorker*, while expending as many column inches on Lindbergh as any other publication of the day, expressed the hope that he would be able to readjust to being a man after becoming a god. Detailing his potential earnings, they advised him to be restrained about capitalizing on his achievements and congratulated him rather backhandedly. Simple admiration for the old-fashioned values of courage, strength and modesty that Lindbergh represented seemed to sit uneasily with their hard-won metropolitan sophistication.

13

The Big Fight

ALTHOUGH HE PROTESTED AGAINST being turned into a 'tin saint', Charles Lindbergh was an image of moral perfection to most 1920s Americans. Other heroes were more fallible, beloved for their vulnerabilities and complexities as much as for their achievements. Charlie Chaplin was one such flawed idol; the salty, sulky baseball star Babe Ruth another. But the greatest sportsman of the 1920s, in terms of drawing power and personal celebrity, was the untamed boxer Jack Dempsey. The total gate receipts for his five big fights between 1921 and 1927 were almost nine million dollars, sums unequalled until the advent of Mohammed Ali forty years later.

Born in 1895, Dempsey came from the small town of Manassa, Colorado, the ninth of thirteen children of poor, itinerant parents of largely Irish stock with a splash of Cherokee blood. He left school after eighth grade and found work as a miner, saying later that his two career options had been mining and cattle-working. Dempsey's adolescence was a rough one, lived in the mines and the hobo 'jungles' where he and other impoverished workers and outlaws camped between catching dangerous but free rides on the undercarriages of cross-country trains.

Soon he found that he had another talent: fighting. Encouraged by his elder brother, who had made a name for himself as a bar-room brawler, Dempsey began taking on all-comers in local saloons. 'I can't sing and I can't dance,' he'd say, in his incongruously girlish voice, 'but I can kick any man's ass.' He chewed pine tar to strengthen his jaw and soaked his fists in brine to toughen them against cuts. By the early 1910s he was touring the bars of the Southwest looking for fights, and at twenty he hired a manager and went professional. Although his real name was William Harrison Dempsey, he used the name Jack Dempsey in homage to a great nineteenth-century middleweight.

The next few years were hard. Managers came and went; a good-for-nothing wife demanded generous support; boxing promoters in New York, where he first arrived in 1916 with less than $30 in his pocket, had no interest in a skinny kid from out west. Only the hard-boiled young sports-writer Damon Runyon, whom he met as a youngster scuffling in Denver, saw Dempsey's potential and encouraged him to continue. Runyon watched one of Dempsey's early fights and gave him his ring soubriquet, the 'Manassa Mauler'.

Finally, after dropping out of boxing for a time and working in the shipyards of Philadelphia, Dempsey was taken on by the manager Jack 'Doc' Kearns and the promoter Tex Rickard, and his career began in earnest. Dapper Kearns was a con man, a master of the 1920s art of marketing 'ballyhoo'. When someone accused him of being a crook, he responded, 'I prefer to be called a manipulator.' Rickard, tall, taciturn and elegant, was cleared in the early 1920s of accusations of abducting and sexually assaulting young girls. Despite this shadow over his reputation, from which he never quite recovered, Dempsey adored him. Rickard was, he said, 'a bourbon-and-branch-water man who could drink all night and not get drunk... a gambler of the old school'. The sports journalist Paul Gallico said Rickard instinctively understood the power of money: 'He knew how to exhibit it, use it, ballyhoo it, spend it, and make it work for him.' Their informal partnership of Dempsey, Kearns and Rickard would make all three rich.

In 1919, under Kearns's management, Dempsey knocked out his opponents in the first round in five consecutive fights. That July he challenged the World Heavyweight Champion, Jess Willard, for his title in Toledo, Ohio. No one in the audience thought Dempsey could win, although sports-writers were starting to take notice of the young boxer. Ring Lardner and Scoop Gleeson came to shake Dempsey's hand before the bout, as well as his old friend Runyon.

At six-foot-five Willard was four inches taller than Dempsey and sixty-five pounds heavier, and far more experienced. But Dempsey was an instinctive fighter, lightning fast and graceful on his feet, possessing a devastating punch with both right and left fists. What set him apart, though, was his savage street-fighter attitude. One journalist called him 'part tiger, part wildcat and all killer'; others described him pursuing his opponents in the ring like a panther, smoldering with the intensity of his desire to win.

'Dempsey was a picture-book fighter,' wrote Paul Gallico in the 1930s. 'He had dark eyes, blue-black hair, and the most beautifully proportioned body ever seen in any ring. He had the wide but sharply sloping shoulders of the puncher, a slim waist, and fine, symmetrical legs. His weaving, shuffling style of approach was drama in itself and suggested the stalking of a jungle animal. He had a smoldering truculence on his face and hatred in his eyes. His gorge lay close to the surface. He was utterly without mercy or pity, asked no quarter, gave none. He would do anything he could get away with, fair or foul, to win.

'This was definitely a part of the man, but was also a result of his early life and schooling in the hobo jungles, bar-rooms, and mining camps of the West. Where Dempsey learned to fight there were no rounds, rest intervals, gloves, referees, or attending seconds. There are no draws and no decisions in rough and tumble fighting. You had to win. If you lost you went to the hospital or to the undertaking parlour. Dempsey, more often than not, in his early days as hobo, saloon bouncer, or roustabout, fought to survive. I always had the feeling that he carried that into the ring with him, that he was impatient of rules and restrictions and niceties of conduct, impatient even of the leather that bound his knuckles.'

Dempsey knocked Willard down seven times in the first round alone. By the time the dazed, defenceless Willard was forced to retire, at the end of the third round, he looked like he was sleep-walking. He had lost several teeth and his jaw, cheek-bone and some ribs had been broken. The scale of Dempsey's victory was such that rumours that he had worn loaded gloves to gain his title swirled around him for the rest of his career.

The Manassa Mauler's success in the ring was marred by allegations outside it of his having dodged the draft during the First World War. Harold Ross, who had known Dempsey as a kid in Colorado, led a campaign against 'Slacker' Dempsey in the US Army magazine, *Stars and Stripes*, of which he was then editor. Dempsey's estranged wife, Maxine, whom he had married at twenty-one when she was well into her thirties, had accused him of beating her and of falsifying his draft papers; she was hoping for a large pay-out.

In court in June 1920 Dempsey testified that he had tried to enlist but been turned down by the army; his appeal had not come through by the time peace was declared. He said he had spent the war years supporting his wife and parents, and helped the war effort by working in a shipyard and recruiting other workers. Although he won his case against Maxine, the photograph he supplied the court of himself working in the shipyard was rendered suspect by the fact that patent leather boots and pin-striped trousers were visible underneath his overalls. It would take Dempsey many years to shake off his slacker reputation.

Tex Rickard capitalized on Dempsey's unfavourable publicity to promote his fights. After Dempsey had twice defended his title, Rickard set up a bout with the French light heavyweight Georges Carpentier in July 1921. No image could have been in greater contrast to Dempsey's than Carpentier's: he was a former flying ace, a decorated war-hero whose nickname was Gorgeous Georges, graceful, clean-cut, sophisticated, well-dressed, a good dancer. Ring Lardner said he was 'one of the most likeable guys you'd want to meet – even if he did have a Greek profile and long eyelashes'. Rickard had no scruples about presenting Dempsey in a negative light as compared to this paragon. As he said, 'hatin' is as good for box office as lovin''.

Rickard's marketing genius was to draw in his audience by making each fight he promoted into a narrative, pitting a hero against a villain, turning a boxing match into an elemental struggle between glory and humiliation, triumph and disaster, good and evil. He expanded boxing's appeal far beyond its traditional audience of working-class men, the kind of people who would have crowded the sawdust floors of Colorado bars to watch the young Dempsey take on all-comers. Having never watched boxing before, respectable and respected public figures – even women – attended the spectacles Rickard staged.

Dempsey's fights generated extraordinary popular interest, even at a time when sportsmen were acknowledged heroes. Sports-entertainers like Dempsey, Babe Ruth, the golfer Bobby

Jones and the tennis player Bill Tilden were idolized for their courage, heroism and strength. Sport provided a vicarious release for the new generation of white-collar workers who spent their days sitting behind desks, as well as an outlet for the surplus money they were earning and their newly acquired leisure time. Managers used sport as a business model, encouraging teamwork and a sense of competition among their workers. Like movies, radio and advertising (to all of which sport was closely linked), great sporting events helped create a sense of national identity and unity over and above differences in ethnicity, class and religion.

The tickets to the Dempsey–Carpentier fight were beautifully made, oversized, engraved and gold-embossed. They brought in the first ever million-dollar box-office take (of which Dempsey and Kearns were to receive a third each), and the audience of 80,000 was as starry as Rickard could have hoped, including tycoons like Henry Ford, John Rockefeller, various Vanderbilts and Astors, diplomats, politicians, musicians, movie stars and three of former President Roosevelt's children. Alice Roosevelt Longworth recalled playing poker on a special train with the Vice-President, Calvin Coolidge, and his party all the way from Washington to New York, where the fight was being held.

Despite the public rivalry Rickard encouraged between his two fighters, when they met Carpentier and Dempsey took to one another immediately. Carpentier thought Dempsey was 'a man made expressly to be a fighter' with his high Native

American cheekbones and dark narrow eyes. His smile, said Carpentier, was almost childlike and lit up his face. Although Dempsey said little except to express the hope 'that we would both make a packet' out of the fight, Carpentier found him immensely likeable. 'Under the traditional rough exterior,' he wrote, Dempsey had 'the equally traditional heart of gold'.

But Dempsey, dark and glowering, was cast as the villain. Even though Carpentier was a foreigner the crowd hoped he would win – he was smaller than Dempsey and it was so clearly an uneven match – and Dempsey sensed their antagonism. Carpentier looked like a statue, said Dempsey, while he was just a street-fighter.

The street-fighter knocked the statue out in the fourth round. Even the press reports afterwards favoured the loser. 'The more powerful but not the better man won,' said the *Morning Telegraph*. The *New York Times* stated that 'Carpentier was quite rightly the more popular of the two men. He was beaten as a fighter but he remains superior as a boxer... Carpentier was the spirit of the fight; Dempsey was its body. Carpentier lost like a gentleman.'

Ring Lardner's short story of 1921, 'The Battle of the Century', was a fictionalized account of the meeting between the hungry young American and the urbane foreigner. It focused less on the good-natured Jim Dugan (Dempsey) than on his wheeler-dealer manager, Larry Moon, a portrait of Kearns, whose pursuit of a triumph for his champion had brought about such a dangerously mismatched competition.

The next fight Rickard organized for Dempsey was against the Argentinian champion, Luis Angel Firpo, in September 1923. Paul Gallico remembered Dempsey's training camp at Saratoga Springs before this meeting as 'the most colourful, exciting, [and] picturesque' of gatherings. Sitting at a rickety wooden table with an illicit beer and a steak sandwich in front of him, Gallico joined the ribald, thrill-seeking gang of Dempsey's supporters: 'lop-ears, stumble-bums, cheap, small-time politicians, fight managers, ring champions, floozies, gangsters, Negroes, policemen and a few actors thrown in for good measure'.

Jack Kearns, 'smart, breezy, wise-cracking, scented', guarded access to his champion. 'Doubtful blondes who wandered in and out of the layout of wooden hotel and lake-front bungalows, and blondes about whom there was no doubt at all' mingled with sports-writers and ageing boxers 'with bent noses and twisted ears'. Dempsey himself, blue-black hair gleaming, 'dressed in trousers and an old gray sweater, [played] checkers on the porch of his bungalow with a sparring partner'. Gallico was moved by the moments of beauty he glimpsed amid the organized chaos of the camp, 'the smooth swivelling of Dempsey's shoulder as he punched a rataplan on the light bag'.

For the editor of *The Ring* magazine the Dempsey–Firpo bout was the most exciting fight he witnessed in fifty years. The two men fought like animals, wrote another commentator, with 'abysmal, unreasoning fury'. 'Firpo came at me as no other living man ever did before, or since', remembered Dempsey. The Argentinian matched Dempsey's aggression, responding to his initial onslaught by knocking Dempsey out of the ring in the first minutes of the fight, only for Dempsey to be pushed back through the ropes by the ringside reporters on to whom he'd fallen. There were eleven knockdowns in the first round. Dempsey knocked Firpo out for a count of ten in the second, and then helped him up as he was declared the winner.

Dempsey's no-holds-barred approach was becoming legendary. His rage in the ring seemed to express all the frustration of America's marginalized underclasses, humiliated by the injustices of the society in which they scraped survival. Dempsey 'seemed to have a constant bottomless well of cold fury somewhere close to his throat'. The champion of the underdog, the victim, the ignored and the hungry, his furious fighting style and rugged individualism reflected where he had come from and what he continued to battle against. He represented the desire for rebellion against the demands of an increasingly modern, stratified, bureaucratizing society, the impulse to smash and destroy the things that a man cannot control.

Some observers said that Dempsey fought foul, but it was more that he recognized that any ideas of fair and foul were irrelevant in the ring, where all that mattered was winning or losing. 'Sometimes, with a touch of macabre humor, he liked to test out the courage and opposition of his opponent with a few low ones,' said Gallico, 'but he was simply unconcerned with such niceties and obvious decencies as a belt line... When the bell rang he ran out and began to attack his opponent, and he never stopped attacking him, trying to batter him to the floor, until the bell ended the round.'

'Many said I was ruthless in the ring,' said Dempsey, looking back on his career. 'How I'd stand over a fellow who was down and clout him again as he tried to rise. How I would get behind an opponent staggering back to his feet and flatten him with a sucker punch as he turned to face me. Guilty!... Why shouldn't I have been adept at such tactics?... It was part of the rules – or lack of rules – through many of my ring years. I've been beaten into a coma in rings. I've been knocked down too often to remember. I've been knocked out... But I never lost a fight on a foul. Nor was I ever thrown out of a ring for not trying.'

In the 1920s stardom beckoned anyone with a saleable talent. America was looking for idols, and when it found them, it sent them to California. Increasingly celebrities were 'normal' individuals who had transformed their circumstances through their own efforts, rather than men who had greatness conferred upon them by their rank or office. Few people in the 1920s would have called politicians or industrial magnates 'great'; instead they venerated popular heroes like Charles Lindbergh, Charlie Chaplin, Babe Ruth or Jack Dempsey as their own. But while high-minded Lindbergh resisted

Hollywood's siren calls, Dempsey was utterly seduced by them.

After winning his title in 1919, Dempsey had starred in a series of short films called *Daredevil Jack*. In late 1923 he returned to the West Coast and resumed his career as an entertainer. He had always done travelling vaudeville work – shadow boxing, rope skipping, laying out a stooge from the audience, offering $1,000 to anyone who could knock him out – but now a circus paid him $45,000 for a three-week tour.

In Hollywood, Dempsey found a group of people like himself from poor backgrounds who had suddenly made it big. As he put it, they were all just 'freaks of nature', handed success, vast wealth and popular adulation because of a good profile or a pretty mouth, or in his case a mighty punch. Until he died of a heroin overdose in 1923, Dempsey's best friend in the film business was the matinee idol Wally Reid, 'the best looking and most reckless of them'. Douglas Fairbanks took Dempsey under his wing; he made friends with Rudolph Valentino and Charlie Chaplin, and went to Marion Davies and W. R. Hearst's parties at San Simeon.

Dempsey was becoming more of an entertainer than a boxer, a product of the press and the movies rather than the world of the ring. The only fight Rickard planned for Dempsey in 1923 after his meeting with Firpo was against Harry Wills, a black contender for the heavyweight title, but fears that a mixed-race bout would cause riots resulted in its being called off. Rickard was content for Dempsey not to fight because he realized that the less often people saw Dempsey in the ring, the more they would pay when he did defend his title; Doc Kearns, milking Dempsey's new Hollywood income, was equally happy to let him enjoy the softer side of success.

Dempsey made half a million dollars in 1924 although he did not fight once, leaving himself open to accusations that he wanted to retain his title without bothering to defend it. By contrast the other sporting legend of the 1920s, Babe Ruth, was paid a yearly salary of $52,000 by the New York Yankees, over three times what the next highest-paid baseball player made.

In 1925 Dempsey married an actress called Estelle Taylor and moved with her to an expensively decorated hacienda-style house complete with its own pool, golf-course, bridle paths and Rolls-Royce in the garage. Estelle persuaded Jack to have his nose fixed. When Dempsey and Kearns fell out over Doc's spending of Dempsey's winnings, Estelle, hoping Jack would give boxing up altogether, encouraged him to sack his manager.

Kearns had been taking half of all Dempsey's earnings, when the legal limit for an agent was a third, without declaring his income or paying tax on it. At first, Dempsey admitted, he had been so thrilled to be making so much money that he had not thought to question Kearns's high-handed appropriation of his earnings, but when he began to feel that Kearns was mistaking 'gratitude for stupidity' he had no choice but to get rid of him (while maintaining his links with Rickard).

One of the early issues of the *New Yorker* in the spring of 1925 carried a typically arch profile of Dempsey whom it described as having 'learned that the camaraderie of poverty cannot survive the blight of wealth. Splitting the first dollar with a friend is not so much, but sharing the first million is a large contract.' Dempsey, the *New Yorker* reported, had the high, piping voice of a teenage boy and could not sit still. He didn't take himself seriously and – hardly surprisingly – he didn't read much. His appeal to women was admiringly noted, and his apparently happy surrender to the trappings of respectability commented upon. 'If he is ever invited to become a Rotarian, he will accept, eagerly.'

Paul Gallico saw Dempsey's Hollywood years rather differently. The wild animal had been 'caged in a silken boudoir… He moved in those days through those absurd frills like a tiger in the circus, dressed up for the show in strange and humiliating clothes.' Dempsey was as intimidated as he was attracted by his beautiful, ambitious wife and her sparkling friends. Every now and then he'd realize that he 'didn't know what the hell they were talking about'. 'I tried like the devil to fit in and couldn't,' he admitted. He felt excluded and lonely; Estelle worried that 'being married to a pug' was ruining her career.

While from a boxing point of view, Dempsey had been softened by the luxurious life he was leading, from a domestic point of view he was still too close to what Gallico called 'the disgusting things that every prize-fighter needs in his trade'. He could not leave behind the savagery that he had once relied upon to win, and that had brought him his success; but it terrified Estelle. That was why she put so much pressure on him to retire – and that, ultimately, was why their passionate, turbulent marriage was doomed to failure.

For Gallico, Dempsey's wildness only 'added to the picture rather than detracted from it, because I like my prize-fighters mean. Cruelty and an absolute lack of mercy are an essential quality in every successful prize-fighter... His brutality and viciousness are carefully cultivated, fed, and watered like a plant, because they are a valuable business commodity'. But the qualities Gallico so admired in Dempsey's fighting were gradually being eroded by his comfortable new life. By the time Dempsey agreed to defend his title in 1926 he had virtually retired, having fought professionally only twice (against Carpentier and Firpo) in the past five years.

The man Tex Rickard pitted against his 31-year-old world champion was Gene Tunney, a First World War veteran from Greenwich Village billed as the 'Fighting Marine'. As with Carpentier, this was a gladiatorial battle of opposites. Twenty-nine-year-old Tunney was a sensitive, intellectual type as compared to Dempsey's vicious tough-guy. While Dempsey, in Tunney's words, 'depended on his wallop', Tunney was a highly disciplined, intelligent technician who relied on tactics and skills.

Tunney's wholesome public image blended 'self-improvement, social idealism, and physical toughness' in contrast to the perceived hedonism and immorality of his era. Like

Charles Lindbergh, Tunney managed to reassure his fans that old-fashioned values could coexist alongside the positive aspects of modernity and science. He attributed his success in the ring to his study of physiognomy, psychology and boxing technique. Where Dempsey was unruly, self-indulgent, passionate and spontaneous, Tunney was controlled, disciplined, methodical... and just a little boring.

The mood had changed at Dempsey's training camp from the louche, carefree days in Saratoga Springs. Kearns was noticeably absent and the rich and famous Dempsey was guarded by detectives night and day. His relationship with Estelle was strained and he was suffering from eczema and intestinal flu, both brought on by stress. His retinue made excuses for him as he failed to land punches on his sparring partner, telling one another that he was taking it easy on his friend – but the truth was that Dempsey was not in ring condition. Physically and mentally he was no longer the 'jungle fighter' of the old days, but because Rickard persuaded him he could beat Tunney, Dempsey carried on. Dempsey's reputation alone ensured that he was the favourite.

A confident Tunney arrived in Philadelphia in an aeroplane for the fight, smiling and waving for the crowds. Over 120,000 people had come to the Sesquicentennial Stadium on a dark, damp September night, among them W. R. Hearst, Babe Ruth, Norma Talmadge (Constance's sister), Florenz Ziegfeld, Charlie Chaplin, and the usual gathering of Astors, Rockefellers, Whitneys and Roosevelts in the $27.50 ringside seats, alongside the sports-writers and commentators. Associated Press assigned first eight and then ten men to cover the contest; the *New York Times* devoted seven pages of its central section (rather than its sports pages) to its coverage of the fight. Gate receipts totalled nearly $2 million.

Tunney's game plan was to psych Dempsey out before the fight by a demonstration of bluff self-belief. As they got ready to enter the ring, Tunney made an impatient Dempsey wait, taking as long as he could to bandage his fists. Once they started fighting Tunney hung back, allowing Dempsey to think he was afraid of him, waiting for the moment when a newly over-confident Dempsey would make a mistake that would allow Tunney to strike. Dempsey said later that he knew he was beaten from Tunney's first blow. Out of fight-practice, flat-footed, his timing off, the champion lost on points in a unanimous decision by the judges.

In defeat, though, Dempsey discovered something he had never known before: the support of the crowd. Always in the past his audiences had booed him while they bet on him to win, but never until the Tunney fight had they taken him to their hearts. 'Losing was the making of me,' he said later. 'I had never been cheered before.'

Paul Gallico described the moment when Dempsey made the transition from 'most unpopular and despised' of sports-men to best-loved. In the early hours of the morning the former champion made his way back to his room at the Ritz-Carlton Hotel where his wife, who could not bear to watch him fight, was waiting for him. Estelle took him in her arms and touched his purple, shapeless face tenderly. 'What happened, Ginsberg?' she asked, using her pet name for him. 'Dempsey grinned out of the good corner of his mouth,' wrote Gallico: '"Honey, I forgot to duck."' Gallico believed that this dichotomy between Dempsey's self-effacing gentleness outside the ring and his toughness inside it was the key to his appeal. 'How wonderful to be so quiet, so gentlemanly – and yet so terrible!'

Moved by the crowd's reaction to his defeat, yet devastated by the loss of his title, Dempsey returned to Hollywood. Babe Ruth, whom he had first become friends with in the early 1920s, sat him down and told him to fight to regain his title. Spindly-legged Ruth, 'a connoisseur of booze, food and dames', was another sportsman-entertainer who understood the importance of giving everything to a competition. The following summer he would hit the still unbeaten record of 60 home runs in the season for the Yankees.

Rickard scheduled a rematch for 364 days after the two boxers' first meeting, for 22 September 1927, this time in Chicago. Dempsey's final training camp was 'the quietest and dullest of all', said Gallico. Estelle was heavily medicated, teetering on the brink of a nervous breakdown; Dempsey just wanted to win.

Dempsey met the young heavyweight Jack Sharkey in an elimination round for the title bout in July. He knocked Sharkey out cold in the seventh round. Damon Runyon was more impressed by the audience which included an Indian maharajah, the circus impresario John Ringling and Franklin Delano Roosevelt. As Runyon made his way to his seat, he said, he 'fell under the hurrying hoofs of fourteen kings of the world of finance, twenty-nine merchant princes, six bootleggers and five ticket speculators, all owners of estates on Long Island and of Rolls-Royce cars'.

Given that the Dempsey–Tunney rematch was taking place in Capone's Chicago, Rickard's greatest challenge was finding a straight referee – and there are still questions about whether or not he managed to. Capone had been a fan of Dempsey's since 1919, when he had offered him whatever he wanted to stage an exhibition fight at his private club. This time he offered to ensure Dempsey's win. As Jack told it, when he refused, Capone sent him an extravagant bunch of flowers. The note read, 'In the name of sportsmanship.' Capone was rumoured to have bet $45,000 on Dempsey to beat Tunney. It was said that $2 million was wagered on the fight in New York alone.

Just before ten o'clock on the evening of 22 September 1927, the honeyed baritone of Graham McNamee came over the wire: 'Good evening, ladies and gentlemen of the radio audience. This is the night.' Seventy independent stations across the country had bought rights to McNamee's presentation of the fight; even the inmates of Sing-Sing prison had been given permission to listen. The fight was the first radio programme to be broadcast worldwide, bringing in an estimated total audience of fifty million people. The trajectory of Dempsey's career had run in parallel to the burgeoning radio industry. In 1920, when fewer than one house in ten thousand had a radio set, the first radio station received its licence in Pittsburgh. Two years later, 576 stations were transmitting and the industry was worth $60 million annually. Tens of millions of Americans heard Dempsey floor Firpo in 1923.

Once again the huge audience of over a hundred thousand was packed with celebrities, many of them Dempsey's friends from Hollywood, including Charlie Chaplin, the disgraced Fatty Arbuckle, W. R. Hearst, Gloria Swanson, Irving Berlin, Doug Fairbanks and Mary Pickford. Auto-magnate Walter Chrysler was there, as was Treasury Secretary Andrew Mellon. Al Capone sat with Damon Runyon. The box-office take was $2.5 million.

Perhaps for the first time, the public were overwhelmingly pulling for Dempsey to win. Boxing fans had begun to tire of Tunney's know-it-all attitude, his use of over-long words, his self-regarding superciliousness; they were no longer impressed by the volume of Omar Khayyam's poetry that he liked to carry around with him to show that he was something more than a mere boxer.

Dempsey was better prepared for this second fight, in better health and hungrier to win, but once again Tunney outboxed him, exploiting Dempsey's raw, undisciplined style. Dempsey was losing on points when he knocked Tunney to the ground with a left hook to the chin in the seventh round. As he always had done, Dempsey instinctively stood glowering over his opponent, waiting for him to get up so he could knock him down again.

But a recently introduced (and not yet universal) rule specified that when a boxer was knocked down, his adversary must retreat to a neutral corner before the referee began the count. Only after Dempsey had reluctantly allowed himself to be escorted to the corner did the official begin counting, buying Tunney additional time to recover from Dempsey's blow. Tunney, after a few seconds seeming fully alert as he sat on the canvas, waited to get back on to his feet until the count of nine, although he had actually been down for between fourteen and seventeen seconds; he knew as well as Dempsey did that there was no need to get up before the official count reached nine. This controversial decision became known as the Long Count.

Back up, Tunney retreated before Dempsey's furious advance, well aware that all he had to do to win was wait. 'Over his swarthy, blue-jowled fighter's face there spread a look which will never leave me as long as I live,' wrote Gallico of Dempsey as he sensed his victim slipping out of his grasp. 'First it was the expression of self-realization of one who knows that his race is run, that he is old and that he is finished. And then through it and replacing it there appeared a glance of such bitter, biting contempt for his opponent that for the moment I felt ashamed for the man who was running away. With his gloves Dempsey made little coaxing pawing motions to Tunney to come in and fight. That was it. Don't run. Come in and fight. This is a fight. For that is what Dempsey would have done.'

Tunney easily won the next three rounds and retained his title on points by the judges' unanimous decision. Dempsey knew why he had lost: Tunney was such a formidable opponent because he lacked (or could control) the 'fighting instinct' by which most boxers are governed. He couldn't be tricked into the attack, wouldn't take a chance, wouldn't play to the crowd – just relied on being able to evade and outlast his opponent.

Some observers suspected that both fights had been fixed, although few dared to say so publicly. Anyone betting on Tunney in either fight would have made a handsome profit. Both fighters had criminal connections. Leo Flynn, the manager with whom Dempsey had replaced Doc Kearns, was thought to be an associate of Al Capone's. Despite his clean-cut image, Tunney had borrowed large sums from the Philadelphia mobster Boo Boo Hoff. Having watched their first fight in Philadelphia, Ring Lardner said, 'Tunney couldn't lick Dempsey if Dempsey was trying.'

After his loss there was nothing else for Dempsey to do but retire. Tex Rickard died in his arms in early 1929, having refused an operation for appendicitis. Later that year Dempsey and Estelle were divorced. For a while he promoted fights for Al Capone, but when Capone 'started giving orders [about] who was going to win and who was going to lose – and naming the round', Dempsey quit.

The ballyhoo that had surrounded Dempsey abated and he

managed to build a life after his boxing career. In the 1920s a hero one day could be a nobody the next, but Dempsey's vulnerability, as much as his invincibility, had earned him a lasting place in American hearts. 'Nothing ever went to Dempsey's head – not his money, not his title, and not the amazing change in his social position,' wrote Paul Gallico. He always 'remained unspoiled, natural and himself'.

Dempsey continued to fight in exhibition matches, wrote about boxing technique and, in the 1930s, opened a bustling chophouse in New York. He was luckier than some other sporting celebrities: the college football hero Red Grange, who in 1925 had been paid $12,000 for his first professional game with the Chicago Bears and soon afterwards signed a $300,000 movie contract, was by 1930 working at a Hollywood nightclub.

Looking back on Dempsey's extraordinary career a decade later, Paul Gallico said that though Dempsey overshadowed his age, 'we were all part of the Dempsey cult and we were blinded by our own ballyhoo'. Dempsey was a victim of the American dream just as much as a symbol of it, puffed up by his promoters, and the hunger of the decade for heroes, into an expendable commodity rather than a man.

'I have seen the coming of the million-dollar gate, the seventy-thousand-dollar horse-race, the hundred-thousand-dollar football game, the millionaire prize-fighter, and the fifty-thousand-dollar golfer. I have witnessed an era of spending in sport such as has never been seen before and which may not be matched again, when the box-office prize for a single ringside seat for a heavyweight championship prize-fight was fifty dollars, and fetched as high as two hundred and fifty dollars a pair from speculators,' wrote Gallico. 'And I have seen the bubble collapse as sharply and completely as did the great stock boom, and watched prize-fighting go downhill from a million-dollar industry back to the small-time money from which it came.'

14

Crash

JACK DEMPSEY WAS JUST ONE OF many Americans coasting to easy wealth on the boom years of the 1920s. While salaries and prices remained largely static, production increased steadily, costs fell and corporate profits rose by 62 per cent, feeding a national sense of optimism. Certain niche groups like farmers and textile workers excepted, most people had more money to spend and, as vacations became more common and working weeks shorter, more time to spend it on each new product the advertisers told them they couldn't live without: wrist-watches, *Reader's Digest* subscriptions, nylon stockings, cigarette lighters, ice-cream bars, movie tickets and crossword-puzzle books.

'Society obeyed the impersonal law of progress,' wrote Malcolm Cowley. 'Cities expanded relentlessly year by year; fortunes grew larger; more and more automobiles appeared in the streets; people were wiser and better read than their ancestors – eventually, by automatic stages, we should reach an intolerable utopia of dull citizens, without crime or suffering or drama.'

In January 1929 *Ladies' Home Journal* published an article entitled, 'Everybody Ought to be Rich' by John Jakob Raskob, self-made financier and former vice-president of General Motors, reportedly worth $100 million in 1928, who listed his occupation in *Who's Who in America* as 'capitalist'. He advised readers to save $15 a month, invest it in the stock market — and find $80,000 in their bank accounts in twenty years' time. Anything felt possible; everything fed the mood of buoyancy. Even Lindbergh's successful landing in Paris prompted the stock market to shoot up another few notches.

Herbert Hoover, campaigning for president in the summer of 1928, declared that America was closer 'to the final triumph over poverty than ever before in the history of any land' and that soon poverty would be 'banished from this nation'. His message was so popular that 58 per cent of the electorate voted for him. But perhaps Hoover had not seen the figures showing nearly three-quarters of the population living at or below the official minimum standard for a working-class family, $2,500 per year. Despite the illusory grandeur of Hoover's ambitions and the general sense of prosperity and advancement throughout the country, inequalities in wealth were vast and increasing. America's thirty-six-thousand richest families collectively received as much per annum as the twelve million families (or nearly half the population) who scraped by on less than $1,500.

Not everyone was as bullish on America – to quote one of the phrases Frederick Allen said characterized the boom philosophy – as Raskob and Hoover. The problem was that as the economy continued its apparently inexorable rise the doom-sayers and disbelievers seemed so patently mistaken. 'I wish to record my utter inability to understand why a lot of folks don't go broke,' said the Supreme Court Justice Louis Brandeis, as early as 1926. 'These consolidations and security flotations plus the building boom, beat my comprehension – unless there is a breakdown within a year.' But despite Brandeis's legal eminence, his prediction of a financial collapse was (to say the least) premature, and no one heeded his warning.

In 1927 Scott Fitzgerald was interviewed by the *New York World*. 'The idea that we're the greatest people in the world because we have the most money is ridiculous. Wait until this prosperity is over!' His interviewer was shocked to confusion: 'In a pleasant corner of the Plaza tea garden he sounded like an intellectual Samson prophesying the crumbling of its marble columns'.

Fitzgerald was an admirer of the historian Oswald Spengler, who, in *The Decline of the West*, published between 1918 and 1923, outlined his theory that the United States had reached a stage comparable to that of Rome in the centuries after Christ's birth – achieving a flowering of civilization that was nothing more than the precursor of its own destruction. According to Spengler, the modern 'Cosmopolis' was the high point of this last stage, 'vast, splendid, spreading in insolence... Here money and intellect celebrate their greatest and their last triumphs'.

The 'greatest and last triumphs' Spengler was picturing may well have been skyscrapers, the radiant symbols of energy, wealth and modernity for 1920s America. As one successful building contractor put it in 1928, skyscrapers were 'the most distinctively American thing in the world... [epitomizing] American life and American civilization... the spontaneous product of a virile and progressive people', requiring all their courage, daring and ingenuity. In that boom year Americans spent $6 billion constructing new buildings, with the epicentre of the real estate bubble on the tiny island of Manhattan. There was nowhere else to go there but up. Estate agents, like stockbrokers, could foresee no end to the soaring prices.

Oswald Spengler saw the huge proportions of the skyscrapers, and their lofty disregard for nature, as swaggering signs of over-confidence. As the city grows from 'primitive barter-centre to culture-city and at last to world-city', he wrote, 'it sacrifices first the blood and soul of its creators to the needs of its majestic evolution, and then the last flower of that growth to the spirit of civilization – and so, doomed, moves on to final self-destruction'.

This fateful transition from barter-centre to doomed cosmopolis was well under way. By 1920, less than half of the American population still lived on farms or in small rural communities. An ideological division between go-getting city-dwellers and upstanding country-dwellers was becoming more marked, but there was ambivalence on both sides. Urbanites were nostalgic for the simple peace of farm life; countrymen were lured into the city by promises of easy money and high living. Middletown exemplified this trend. Its population was steadily boosted throughout the period of the Lynds' study by people from nearby villages and farming communities, but its most successful citizens tended to leave for even bigger cities.

New York was the pinnacle of American urban culture, the place where the ambitious dreamer from every small town believed that he, too, could make it big. The approach by sea produced the most dramatic effect on hopeful newcomers. Langston Hughes described the thrill of his first glimpse of Manhattan's towers 'with their million golden eyes, growing slowly taller and taller above the green water, until they looked as if they could touch the sky!' John Dos Passos watched the buildings grow denser, forming 'a granite mountain split with knifecut canyons... Steel, glass, tile, concrete will be the materials of the skyscrapers. Crammed on the narrow island the millionwindowed buildings will jut, glittering pyramid on pyramid, white cloudsheads piled above a thunderstorm'.

From 1857, when the first building with passenger lifts was successfully completed in New York, architects had been using new materials like iron, steel and glass to create structures of dramatic and astonishing height. The first steel-framed building, using a riveted skeleton, was built in Chicago by

William Holabird in the late 1880s. By 1900 all the industrial components required to create skyscrapers – steel framing and riveting, cable suspension, concrete – were in use and buildings of twenty storeys and more were under construction in New York and Chicago.

The birthplace of the skyscraper, the Chicago school of the late nineteenth century, was utilitarian, distrustful of historical allusion, powerful, simple and direct. Chicagoan architects created buildings to reflect the work that went on inside them. Form did not just follow function, but dramatized it. The skyscraper's 'dominant chord must be tall, every inch of it tall', wrote Louis Sullivan, a prominent Chicago architect, in 1896. 'The force and power of altitude must be in it, the glory and pride of exaltation must be in it. It must be every inch a proud and soaring thing.'

Because America was such a new country, with no established architectural traditions of its own, designers at the start of the century were granted extraordinary freedom to create, unhampered by existing forms or 'ignoble history'. Spurred onwards by America's burgeoning industrial and financial wealth, architects proclaimed their clients' prestige, power and wealth through height, creative use of colour and form and dramatic night-time illumination.

In 1925, New York claimed 522 buildings of ten storeys or more. Thirty new office buildings went up in the city the following year. By 1929, there were seventy-eight buildings above twenty storeys and nineteen above forty. 'The appeal and inspiration lie, of course, in the element of loftiness, in the suggestion of slenderness and aspiration, the soaring quality as of a thing rising from the earth as a unitary utterance,' wrote Sullivan.

America was in thrall to these cathedrals erected to their new god, success. Elinor Glyn was content simply to enjoy her stay at the Ritz Tower in 1927, then the highest inhabited building in the world; two years later Harry Crosby was so overwhelmed by staying on the twenty-seventh floor of the Savoy that he tried to persuade his wife to jump out of their hotel window with him.

But some commentators thought the buildings were 'appropriate to an age of complacency', their extraordinary steel frames plastered with a jumble of derivative architectural styles intended to exalt the businesses who paid for them rather than extend creative endeavour. 'Up to the present all that we can call a modern style consists of misappropriated fragments of antiquity,' observed the architectural critic Louis Mumford derisively in 1921.

Frank Lloyd Wright, largely unappreciated during the 1920s, bewailed the lack of integrity in modern architecture, calling skyscrapers a triumph of 'business-building' and damning the rise of 'the suburban house-parade... chateaux, manor houses, Venetian palaces, feudal castles and Queen Anne cottages'. He called in vain for a new architecture that would 'broaden, lengthen, strengthen and deepen the life of the simplest man'.

In an era dominated by business interests, domestic architecture floundered, true architectural innovation replaced by flash and derivation. The sleeping-porch so beloved by George Babbitt was considered the height of suburban design ingenuity. Far more attention was paid to the construction of highways, bridges, motels, airports and petrol stations than to the millions of new residential areas sprawling out across the country.

Perhaps the most beautiful and whimsical of the skyscrapers of the building boom of the late 1920s was the chrome-topped Chrysler Building, designed by William van Alen for Walter Chrysler's three-year-old Chrysler Corporation, soon to be renamed Chrysler Motors. Chrysler had just been voted *Time* magazine's Man of the Year (the first Man of the Year, the previous year, had been Charles Lindbergh), and the car industry in general, and Chrysler Motors specifically, was thriving. The Chrysler Building, intended to be the tallest building in the world, was to be a monument to their success as well as the most breathtaking of advertising hoardings.

Chrysler asked Van Alen to create 'a cathedral of modern industrial design'. Van Alen was a proponent of Art Deco, embracing colour, pattern and texture, as romantic and eclectic as he was modern and utilitarian. He had studied architecture in Paris between 1908 and 1911 at the Ecole des Beaux-Arts, and would attend the annual Society of Beaux-Arts Architects' Ball in 1930 triumphantly dressed as his lofty, shimmering creation. While other Art Deco buildings incorporated Gothic or Mayan motifs, Van Alen used a modernist, theatrical 'machine aesthetic' for the Chrysler Building. His design embodied 'the emblazonment of automotive progress', adorning the building with winged radiator caps and a frieze of stylized mudguards and hubcaps. The reflective chrome vertex was planned to seem to melt into the sky. But most mesmeric of all was the Chrysler Building's height. From its uppermost point, wrote one visitor nearly sixty years after its completion, 'the city below appears as dreamy, distant, and unneccessary as the mercury-colored sea must look to an enraptured diver.'

Like the building itself, the four monumental murals in the lobby were designed to exalt the automotive industry and its commitment to progress and civilization. The first mural uses a single worker to signify strength; the second portrays the natural materials of energy and how man harnesses it; the third, representing craftsmanship, is a group of portraits of fifty labourers who worked on the building itself: masons, riveters and riggers; the fourth is a paean to transportation, picturing ocean liners, dirigibles, trains and Lindbergh's *Spirit of St Louis* – but no cars. Surmounting them all is the image of a virtuous knight, symbol of the good faith and sense of responsibility felt by the worthy industrialist towards the people whose lives his products were transforming.

Workers began their excavations into Manhattan's mica bedrock in November 1928 and the first steel billet was set five months later. In September 1929, as brokers and office workers returned from their Labor Day break, the building was topped and installation commenced of the chromium-clad dome, spire and eagle-headed and -winged finials. Van Alen's technical ingenuity and engineering were long-lasting; seventy years later, when the building was restored, none of the spire's cladding needed replacing. The building was also noteworthy for its safe working conditions. At a time when on average one labourer died for every floor that was erected above the fifteenth, not one of the 2,400 men who worked on the thousand-foot-tall Chrysler Building was killed in its construction.

When it was finished, *Architectural Forum* hailed the Chrysler Building as 'simply the realization, the fulfilment in metal and masonry, of a one-man dream, a dream of such ambition and such magnitude as to defy the comprehension and the criticism of ordinary man or by ordinary standards'. It represented not just the triumph of industry, but the triumph of aspiration.

The first office workers began moving into the Chrysler Building in April 1930, the month before its official opening. By the time it had been completed, that July, it had a 65 per cent occupancy rate. Tenants included Henry Luce's Time Incorporated empire (whose *Time* magazine had hailed Walter Chrysler as Man of the Year) and the oil company Texaco as well as Chrysler Motors itself.

Considering the economic background, the Chrysler Building was an incredible success. Even in 1935, 70 per cent of its office space was full. By contrast the nearby skyscraper that overtook it as the tallest building in the world in 1931, the 102-

storey Empire State Building, was a flop. Built by John Raskob as a direct challenge to Walter Chrysler's building, it cost over $26 million to construct (as opposed to $14 million for the Chrysler Building) and its offices were less than a quarter full when it was finished in 1931. It was not until the 1940s that it began to make money. New Yorkers nicknamed it the Empty State Building.

Walter Chrysler commissioned the Chrysler Building at precisely the moment when the great 'Bull Market' of the late 1920s was rising to its frenzied peak. It was no accident that the era's monument to success should have been raised by a car manufacturer. The stock market's dramatic rise in 1928 and 1929 was fuelled by the ever-increasing profits and expansion of companies like General Motors and Chrysler Motors.

By the late 1920s the automotive industry paid nearly a tenth of America's manufacturing wages and made over a tenth of all her manufactured goods. Intoxicated by their own aggrandisement, automotive bosses had ceased, according to one commentator, 'to worry about the saturation point'. Walter Chrysler triumphantly declared that he and his associates were 'making the first machine of considerable size in the history of the world for which every human being was a potential customer'. 'Our present progress is but a beginning,' he told the *Chicago Tribune* in 1928. 'We have but culled the first fruits.'

The Bull Market began in the spring of 1928 when General Motors' stock price rose dramatically against Ford's, following the delayed introduction of the Model A. Observers realized that General Motors would profit from Ford's slowness. John Raskob, then vice-president and treasurer of General Motors, gave an interview in which he said he thought General Motors stock was undervalued. Its price rocketed ten points in a matter of days, accounting on Monday 5 March for a third of all stock trades.

Chrysler Motors stock was also soaring: the Maxwell Company stock which Walter Chrysler had bought for $16 when he took over the company in 1921, and which became the Chrysler Corporation four years later, was worth $563 in 1928. Financiers and industrialists like Raskob and Chrysler publicly pronounced that selling stock was 'selling America short' – not just foolish but unpatriotic and possibly unchristian.

In the same month that Raskob kick-started the boom, and the same month that Cadillac sales in New York reached an all-time high, speculator Billy Durant headed a pool which invested heavily in the Radio Corporation of America (RCA). RCA had recently been acquired by the young buccaneer Joseph Kennedy. Durant's well-connected consortium included John Raskob, committing $1 million; Walter Chrysler, investing $500,000; the steel magnate Charles Schwab; Percy Rockefeller, nephew of John D.; Joseph Tumulty, former aide to President Wilson; and the wife of the head of RCA. They raised a total of $12 million and made $5 million in a week. RCA stock went up from $85 at the start of 1928 to $420 by the end of the year.

Durant, the former head of General Motors, reportedly made $100 million during the boom years. He headed a group of Midwestern stock speculators with backgrounds in the Chicago grain pit or the automotive industry who became known as the 'prosperity boys'; the press called him 'the leading bull'.

Pools – essentially market manipulation – were a special feature of the suggestible 1920s Bull Market. In 1927 pools sold to the public $400 million worth of securities; the following year that number had almost doubled to $790 million. Techniques used to raise the price of pool stocks included hiring publicity agents to spread positive news about a company, paying financial journalists to promote specific stocks, distributing biased 'tipster sheets' to investors and using prominent investors' celebrity glitter to lure in smaller fish. Unscrupulous business practices were the norm in a virtually unregulated industry. Phrases like, 'The possibilities of that company are *unlimited*,' and 'Never give up your position in a good stock,' were repeated like mantras.

In late 1928 the National City Bank created a pool for Anaconda Copper (a Montana mine owned by investor Percy Rockefeller's father, William) and started pushing its stock, then priced at $40, even though underwriters knew that copper was fetching weak prices in Chile. The share price leapt to $128 in three months and at its peak in October 1929 was selling for $150. Anaconda Copper became one of the magic phrases of the boom years, whispered like a talisman from one gullible investor to the next. A huge number of Anaconda's ill-informed small investors went bust while benefiting members of the $32 million pool, who included Percy Rockefeller, Billy Durant and John Raskob – associates from the RCA pool of the previous year. They were involved in another type of short-selling speculation, later made illegal, known as 'pump and dump', which was one of the great banking scandals of American history. In the trough of the Depression in 1932, Anaconda Copper stock was worth just $4.

When a Senate committee conducted what became known as the Bear Hunt in 1932, seeking evidence on which to base regulation of the stock market following the 1929 crash, the brash trader Matthew 'Bear' Brush was asked if he had known about practices comparable to Al Capone's in the Wall Street of the late 1920s. 'Al Capone is a piker compared to that racket,' Brush replied.

All America seemed caught up in what economist John Galbraith later called a 'mass escape into make believe'. Everyone talked stocks and shares: the market had replaced sex as the national conversational obsession. Having grown accustomed to borrowing to finance buying a car or a washing machine, it was a short step to borrowing to invest in stocks that apparently could not lose value. Wall Street investment houses started opening branch offices in small cities – 1,192 of them by October 1928 – to capitalize on the national mania for buying stock. A travelling salesman told the business writer Edwin Lefèvre that nine-tenths of the people he saw in city nightclubs as he travelled across country were spending uncashed stock-market profits. He was struck by the thought 'that these people had acquired the worst habits of the idle rich, without the riches'.

'The basic delusion was that we had entered a fourth-dimension economic world,' said the economics journalist Garet Garrett, looking back on the boom years from the perspective of the 1930s. Even the children in John Dos Passos's *Manhattan Transfer* played at 'stock exchange': 'I've got a million dollars in bonds to sell and Maisie can be the bulls an' Jimmy can be the bears.' Groucho Marx loved stock-speculating. He took tips from elevator boys and passed them on to his brothers. As he bustled over to his brokers' office to organize another transaction he chortled to himself, 'What an easy racket.' The psychic Evangeline Adams charged $20 for her financial advice newsletter.

But pundits crying, 'Buy! Buy! Buy!' were choosing to ignore warning signs that the economy was slowing down – and in some cases had never been booming. The United States was sustaining the world's slow post-war economy by investing dollars abroad but purchasing little in return. Farmers, untouched by urban prosperity, had been going bust in unprecedented numbers throughout the 1920s. In ten years Georgia's bankruptcy rate had gone up 1,000 per cent. Florida had never recovered from its property crash in 1926 after the Great Miami Hurricane. Seven hundred thousand people were displaced in the Southwest when the Mississippi River flooded in 1927. The Government had been encouraging people to use mortgages to buy their own homes but by 1926 the housing market was glutted. Mortgage indebtedness, which had more than doubled between 1922 and 1929, stood at $27.1 billion. Residential construction work abated and the automotive industry cooled off. Only the stock market continued to soar; by 1928 it was carrying the whole economy on its inflated shoulders.

Mini price collapses occurred in June 1928, December 1928 and March 1929, but each time the market recovered and carried on rising. Interest rates went up, but bankers defied the Federal Reserve to continue to provide affordable loans to one another, and the stock boom continued. On the first working day after the Labor Day long weekend, market averages reached peaks that would not be bettered for twenty-five years. Evangeline Adams predicted that the Dow could climb all the way to heaven.

But gradually the bears began to outnumber the bulls. As John Galbraith later wrote, panic began to rise 'in dozens and then in hundreds and finally in thousands of breasts'. And so the crash came, arriving 'with a kind of surrealistic slowness – so gradually that, on the one hand, it was possible to live through a good part of it without realizing what was happening, and, on the other hand, it was possible to believe that one had experienced and survived it when in fact it had no more than just begun'.

Some got out in time. Joe Kennedy was one of the clever

ones. Having made a fortune from RCA and various other movie and property interests he sold quietly well before the crash, saying, 'Only a fool holds out for top dollar.' He was less successful handling his profligate mistress Gloria Swanson's financial affairs. Gloria Productions brought out its last film in 1930, at about the time their affair came to an end.

Others refused to believe that a fall in prices was even possible. A Professor Dice published *New Levels in the Stock Market* in the autumn of 1929. 'Among the yardsticks for predicting the behaviour of stocks which have been rendered obsolete are the truism that what goes up must come down, that the market will be at the end of a major advance after twenty to twenty-four months of climbing, that major declines will run from eleven to fifteen months, that stock prices cannot safely exceed ten times the net earnings.' On 15 October, the celebrity economist Irving Fisher declared that stock prices stood on 'what looks like a permanently high plateau'. On 23 October, the Chrysler Building's lofty silver dome was fitted into place.

The next day, on what became known as Black Thursday, after a slow but steady decline in prices the market plunged into free fall. Winston Churchill, visiting New York, watched the prices plummet from the visitors' gallery of the New York Stock Exchange. A group of elder statesmen from the financial world tried to arrest disaster by pouring millions back into the market as a show of faith, but succeeded only in staving off collapse for two days. General panic ensued on Black Tuesday, 29 October, when the market lost $14 billion in value.

Groucho Marx's broker called him that day. 'Marx,' he said, 'the jig is up!' and put down the telephone. Groucho was philosophical. 'All I lost was two hundred and forty thousand dollars... I would have lost more but that was all the money I had.' His brother Harpo said his remaining holdings, post-crash, 'were probably worth a medium-size bag of jelly-beans'.

Within two weeks the total value of the New York Stock Exchange was down by half. Nearly 13 million stocks changed hands in October and by the end of the month the market had fallen 43 points – the amount it had gained in the previous year. Plummeting stock and share prices lost their owners over $40 billion. Jack Dempsey lost $3 million.

'On the whole, the greater the earlier reputation for omniscience, the more serene the previous idiocy, the greater the foolishness now exposed,' wrote John Galbraith some forty years later. It was a total, ruthless liquidation of the market. Speculators who thought they could outwit it lost heavily; among them was 'the leading bull', Billy Durant. Generally speaking, customers fared worse than brokers, who sold their own stocks first and thus made smaller losses than their clients, and who also had access to longer grace periods from their lenders and cheaper credit.

It is a myth that streams of suicidal traders and investors leapt to their deaths from the skyscrapers that had once represented their success, but, as Galbraith commented, the public seized on accounts of suicides 'to show that people were reacting appropriately to their misfortune'. Everybody could see that the crash was not simply an economic disaster – it was a revolution that would affect the life of every single American, whether they had been actively involved in the stock market boom or not. Galbraith called it a 'levelling process comparable in magnitude and suddenness to that presided over a decade before by Lenin'.

The crash did not cause the Depression; that was part of a far broader malaise. What it did was expose the weaknesses that underpinned the confidence and optimism of the 1920s – poor distribution of income, a weak banking structure and insufficient regulations, the economy's dependence on new consumer goods, the over-extension of industry and the Government's blind belief that promoting business interests would make America uniformly prosperous. President Hoover, who had warned against over-speculation, was not to blame for the crash, but his response to it, over the next few years, was leaden and inadequate. Limited government was useless when confronted by a disaster on this scale.

The international situation had also been an important contributory factor. The United States was a creditor nation; it exported far more than it imported; its sturdy protectionism hindered poorer countries, especially in war-torn Europe, from rebuilding their economies. Ultimately, though, the shoddy market practice and excessive speculation that stimulated the boom and then brought America crashing to its knees was derived from Wall Street itself.

People saw the crash and the Depression as the inevitable

result of the selfish debauchery of the 1920s. It was a punishment for their profligacy, a necessary correction. President Hoover said that his austere (but very rich) Financial Secretary, Andrew Mellon, commented simply, 'They deserved it,' when the boom broke. 'Liquidate labor, liquidate stocks, liquidate the farmers, liquidate real estate,' Mellon declared. He believed that letting economic events run their course would 'purge the rottenness out of the system. High costs of living and high living will come down. People will work harder, live a more moral life. Values will be adjusted, and enterprising people will pick up the wrecks from less competent people.' But it would be a long time before the wrecks were picked up.

Over the next two decades, struggling to cope with unemployment, hunger, homelessness and war, there was little room in the American consciousness for the violet strains of a jazz orchestra floating on warm summer air. But something about the twenties – its energy and youthfulness, its 'sparkling cynicism' alongside its overwhelming self-belief – has endured to this day.

Concluding an essay entitled 'Echoes of the Jazz Age' in November 1931, as ever Scott Fitzgerald summed up his age best. 'Now once more the belt is tight and we summon the proper expression of horror as we look back at our wasted youth. Sometimes, though, there is a ghostly rumble among the drums, an asthmatic whisper in the trombones that swings me back into the early twenties when we drank wood alcohol and every day in every way grew better and better, and there was a first abortive shortening of the skirts... and people you didn't want to know said "Yes, we have no bananas," and it seemed only a question of years before the older people would step aside and let the world be run by those who saw things as they were – and it all seems rosy and romantic to us who were young then, because we will never feel quite so intensely about our surroundings any more.'

Bibliography

Chapter 1 'You Cannot Make Your Shimmy Shake on Tea'
The best near-contemporary account of Prohibition – and indeed the period as a whole – is the journalist Frederick Lewis Allen's 1931 *Only Yesterday*. Professor William Leuchtenberg's 1958 *The Perils of Prosperity* is another classic but with greater historical context. Among other books listed in the bibliography, I used Laurence Bergreen and John Kobler's biographies for my portrait of Al Capone and Thomas Coffey's 1975 *The Long Thirst* and Herbert Asbury's 1950 *The Great Illusion for Prohibition*.

Chapter 2 'The Rhythm of Life'
Kathy Ogren's 1989 *The Jazz Revolution: Twenties America and the Meaning of Jazz* is the most fascinating account of jazz in the 1920s. Louis Armstrong's memoirs and Chris Albertson's *Bessie*, with its interviews with Bessie Smith's niece Ruby,

were invaluable. Nathan Huggins's account of *The Harlem Renaissance* and Langston Hughes's biography by Arnold Rampersad are good, although the best sources as ever are the primary ones: autobiographical writing, novels and poetry by Hughes, Zora Neale Hurston, Claude Mackay, even Carl Van Vechten, and the broader non-fiction writings and collections of Alain Locke and James Weldon Johnson.

CHAPTER 3 FEMME FATALE

Throughout the book I relied heavily on *Middletown*, the sociologists Robert and Helen Lynd's classic study of small town American life in the 1920s, but perhaps it is most relevant to the chapter on women and how their lives were changing during this period. Paula Fass's 1977 examination of American youth in the 1920s, *The Damned and the Beautiful*, was also useful. Anita Loos and Tallulah Bankhead, both emancipated and ambitious women who exemplified their age almost as much as Zelda Fitzgerald did, wrote memoirs. There have been several joint biographies of Scott and Zelda Fitzgerald, but as far as I know only one, published by Nancy Milford in 1970, on Zelda alone – though the Fitzgeralds' stories and novels are the best introduction to their lives. Other evocative popular novels of the period include Edith Hull's *The Sheik*, Katherine Brush's *Glitter*, David Garnett's *Dope Darling* and Warner Fabian's *Flaming Youth*.

CHAPTER 4 'FIVE AND TEN CENT LUSTS AND DREAMS'
Marion Davies, Charlie Chaplin, Cecil Demille, Gloria Swanson, Lillian Gish and Eleanor Glyn are among many Hollywood luminaries who wrote memoirs, although those of the professional writers like Anita Loos and the journalist Adela Saint John are generally more polished and accessible. Kenneth Anger's sensationalist *Hollywood Babylon* dishes the dirt on Hollywood scandals and Marjorie Rosen's 1973 *Popcorn Venus* explores women's role in the movies. I used Stuart Oderman's 1994 biography of Fatty Arbuckle for my account of his rise and fall.

CHAPTER 5 'MY GOD! HOW THE MONEY ROLLS IN!'
Journalist William Allen White provides the best public portrait of the troubled Warren Harding, while rival Washington hostesses Evalyn McLean (*Father Struck it Rich*, 1936) and Alice Roosevelt Longworth (*Crowded Hours*, 1933) give insights into his and Florence's private lives. Two books published in 1998 were also helpful: a biography of Edward Doheny (*Dark Side of Fortune* by Margaret Davis) and, especially, *Florence Harding* by Carl Anthony.

CHAPTER 6 'THE BUSINESS OF AMERICA IS BUSINESS'
While I highly recommend Stephen Fox's history of advertising in America (*The Mirror Makers*, 1984), Robert Lacey's *Ford: The Men and the Machine* (1986) and Vincent Curcio's 2000 biography of Walter Chrysler, without doubt the best book on

smugly industrious middle-class America is Sinclair Lewis's brilliant 1922 novel, *Babbitt*.

CHAPTER 7 FEAR OF THE FOREIGN

Sinclair Lewis, a passionate defender of Sacco and Vanzetti, also wrote a semi-fictionalised account of their ordeal, *Boston* (1928). Another of their defenders, the novelist John Dos Passos, collected information for their defense in *Facing the Chair* (1927). Sacco and Vanzetti's letters were collected in 1927 and republished with a good summary of the trials, evidence and its later ramifications by Penguin Classics in 1997.

CHAPTER 8 THE KU KLUX KLAN REDUX

Henry Fry's 1922 expose of the Ku Klux Klan's resurgence is still fascinating, though fuller and clearer accounts of the Klan's rise and fall in the 1920s can be found in Wyn Wade's 1987 *The Fiery Cross* and Nancy Maclean's 1994 *Behind the Mask of Chivalry*. I found Kathryn Blee's 1991 *Women in the Klan*, a detailed exploration of the role of women in the Klan, particularly interesting.

CHAPTER 9 IN EXILE

Harry Crosby's extraordinary and vivid diaries (published as *Shadows of the Sun* in 1977) and Caresse's later memoirs (*The Passionate Years*, 1955) are their own testimony. Janet Flanner's articles as the *New Yorker*'s Paris correspondent (collected in 2003 as *Paris was Yesterday*) give a flavour of how Americans experienced Paris in the 1920s, as does Amanda Vaill's wonderful 1998 *Everybody Was So Young*, about Gerald and Sara Murphy. In fiction, Kay Boyle's 1934 *My Next Bride*, though not much of a read, is interesting as a resentful *roman a clef* about the Crosbys to whom she had once been close, while Ernest Hemingway's 1927 *The Sun Also Rises* is the ultimate novel about Americans in Paris.

CHAPTER 10 THE NEW YORKER

Malcolm Cowley's 1934 *Exile's Return* gives a good flavour of the literary world in 1920s America, as do old copies of the periodicals of the day – the *Saturday Evening Post*, the *American Mercury*, *Vanity Fair*, *Harpers*, the *Nation* and of course the *New Yorker*. Harold Ross's ex-wife Jane Grant (*Ross, the New Yorker and Me*, 1968) and his employee and friend James Thurber (*The Years with Ross*, 1959) both wrote excellent accounts of their lives with him and the *New Yorker*.

CHAPTER 11 'YES, WE HAVE NO BANANAS TODAY'

In their different ways, the two best journalistic accounts of the Scopes trial are Joseph Wood Krutch's 1962 *More Lives than One* and Henry Mencken's bitterly funny articles for the Baltimore *Evening Sun*. The 1997 Pulitzer Prize-winning *Summer for the Gods: The Scopes Trial and America's Continuing Debate over Science and Religion* by Edward Larson is a fantastic modern retelling of the events.

Chapter 12 The Spirit of St. Louis

Lindbergh told the story of his flight with passion and eloquence in 1927 with *We* and in 1953 with *The Spirit of St. Louis*, which won the Pulitzer Prize in 1954. For an overview of his life, Scott Berg's 1998 biography is unbeatable.

Chapter 13 The Big Fight

Jack Dempsey, Gene Tunney and Georges Carpentier all wrote their own life stories, although I also used the sportswriter Paul Gallico's 1938 memoirs, *Farewell to Sport*. The best recent accounts of Dempsey's rivalry with Tunney are Bruce Evensen's 1996 *When Dempsey Fought Tunney* and an article in the *Journal of American Studies* 19 by E. J. Gorn, 'The Manassa Mauler and the Fighting Marine'. I was also delighted to find that most of Dempsey's fights (as well as footage of Charles Lindbergh) can be found on Youtube.

Chapter 14 Crash

Neal Bascomb's 2003 *Higher* traces the race between the Chrysler and Empire State Buildings to be the tallest building in the world. Although Maury Klein's 2001 *Rainbow's End: The Crash of 1929* is excellent, nothing can surpass John Kenneth Galbraith's 1961 *The Great Crash*.

Bibliographic References

Albertson, C., *Bessie* New Haven, CT 2003

Allen, F. L., *Only Yesterday* New York, NY 1964

American Mercury

Andrews, W., *Architecture, Ambition and Americans* London 1984

Anger, K., *Hollywood Babylon* Phoenix, AZ 1965

Anthony, C. S., *Florence Harding* New York, NY 1998

Armstrong, L., *Swing That Music* New York, NY 1936

Asbury, H., *The Great Illusion: An Informal History of Prohibition* Garden City, NJ 1950

Bankhead, T., *Tallulah: My Autobiography* New York, NY 1952

Barton, B., *The Man Nobody Knows* New York, NY 1924

Bascomb, N., *Higher: A Historic Race to the Sky and the Making of a City* New York, NY 2003

Basinger, J., *Silent Stars* Middletown, CT 2001

Benchley, R., *After 1903 – What?* New York, NY 1938

Berg, A. S., *Lindbergh* New York, NY 1998

——, *Max Perkins: Editor of Genius* New York, NY 1978

Bergreen, L., *Capone: The Man and the Era* New York, NY 1992

Bernstein, I., *The Lean Years: A History of the American Worker, 1920–1933* Boston, MA 1966

Blee, K. M., *Women of the Klan* Berkeley, CA 1991

Boyle, K., *Words That Must Somehow be Said* San Francisco, CA 1985

Breslin, J., *Damon Runyan: A Life* London 1992

Broer, L. & J. D. Walther, eds., *Dancing Fools & Weary Blues* Bowling Green, OH 1990

Brooks, J., *Once in Golconda: A True Drama of Wall Street 1920–1938* New York, NY 1969

Brooks, V. W., *Days of the Phoenix: The 1920s I Remember* New York, NY 1957

Burchard, J., and A. Bush-Brown, *The Architecture of America: A Social and Cultural History* Boston, MA 1961

Cannadine, D., *Mellon* New York, NY 2003

Carey, G., *Doug & Mary: A Biography of Douglas Fairbanks* New York, NY 1978

Carpentier, G., *Carpentier by Himself* London 1955

Cashman, S. D., *America in the Twenties and Thirties. The Olympian Age of Franklin Delano Roosevelt* New York, NY 1989

Chaplin, C., *My Autobiography* New York, NY 1964

Chesler, E., *Woman of Valor: Margaret Sangster & the Birth Control Movement* New York, NY 1992

Chilton, J., *Who's Who of Jazz: Storyville to Swing St* Philadelphia, PA 1972

Chrysler, W. B., *Life of an American Workman* New York, NY 1937

Churchill, A., *The Year the World Went Mad* New York, NY 1990

Coben, S., *Rebellion Against Victorianism. The Impetus for Cultural Change in 1920s America* New York, NY 1991

Cockburn, C., *In Time of Trouble* New York, NY 1957

Coffey, T. M., *The Long Thirst: Prohibition in America, 1920–1933* New York, NY 1975

Condit, C. W., *American Building Art in the Twentieth Century* New York, NY 1961

Coward, N., *Present Indicative* London 1937

——, *The Vortex* London 1924

Cowley, M., *Exile's Return* New York, NY 1934

Crane, H., *The Bridge* New York, NY 1930

Cronon, E. D., *Black Moses: The Story of Marcus Garvey and the UNIA* Madison, WI 1970

Crosby, C., *The Passionate Years* London 1955

Crosby, H., *Shadows of the Sun* Santa Barbara, CA 1977

Crunden, R. M., *From Self to Society: Transition in American Thought, 1919–1941* Englewood Cliffs, NJ 1972

Cummings, e. e., *The Enormous Room* New York, NY 1922

Cunard, N., ed., *Negro: An Anthology* New York, NY 1970

Curcio, V., *Chrysler: The Life and Times of an Automotive Genius* Oxford 2000

Darrow, C., *The Story of My Life* New York, NY 1932

Davies, Marion, *The Times We Had* Indianapolis, IN 1975

Davis, M. L, *Dark Side of Fortune* Berkeley, CA 1998

DeMille, W., *Autobiography* London 1960

Dempsey, J. and B. P., *The Name's Dempsey* New York, NY 1977

Dempsey, J., *Massacre in the Sun* London 1960

——, *Round by Round* New York, NY 1940

Dos Passos, J., *Facing the Chair* Boston, MA 1927

——, *Manhattan Transfer* London 1987

Einstein, I., *Prohibition Agent No. 1* New York, NY 1932

Eisenberg, D., U. Dan, and E. Landau, *Meyer Lansky: Mogul of the Mob* London 1979

Evensen, B. J., *When Dempsey Fought Tunney* Knoxville, TN 1996

Everdell, W., *The First Moderns* London 1997

Fass, P., *The Damned and the Beautiful* New York, NY 1977

Feinstein, E., *Bessie Smith* Harmondsworth 1985

Flamini, R., *Thalberg: The Last Tycoon and the World of MGM* London 1994

Flanner, J., *Paris Was Yesterday 1925–1939* London 2003

Flink, J. J., *The Car Culture* Cambridge, MA 1975

Foner, E., *The Modern Temper* New York, NY 1995

Fox, S., *The Mirror Makers: A History of American Advertising and its Creators* New York, NY 1984

Freeman, D., *The Fateful Hoaxing of Margaret Mead* Boulder, CO 1999

French, P., *The Movie Moguls: An Informal History of the Hollywood Tycoons* London 1969

Fry, H., *The Modern Ku Klux Klan* Boston, MA 1922

Galbraith, J.K., *The Great Crash* Boston, MA 1961

Gallico, P., *Farewell to Sport* New York, NY 1938

Geisst, C. R., *Wall Street: A History* New York, NY 1999

Gerstle, G., *American Crucible: Race & Nation in the 20th Century* Princeton, NJ 2001

Gish, L., *The Movies, Mr Griffith and Me* Englewood Cliffs, NJ 1969

Glyn, E., *Romantic Adventure* London 1936

Goldberg, D. J., *Discontented America: The United States in the 1920s* Baltimore, MD 1997

Goldberg, R. A., *America in the Twenties* Syracuse, NY 2003

——, *Hooded Empire: The Ku Klux Klan in Colorado* Urbana, IL 1981

Gorn, E. J., 'The Manassa Mauler and the Fighting Marine' *Journal of American Studies* 19 1985

Grant, J., *Ross, the New Yorker and Me* New York, NY 1968

Grant, M., *The Passing of a Great Race* New York, NY 1916

Griffith, R., A. Mayer & E. Bowser, *The Movies* New York, NY 1971

Hamalian, L., *The Cramoisy Queen: A Life of Caresse Crosby* Carbondale, IL 2005

Harpers

Harriman, M. C., *The Vicious Circle* New York, NY 1951

Hemingway, E., *A Moveable Feast* New York, NY 1964

Herman, A., *The Idea of Decline in Western History* London 1997

Hitchcock, H. R., *Modern Architecture* New York, NY 1929

Hoffman, F. J., *The 1920s: American Writing in the Postwar Decade* New York, NY 1954

Hoover, H. C., *Memoirs* New York, NY 1951–2

Huggins, N. I., *The Harlem Renaissance* New York NY 1971

Hughes, L., *The Big Sea* New York, NY 1940

——, *Fine Clothes to the Jew* New York, NY 1927

——, *Weary Blues* New York, NY 1926

Jackson, K. T., *The Ku Klux Klan in the City 1915–1930* New York, NY 1967

Jarrett, J., *Gene Tunney. The Golden Guy Who Licked Jack Dempsey Twice* London 2003

Johnson, J. W., *Selected Writings* Oxford, 1995

Klein, M., *Rainbow's End: The Crash of 1929* New York NY 2001

Kobler, J., *Capone: The Life and World of Al Capone* New York, NY 1971

Krutch, J. W., *More Lives Than One* New York, NY 1962

Kunkel, T., *Genius in Disguise: Harold Ross of the New Yorker* New York, NY 1995

Lacey, R., *Ford: The Men and the Machine* Boston, MA 1986

Lardner, R., *The Story of a Wonder Boy* New York, NY 1927

Larson, E. J., *Summer for the Gods: The Scopes Trial and America's Continuing Debate over Science and Religion* New York, NY 1997

Lears, J., *Fables of Abundance: A Cultural History of Advertising in America* New York, NY 1994

Leuchtenberg, W., *The Perils of Prosperity* Chicago, IL 1958

Lindbergh, C., *The Spirit of St. Louis* London 1953

——, *We* London 1927

Lippmann, W., *Preface to Morals* New York, NY 1929

Locke, A., *The New Negro: An Interpretation* New York, NY 1925

Lomax, A., *Mister Jelly Roll* Berkeley, CA 1973

Longworth, A. R., *Crowded Hours* London 1933

Loos, A., *Kiss Hollywood Goodbye* London 1974

——, *The Talmadge Girls* New York, NY 1978

Loucks, E. H., *The Ku Klux Klan in Pennsylvania* Harrisburg, PA 1936

Lynd, R. & H. M., *Middletown* New York, NY 1929

Lynn, K. S., *Charlie Chaplin and His Times* New York, NY 1997

MacLean, N., *Behind the Mask of Chivalry* New York, NY 1994

Macleish, A., *Riders on the Earth* Boston, MA 1978

MacManus, T. F., and N. Beasley, *Men, Money and Motors* New York, NY 1929

Maland, C. J., *Chaplin and American Culture* Princeton, NJ, 1989

Mast, G., *A Short History of the Movies* New York, NY 1971

McAlmon, R., & K. Boyle *Geniuses Together, 1920–1930* London 1970

McKay, C., *A Long Way From Home* New York, NY 1969

McLean, E. W., *Father Struck it Rich* London 1936

Mead, M., *Coming of Age in Samoa* New York, NY 1927

Meade, M., *Bobbed Hair and Bathtub Gin* New York, NY 2004

Means, G., *The Strange Death of President Harding* London 1930

Mecklin, J. M., *The Ku Klux Klan* New York, NY 1924

Mencken, H. L., *The American Language* London 1923

Mezzrow, M., *Really the Blues* New York, NY 1946

Milford, N., *Savage Beauty: The Life of Edna St Vincent Millay* New York, NY 2001

——, *Zelda: A Biography* New York, NY 1970

Miller, N., *New World Coming* New York, NY 2003

Moore, L. J., *Citizen Klansmen* Chapel Hill, NC 1991

Mowry, G., *The Urban Nation, 1920–60* New York, NY 1965

Mumford, L., ed., *Roots of Contemporary American Architecture* New York, NY 1952

Murray, R. K., *Red Scare: A Case Study in National Hysteria* Minneapolis, MN 1955

The Nation

The New Yorker

Nichols, B., *All I Could Never Be* London 1949

——, *The Star Spangled Manner* London 1928

Noggle, B., *Teapot Dome: Oil & Politics in the 1920s* New York, NY 1962

Oderman, S., *Roscoe 'Fatty' Arbuckle: A Biography of the Silent Film Comedian 1887–1933* Jefferson, NC 1994

Ogren, K. J., *The Jazz Revolution: Twenties America and the Meaning of Jazz* New York, NY 1989

Oliver, P., *Blues Fell This Morning: The Meaning of the Blues* New York, NY 1969

Peiss, K., *Hope in a Jar. The Making of American Beauty Culture* New York, NY 1998

Perret, G., *America in the Twenties* New York, NY 1982

Pound, A., *The Turning Wheel* New York, NY 1934

Rampersad, A., *The Life of Langston Hughes, 1902–1941* New York, NY 1986

Roberts, R., *Jack Dempsey: The Manassa Mauler* Baton Rouge, LA 1979

Robinson, C. and R. Bletter, *Skyscraper Style: Art Deco New York* Oxford 1975

Robinson, D., *Hollywood in the Twenties* New York, NY 1968

Rosen, M., *Popcorn Venus* London 1973

Russo, G., *The Outfit: The Role of Chicago's Underworld in the Shaping of Modern America* New York, NY 2001

Rutland, R., *The Newsmongers: Journalism in the Life of the Nation* New York, NY 1973

Sacco, N., and B. Vanzetti, *Letters* London 1929

Sampson, A., *Empires of the Sky* New York, NY 1984

——, *The Seven Sisters* New York, NY 1978

Seldes, G., *The Seven Lively Arts* New York, NY 1924

Shapiro, N., and A. McCarthy, eds., *Hear Me Talkin' to Ya* New York, NY 1955

Siegfried, A., *America Comes of Age* New York, NY 1927

Spengler, O., *The Decline of the West* Oxford 1991

Starrett, W. A., *Skyscrapers and the Men Who Build Them* New York, NY 1928

Stearns, H., ed., *Civilization in the United States* New York, NY 1922

Stein, G., *The Autobiography of Alice B. Toklas* New York, NY 1933

Stevenson, E., *Babbitts & Bohemians: The American 1920s* New York, NY 1967

St Johns, A. R., *Love, Laughter and Tears. My Hollywood Story* New York, NY 1978

Stoddard, L., *The Rising Tide of Color* Brighton 1981

Sullivan, M., *Our Times. VI: The Twenties* New York, NY 1935

Swanson, G., *Swanson on Swanson* London 1981

Taylor, D. J., *Bright Young People. The Rise and Fall of a Generation 1918–1940* London 2007

Taylor, K., *Sometimes Madness is Wisdom: Zelda and Scott Fitzgerald, A Marriage* London 2002

Teague, M., *Mrs L.: Conversations with Alice Roosevelt Longworth* London 1981

Thurber, J., *The Years with Ross* Boston, MA 1959

transition

Tunney, G., *A Man Must Fight* New York, NY 1932

Vaill, A., *Everybody Was So Young: Gerald and Sara Murphy, A Lost Generation Love Story* New York, NY 1998

Vanity Fair

Vanzetti, B., *The Story of a Proletarian Life* London 2001

Wade, W. C., *The Fiery Cross – The Ku Klux Klan in America* New York, NY 1987

Weeks, R. B., ed., *Commonwealth vs. Sacco and Vanzetti* Englewood Cliffs, NJ 1958

White, W. A., *Autobiography* New York, NY 1946

——, *Letters of William Allen White, 1899–1943* New York, NY 1947

——, *Masks in a Pageant* New York, NY 1930

Williams, W. C., *Autobiography* New York, NY 1951

Wilson, E., *The Twenties* New York, NY 1975

Wolff, G., *Black Sun: The Brief Transit and Violent Eclipse of Harry Crosby* London 1976

Yagoda, B., *The New Yorker and the World it Made* New York, NY 2000

Index

Acknowledgements

My very grateful thanks to Toby Mundy, Sarah Norman, Fran Owen and everyone at Atlantic Books, to Tif Loehnis and everyone at Janklow and Nesbit, and to my family.